T0247733

KEN MORROW

MIRACLE GOLD, FOUR STANLEY CUPS, AND A LIFETIME OF ISLANDERS HOCKEY

Ken Morrow
with Allan Kreda

TRIUMPH
BOOKS

Library of Congress Cataloging-in-Publication Data available upon request.

This book is available in quantity at special discounts for your group or organization. For further information, contact:

Triumph Books LLC
814 North Franklin Street
Chicago, Illinois 60610
(312) 337-0747
www.triumphbooks.com

Printed in U.S.A.
ISBN: 978-1-63727-643-3
Page production by Nord Compo
Photos courtesy of Ken Morrow's collection unless otherwise specified

CONTENTS

FOREWORD *by Denis Potvin*   **v**

INTRODUCTION *by Allan Kreda*   **xi**

PROLOGUE *by Ken Morrow*   **xv**

CHAPTER 1.   Family Days Then and Now   **1**

CHAPTER 2.   Don Morrow   **11**

CHAPTER 3.   Bowling Green   **19**

CHAPTER 4.   1979–80: 61 Games Before Lake Placid   **33**

CHAPTER 5.   Five Games at Lake Placid   **49**

CHAPTER 6.   The Longest 10 Minutes   **65**

CHAPTER 7.   The Aftermath   **79**

CHAPTER 8.   Herb Brooks   **95**

CHAPTER 9.   From Lake Placid to Long Island: 1980 Stanley Cup Playoffs   **107**

CHAPTER 10.   1980 Stanley Cup Final   **125**

CHAPTER 11.   1981 Stanley Cup Playoffs   **141**

CHAPTER 12.   1982 Stanley Cup Playoffs   157

CHAPTER 13.   1983 Stanley Cup Playoffs:
               "I Love You Guys"   175

CHAPTER 14.   1984 Stanley Cup Playoffs:
               New York Rangers Overtime Goal   195

CHAPTER 15.   1984 Heading for Edmonton—and the End   209

CHAPTER 16.   1985–89 New York Islanders   223

CHAPTER 17.   Al Arbour   239

CHAPTER 18.   Euchre with LaFontaine–Trottier–Bossy   247

AFTERWORD *by Stan Fischler*   263

ACKNOWLEDGMENTS   271

ABOUT THE AUTHORS   279

APPENDIX   283

FOREWORD

I FIRST MET KENNY MORROW less than a week after he won the gold medal at Lake Placid and a day or two before he made his Islanders debut at Nassau Coliseum.

He was this tall and lean bearded guy who arrived with a reputation as a team-first, prototypical defensive defenseman.

Who could have predicted what was ahead for us as partners on the blue line and all the success we would share as Islanders teammates?

As team captain, I was quick to greet Kenny and welcome him to the club. He was very quiet. He may not have said much, but I could quickly see with the quality and tenacity of his play that he didn't have to say much at all.

We were playing our regular schedule during the Winter Olympics and were aware of the unfolding drama in upstate New York. I remember watching the U.S. team beat Finland on that Sunday to clinch the gold medal. But honestly, I wasn't remembering that Kenny was our draft pick and could potentially soon be part of our team.

He had been selected by the Islanders in the fourth round back in 1976, but in those days, there was rarely talk amongst the team about which players might join us after the Olympic Games.

After we led the league in points during 1978–79—only to be upset by the Rangers in the semifinals—the early part of the 1979–80 season was a struggle for the Islanders.

We won only nine of our first 25 games, and I suffered my worst injury in pro hockey in late November of that season in Edmonton, a serious right thumb injury that required surgery. This came after I missed the first eight games with a bruised clavicle.

The recovery cost me more than three months away from the team as I spent day after day working to get flexibility and dexterity back. It was one of the most difficult periods of my career, not being able to play for so long and help lead our efforts on the ice.

So that Saturday afternoon when I was finally able to return— March 1, 1980, at home against Detroit—was especially significant.

And wouldn't you know it, that was Kenny's first game, just five days after he and his Olympic teammates visited President Carter at the White House with their gold medals.

Now Kenny would don his Islanders home white uniform with blue and orange piping for the first time.

And Barb, Ken's loving wife, was surely thrilled to see him in an NHL jersey for the first time after all those games at Bowling Green plus the magical ride at Lake Placid. Barb's pride and satisfaction being there that afternoon at Nassau Coliseum had to be off the charts. What a phenomenal first year of marriage that had to be!

And it had to be surreal and memorable for Ken, too.

I was particularly nervous after missing more than three months, and I needed something positive to help me get back to my game. Without a doubt, it came in the form of this strong American defenseman with a steady and solid game.

Kenny and I found instant chemistry. Then, less than two weeks later, general manager Bill Torrey traded Billy Harris and Dave Lewis to Los Angeles to acquire Butch Goring.

That cemented our balance as a team. We had gotten stronger on the backline by adding Gord Lane in a trade from Washington the previous December, then became even stronger up front by adding Butch.

And the rest, as they say, is history.

Kenny and I often played together as we finished the regular season with a 12-game unbeaten streak heading into the playoffs.

He and I complemented each other very well—with his right-handed shot and mine from the left. His defense-first tendency allowed me to pursue offense when the time was right.

I don't think you can find two more completely different people. As our captain, I was an outgoing personality and public speaker. Ken was the opposite—mild-mannered and reserved—yet we blended very well.

Ken's style of play and his calm personality just fit with our team dynamic right off the bat. Here's a guy who had never played in the NHL who came in and played solidly.

Kenny made the adjustment to playing in the pros without difficulty, and his presence and steady play made a huge difference as we defeated Los Angeles, Boston, Buffalo, and Philadelphia on our way to our first Stanley Cup.

He scored his first overtime winner against the Kings in Game 3 of the opening round at the Forum in Los Angeles, a sign of Kenny's and our good overtime results to come in the years to follow.

When I think of Kenny as a defense partner, I remember how steady and smart he was with the puck. He basically had two plays: passing the puck to me—which was my favorite—or moving it up the boards.

Kenny never thought of himself as an "I'm going to beat this guy" type of player. His first option was always the team-wise choice.

That's Kenny Morrow in a nutshell, fitting his personality well. He simply showed up one day and became a major part of our team, from an unassuming entrance to a powerful presence.

He had played 58 games for the U.S. national team, then seven games at Lake Placid, followed by 18 more with the Islanders in the regular season, and then 20 tense playoff games as an NHL rookie—culminating with the Stanley Cup.

Right into the playoff cauldron and Kenny didn't miss a beat. He was unfazed by all of it. He accepted it and just did what he did. His positioning was perfect. His game was not complicated. You never heard a complaint from Ken, and every one of us knew he was often playing in pain. Yet he never missed a shift or a practice and for that, he surely became beloved.

Because of his full beard, Al Arbour nicknamed him "Moses" upon arrival on Long Island—and the guys called him "The Wolfman," which he accepted with his unique laugh. And Kenny has this real genuine laugh!

The bottom line is that he could not have been a better fit for us at a time when we truly needed it.

We had suffered through two grueling playoff losses in 1978 and 1979 in part because we just didn't have enough balance on the backline. With the addition of Kenny after Gord Lane, our defense was really solidified. We also had Stefan Persson, who played with me on the power play, plus Dave "Bammer" Langevin and Bob Lorimer.

Kenny and I were paired to kill penalties and Kenny and Gord were usually paired during the 1980 playoff run. We needed and benefited from having defensemen like Gord and Kenny in the mix.

Perhaps no situation epitomized that better than the closing seconds of Game 4 of the 1983 Cup Final at Nassau Coliseum.

We were leading the Edmonton Oilers three games to none and certainly wanted to close it out without a trip back to Alberta. Of course, the Oilers would not make it that easy. We were ahead 3–2 with less than 90 seconds remaining and Edmonton had its goalie, Andy Moog, pulled for an extra skater. The pressure was on as the Oilers had their big guns, including Wayne Gretzky and Mark Messier, on the ice pressing for that tying goal.

Kenny blocked a shot by right wing Dave Lumley, then tied up Gretzky briefly behind our net and as time clicked away, I had the puck in our zone after I had intercepted a pass.

I was trying to work it out of danger, but as I was taking a step to move the puck ahead, Gretzky managed to strip it away.

Suddenly, I was sort of skating over the puck. And you can imagine the momentary and immediate panic with the Oilers swarming.

But when I turned around, Kenny was there.

Kenny was always right there.

This time he confidently scooped up the puck, took a few of his signature long strides toward center ice, then shot the puck through traffic and directly into Edmonton's empty net.

I was following him, and that shot was a bullseye!

That ensuing group hug on the ice—with Bob Nystrom, John Tonelli, Kenny, and myself—will always be one for the ages.

Kenny was part of a group of guys who truly rose to the occasion— time and time and time again.

When you consider the players on our team who scored big-time goals, the list is packed with legends. There were Trottier, Bossy, and Gillies plus Tonelli, Nystrom, and without question Kenny Morrow.

That's why when you talk about winning 19 consecutive playoff series, you think of those who scored series-clinching goals.

Because without them, we don't win all those series or those four straight Stanley Cups.

Kenny did it one more time in that epic Game 5 overtime victory over the Rangers in April 1984 at Nassau Coliseum.

That goal against Glen Hanlon had the seeing-eye puck skill Kenny made famous in the playoffs, producing yet another thrilling end for us and complete heartbreak for the Rangers after they came very close to ending our dynasty in that frenetic overtime.

The best way to explain these overtime goals is that Kenny was so well-schooled as a defensive defenseman. When he would get the puck in an area like he did against the Rangers in that overtime along the boards at a sharp angle, his first thought would be to not let the shot get blocked.

There is no way with a wrist shot from the point that you are thinking you will score a goal or beat the goalie. But in that moment, Kenny's shot simply had eyes.

I know this for a fact, having been in the same position. You see a lot of traffic and you want to make sure the puck just gets through, so shooting early or shifting by a half a foot or so is the way to go.

That is always the main mindset of a defenseman in the offensive zone with the puck. Kenny did that and he did that very well.

The euphoria we felt after beating the Rangers in such dramatic fashion that night is right up there with my favorite career moments. To have Ken Morrow be the overtime hero again made it even more special.

Like me, Kenny was a lifetime Islander. I retired in 1988 after 15 NHL seasons—nine of them as his teammate—and Kenny played one more year.

We are forever linked through our shared Stanley Cup championships and—even more importantly—decades of friendship.

Denis Potvin served as New York Islanders captain during the team's record 19 straight playoff series wins and since unmatched four Stanley Cup championships in the 1980s. He won the James Norris Memorial Trophy as the NHL's top defenseman three times. He was elected to the Hockey Hall of Fame in 1991.

INTRODUCTION

I FIRST MET KEN MORROW during the 1985–86 NHL season in one of my earliest forays into the New York Islanders locker room as an intern for SportsChannel.

I was on the quiet side, and Ken was a man of few words. Our first interaction was certainly not dramatic. It probably consisted of me listening closely and scribbling down several postgame comments from the players available to the media.

A few words may have been exchanged between us, but my enduring memory is the respect I felt encountering a player of Ken's stature.

As a 14-year-old in early 1980, I was obsessively immersed in hockey. Keeping track of the Rangers, the Islanders, and the NHL overall was as integral to my daily routine as breathing. So of course, I followed every minute of Team USA's play at the Olympics in Lake Placid.

The tall, bearded defenseman had achieved something thoroughly amazing—winning a gold medal and a Stanley Cup within three months, then earning three more consecutive Cups after that. Ken was a player in a class by himself amid the assemblage of Islanders who had won those four Stanley Cups together.

And there was something inherently stylish and artistically pleasing in the seamless way Ken fit into the Islanders lineup straight from Lake Placid—as if he had been there all along.

Quiet consistency is a trademark of mine, which made it easy to relate to Ken. This particular trait is likely what connected us so well for this project decades later.

My personal hockey history goes back to growing up in Brooklyn in the early 1970s, when my older brother, David, and father, Bert, had Rangers season tickets from 1971–72 to 1974–75. That was the heyday of the NY Rangers' GAG ("Goal-A-Game") Line, featuring center Jean Ratelle, left wing Vic Hadfield, and Rod Gilbert on the right.

I remember my first game in November 1971, a matinee at Madison Square Garden with the Rangers playing the Buffalo Sabres. The three of us were close to the ice awaiting pregame warm-ups as the Rangers skated out in their gleaming white home uniforms, the second-year Sabres in their dark blues at the other end.

My dad nudged me as those Rangers legends glided onto the ice and skated a few circles then stopped along the boards near us. Faces were so clear in that era before helmets.

"There they are," my dad said softly.

Three words and an unforgettable image that has resonated for me ever since. From that day forward, I was hooked.

Little did I know this grade-school-era hockey fixation would turn into a lifetime passion, far from the prescribed pre-med path that I began years later at Stuyvesant High School in Manhattan.

I was listening to games on the radio and watching them on TV more closely than I was studying chemistry and biology, by that time at Brooklyn College. One newswriting course between physics and calculus classes in my junior year turned the tide, and I found myself immersed in journalism for good.

And then my break came in September 1985 when I started interning for the Hockey Maven, Stan Fischler.

What has proven to be an invaluable education and friendship had begun.

I worked for Stan that '85–86 season and the following year covering Rangers home games before completing a master's degree in print journalism at Northwestern University in Chicago.

Since then—and like Ken's career—my mission has always been one of perseverance. *No one will ever outwork me,* I told myself early in my career.

My signature Ken Morrow moment, however, occurred well before we met.

On April 10, 1984, I was torn between preparation for an absurdly early organic chemistry exam the following morning and a critical Rangers–Islanders playoff game at raucous Nassau Coliseum. This was a decisive Game 5 of an intense opening-round series, with the Herb Brooks–coached Rangers having their best chance to end the Islanders' dynasty.

I went to watch at a friend's apartment, a 20-minute bicycle ride away, because he had the cable channel that broadcast Islanders home games.

The Islanders led 2–1 late in the third and were poised to finish the Rangers in regulation time, but Don Maloney tied the game with a last-minute goal to force overtime. Stunningly, the rivals would play on.

I made a calculated decision to ride home and listen to overtime on my Sony Walkman. I reasoned that with the test's early start time, I couldn't risk triple-overtime drama leading to me getting home well past midnight.

This "dangerous" bicycle journey on the streets of Brooklyn—way before bike lanes existed—couldn't have been more stressful.

Rangers forwards Mikko Leinonen and Bob Brooke had golden chances to score against Billy Smith but could not convert.

So close and still so far.

The nearly nine minutes of overtime was so intense that pundits consider it among the most riveting overtimes ever.

Just as I arrived home safely, the moment happened!

Ken Morrow's knuckleball shot eluded Rangers goaltender Glen Hanlon at 8:56, and the "Drive for Five" was still on.

The Islanders had done it again, to my immense chagrin.

With three-plus decades in the writing business, I have written countless articles for The Associated Press, Bloomberg News, and *The New York Times*, as well as *The Hockey News* and other outlets.

I believe every professional hockey writer started as a fan. For me, maintaining that youthful enthusiasm for the game while developing impartiality early in my career has been key to my professional success.

Memories of those epic early-'80s Islanders playoff games bubbled up when—in early 2023—I was assigned to write a feature for The Hockey News on the Islanders' dynasty players.

Ken Morrow had to be interviewed and included for obvious reasons, as one of 16 Islanders who won four straight Stanley Cups—and he scored the most overtime goals (three) of any Islander in the combined 1980–84 playoff runs.

I had the keen sense while we spoke that Ken's epic career resonates way beyond games and championships. He was more than a vital cog in the machine that won those four Cups and 19 consecutive playoff series with the Islanders after he was part of that legendary American team that achieved the impossible in February 1980.

I suggested that his life stories of tenacity and perseverance should be shared as an enduring legacy of the special career he had and the special person he is.

He agreed, and here we are.

—Allan Kreda

PROLOGUE

FORGED WITH HARD WORK AND DEDICATION, my hockey life has been especially blessed with success in two distinct places.

On May 17, 1983, at Nassau Coliseum, there was less than a minute to go with a one-goal lead in Game 4 of the Stanley Cup Final against the Edmonton Oilers before my Islanders teammates and I would be able to lift the trophy above the Nassau Coliseum ice again.

Somehow the puck was on my stick as I skated out of our zone, and I could see a sliver of daylight between two Oilers defenders backing toward their own empty net.

All that was between us and a fourth straight Cup would be shooting the puck past them and into the empty net to complete a four-game sweep.

I sensed Bobby Nystrom to my right and Johnny Tonelli also ahead of the play to the left. All I could think about was making sure I skated over the red line so there was no risk of icing the puck, considering all the weapons the Oilers would have on the ice for another face-off back in our end. There was no way we could give Wayne Gretzky, Mark Messier, Jari Kurri, or Paul Coffey a chance to tie the game.

This shot had to go in. I fired the puck straight ahead and it fortunately found its way through and the net bulged.

Then, hugs and bedlam ensued.

* * *

It was a similar scene of euphoria in a different setting three years and three months before that celebration on Long Island when relentless patriotic cheering erupted in the tiny town of Lake Placid in upstate New York at the 1980 Winter Olympics.

After we shocked the vaunted Soviet team on Friday, February 22, 1980, then clinched gold with a comeback victory over Finland two days later, we stood together as a bunch of college kids—or "Big Doolies," as Phil Verchota called us and we affectionately became known—celebrating one of the most improbable victories in sports history at any level in any era.

When my kids were growing up, I often would be the show-and-tell subject at school, arriving with my gold medal to share stories about 1980 in Lake Placid.

I loved doing that.

Teachers always had their stories—where they were when we won and who they were with when they watched the games. It is wonderful hearing all those stories, and to this day 40-plus years later I still receive mail from people across the country thanking me for our efforts.

I am truly humbled.

Now with grandkids, the teachers are too young to remember 1980 for themselves. They know the story of Lake Placid more from the 2004 movie *Miracle* or from highlights on YouTube.

I get requests from youngsters wanting to write college or high school papers about a notable and historic event. They often pick our gold medal run as a life lesson, considering everything that was happening in the world back then and how our miraculous win at the Winter Games lifted an entire nation.

Reading letters from people of all ages thanking me and telling their story of what the "Miracle on Ice" and 1980 gold medal meant to them and their families has always been and continues to be amazing and inspiring.

People often say they want another of these events to help unite us—similar to how the end of World War II in 1945 or Neil Armstrong walking on the moon in 1969 brought Americans together.

Our hockey team was able to achieve a standalone victory that continues to grow in stature.

Being part of Team USA at Lake Placid followed by winning four straight Stanley Cups with the New York Islanders has put me in an especially unique and singular place in hockey history.

But none of that would have been possible without my family, teammates, and coaches along the way.

This is my story.

—Ken Morrow

CHAPTER 1

FAMILY DAYS THEN AND NOW

I WAS BORN ON OCTOBER 17, 1956, and raised in Flint, Michigan.

Back then, Flint was an automobile factory town, and being that it was 60 miles north of Detroit, everything revolved around the auto industry. People either worked in the factories or worked a job that serviced the factories and their workers.

In 1969, my parents, Don and Loretta, moved our family of five to nearby Davison, a small town about 10 miles east of Flint. We moved from the city limits to the suburbs as I was entering seventh grade. My brother, Greg, is 18 months older than I am, and my sister, Kathi, is four years younger. She still lives in the Flint area.

Growing up in Flint was about as blue-collar American as you could get in those days. My father, grandfather, uncles, cousins, and friends' parents all worked in the factory or auto industry. It was a way of life and almost everyone followed a similar path—go through high school, get a beginning job in the factory, start making money, take on car and housing payments, get married and raise a family, and then 30 years later repeat the cycle with their own kids.

We didn't have a lot of money, but I never found myself wanting for anything either. My dad worked at Ternstedt, which was part of General Motors as a manufacturing plant. My mom worked various jobs, at a small neighborhood grocery store, as an insurance company secretary, and as a police dispatcher.

Our grandparents and aunts and uncles and cousins shared time together and spent many weekends going "up north" in Michigan, near the lake in the summer and snowmobiling in the winter.

It was in Flint, at our small house on Kellar Avenue in a working-class neighborhood, that my brother and I got started skating and playing hockey. I'm not sure why, but my father took an interest in hockey when my brother and I were young. We started making a homemade rink in our backyard when I was around five years old.

When it snowed, which seemed like every day in Michigan in those days, we would trample down the snow with our boots and pull the hose out of the basement window and start making ice. The rink, which was 25 feet wide and 50 feet long, took up most of the small backyard, and back then it stayed cold enough to stay frozen through most of the winter. We started with small boards around the rink to keep the puck from leaving the ice and eventually, we put up bigger boards and then floodlights as the years went along.

Neighborhood kids and friends would come over to skate, and I remember many days when we would put our skates on in the morning and not take them off until night. The only time we would come in was to eat lunch and dinner—with our skates on! This was our Field of Dreams. What great memories!

My father made small nets for the rink, and he would cut the middle out of pucks when we were too young to stickhandle or shoot with a bigger puck. I remember constantly digging through snowbanks looking for pucks that flew out of the rink into the snow.

Falling in love with hockey skating on our backyard rink led to playing in an organized youth league in Flint when I was around seven or eight years old. Greg and I played on the same teams growing up, and my dad coached most of those teams. All of the ice rinks in Flint were outdoors—Memorial Park, Lincoln Park, and Whaley Park were outdoor rinks where we practiced and played.

A lot of our skating was done in our backyard. It wasn't until I was in my teens that we had an indoor arena in Flint. In those early days of organized hockey, there weren't enough kids of the same age group to have a full team, so each team had one line of the same age group, and during games they would have to match lines by age with the team you were playing against. I remember it being so cold that they had a warming building where you put on your skates, and we would go out for our shift and then go back inside to stay warm until our next shift. I also remember my feet and hands going numb when we skated outdoors and having tears in my eyes because my feet hurt so badly when they thawed out.

Yet there we were the next day, doing the same thing all over again.

People ask me if I always knew I wanted to play in the NHL when I was growing up. The truth is that I fell in love playing hockey on our backyard rink at a young age, and it was all I wanted to do. There were no dreams of playing in college or in the Olympics or in the NHL; I just wanted to be out skating and having fun. If a kid has a passion for playing hockey, then it will show itself. They will want to be at the rink every day or be outside playing street hockey or be shooting pucks in the basement or driveway. If they can't get enough, then they have a love for the sport!

The sacrifices that hockey parents and their kids make to play this sport build great character and develop a strong work ethic and values like teamwork that carry over into life. Between all the early-morning practices in the middle of winter, giving up weekends and driving many hours to play against better competition, plus the cost of gas and travel and hockey equipment and ice time, there is a shared sacrifice that bonds hockey people.

Most of our friends were "hockey" families—the parents and the kids that we grew up with playing hockey. We had good friends and great hockey dads like Gale Cronk and Jay Buckner, and we became close with them and their families. These two men and my dad gave so much of their time and effort to us kids and to youth hockey.

After playing in the Greater Flint Hockey Association (GFHA) in my early youth hockey years, we started looking for ways to play against better competition than what was available in Flint. That would mean having to travel to Detroit or traveling into Canada.

Once the indoor arena opened in Flint in 1969, my father, along with Mr. Cronk and Mr. Buckner, wanted to start a travel team. Forming a travel team would be the only way for a kid from Flint to get an opportunity to play against higher-level hockey competition. This was met with stiff resistance from the GFHA, which only wanted recreational hockey for the kids.

So my father and these two friends broke away and started a new league called the Eastern Michigan Hockey Association (EMHA). All of a sudden, anyone associated with the EMHA was blackballed from renting ice at the new indoor arena, which was home to the GFHA, so we joined a league in Detroit and did a lot of traveling. Then, it just so happened that one of our travel player's father, Dale Dewitt, owned a construction company, and he built a new indoor rink that the EMHA would use as our new home. Without the sacrifice and fortitude and vision of my father and these dedicated hockey dads, I and many others would not have had the opportunity to move ahead in the hockey world.

I have so many memories of time spent in cars, vans, and SUVs with hockey equipment piled in the back, hockey families meeting in parking lots and caravanning to Detroit or Chicago or wherever we were playing.

They broke the mold with Gale Cronk. He was an assistant coach for my dad, but he also managed the team, scheduled our games, and coordinated the travel. And maybe best of all, he was a tremendous promoter. His son Kelly played on those same travel teams that I did growing up. Mr. Cronk had a big Chevrolet Suburban SUV that he would drive to our games, and he rebuilt the engine at least three times because of all the miles he put on it.

He always had room for any players who needed a ride. He would print out maps to the rinks and hand them out to the parents before we left the parking lot. One funny story: we were playing in a suburb of Detroit, and he made copies of a map with directions to the rink, which was over an hour's drive away. This particular time, he happened to make copies that transposed the map so that everything was backward. When we were supposed to turn right, the map showed to turn left. It wasn't until we were way on the opposite side of Detroit that we figured out the problem and barely made it to the game in time to play.

After that trip, we nicknamed him "Wrong Way Cronk," and that good-heartedly stuck with him for many years. One of his creative ideas to promote the team was using a printing shop to make paper placemats with our EMHA travel team schedule and photos of the players on it. He would then carry boxes of these placemats in his car and hand them out whenever we stopped at a diner or restaurant.

The restaurants were happy to get free placemats, and anyone who came in to eat would have a placemat with our schedule on it. He spent his own money on printing, keeping his car on the road, and gas. He gave all his time to us kids and to hockey. He was a truly remarkable man and eventually became owner of the printing shop he was paying to print everything.

In those early travel years, we got our butts kicked many nights playing against better Detroit and Canadian teams. The only way we were going to get better was to play against the best.

There was high school hockey in the Flint area and around Michigan at that time, but the better players were on travel teams. Once the EMHA was formed, we were traveling to Detroit most weekends and many times during the week on school nights. We also traveled to Chicago for games and tournaments, which was a five- to six-hour drive.

My high school in Davison had a hockey team, but my brother and I didn't play for it. The simple reason was that we were looking to play against the best competition we could find, and that would require playing travel hockey.

I was a very quiet and unassuming kid. In high school, I was the "blend in and don't bring any attention to yourself" type. "Shy" and "low maintenance" might be the best descriptions of myself.

For me, there were no other sports that compared to hockey. Basketball was my second-favorite sport. I played a lot of pick up basketball, but because the season ran at the same time as hockey, I couldn't play in high school. With most of my spare time spent playing hockey, I wasn't involved in any high school activities, and I was too awkward and shy to be involved in anything socially.

So playing hockey became my life, and I loved every minute of it!

I never knew what the future would hold and how fortunate I would become.

I had a growth spurt when I was around 13 years old where I shot up six inches in height in one year. In one team photo I was the same height as everybody else, and in the team photo the following year I was a head taller than my teammates.

Having a dad who was 6'5" and a great athlete and having an older brother to try to keep up with helped shape and drive me as a player.

Our dad didn't push us. He was involved and supportive, but he let us dictate, through our passion for hockey, just how far we would push the limits for ourselves.

He was a quiet man, gifted with size and athletic ability, but he never bragged or talked about his accomplishments.

It took hearing many stories over many decades from people who knew my father to find out just how good of an athlete he was. He is in the Greater Flint Area Sports Hall of Fame.

People have told me I have some of those same qualities, reminding them of my dad. It certainly makes me feel proud to hear that. There are players that need to be pushed hard by a coach to get the best out of them. My coaches throughout my career—all the way up to Herb Brooks and Al Arbour—found out I was not that guy.

For me, the only thing was to do my job and do it well—to be dependable. I didn't need the spotlight shining on me. You can say I am a product of my Flint childhood—a working-class mindset and a solid work ethic that set a foundation for me at a young age.

Nothing was easy for our parents, working in the factories and trying to make enough money to pay the bills and raise a family. It may have been a hard life, but there was a simplicity to it that I wish our kids and grandkids would get to experience. There were no cell phones or computers. Distractions were minimal compared with today's world.

We would be outside from morning until night in both winter and summer, playing in the neighborhood and inventing games. Riding bikes and going to the park to play football or baseball was our daily effort. There was no technology or internet to distract you and take away from the fun of being a kid.

When you're out skating on a rink—with the speed of the game, the wind sweeping past your ears with nonstop action—there's no comparison to other sports like baseball and football. I tried baseball as a kid, but I was not very good at it, and it was too boring for me. I never liked just standing there waiting for the ball to be hit your way and sitting in the dugout waiting for your turn to bat.

My mom and sister were part of our hockey life, probably more than they wanted to be. They gave up their weekends and spent way too much time in cold hockey rinks. But having said that, this was family time together, and I will always treasure that.

Hockey—more than any other sport—requires a high level of sacrifice, support, and dedication from families and many others who help along the way. Success cannot be achieved alone, and that is why you always hear hockey players thanking their family when they talk about their hockey life.

My family—especially my brother Greg—understands this life very well.

My sister, Kathi, has two sons and works in a Flint-area school system, and Greg works for the Islanders as a college scout. He played college hockey at Ohio State, a big rival of Bowling Green, where I went

9

to school. We played against each other for three seasons. Growing up playing hockey together and playing Division I college hockey is something of which we can both be very proud. Having Greg also work for the Islanders is a big bonus!

I met my wife, Barb, at Bowling Green, and we were married in August 1979, just before our pre-Olympic season started. She has seen it all and more.

In July 1982, our first daughter, Krysten, was born on Long Island, the summer after our third Stanley Cup win. We have photos of her as a baby sitting in the top of the Cup.

Our second daughter, Brittany, just missed her Cup moment since she was born midway through the 1983–84 season on January 6, 1984.

I actually scored one of my 17 career regular season goals the night after she was born. It came against the Chicago Blackhawks in a 5–3 win at home. I scored in the first period against the great Tony Esposito, who was in his final NHL season.

I was on top of the world, as you would imagine. I scored three goals in 63 games that season and this one happened to come just hours after Brittany was born.

Our son, Evan, came along in 1997. He played Division II college soccer at a school near Charlotte, North Carolina, and graduated with a degree in sports management and business. He played four sports growing up and was on the drumline and student council in high school. He certainly was much more balanced in his life and more involved in activities than I was in high school.

Barb and I have always preached balance with our kids—to be active, to be engaged, and to pursue your passions, whatever they may be.

All three of our kids live within 15 minutes of us in Kansas City, and Barb and I are so grateful that we get to see them and our six grandkids almost every day.

The hockey life has given me so much, and I always remind myself how lucky I am.

CHAPTER 2

DON MORROW

AT 6'5" AND BEING A VERY QUIET GUY, my dad was a gentle giant. So when he did say something, he had your attention. I have been told that I have some of those same qualities—in fact, I had been compared to Abraham Lincoln in the media throughout my playing career because of my 6'4" frame, my beard, and being soft spoken. As I have grown older, I have become more comfortable in opening up more.

My dad, however, didn't develop that same comfort. He kept his childhood, his life, his accomplishments, and his struggles mostly to himself. His generation—the Greatest Generation—lived through the Depression and WWII, and they kept things to themselves. They tackled adversity and challenges and didn't complain or burden anybody else. That describes my father. He didn't tell us much about his life growing up. The sad part of it all is that he died way too young, at just 48 years old, in 1976 when I was a freshman at Bowling Green.

What I do know about my father is that he was a great athlete, both in baseball and basketball. Baseball was *the* sport in America back in that era and my dad excelled. He was a shortstop, essentially Cal Ripken Jr. before Cal Ripken Jr. because of his size and power. After digging through scrapbooks, newspaper articles, and old photos stored away in my basement and in closets, plus what I learned while growing up, this is what I have pieced together about my dad's life.

13

Don Morrow was born in 1928 and graduated from Flint Central High School in 1946, where he lettered in baseball and basketball. He played City League baseball in the summer and was making a name for himself and getting noticed by local scouts in the Detroit Tigers organization.

He received a scholarship and enrolled at Michigan State University, which was just an hour away from Flint, where he would play both baseball and basketball. After playing at Michigan State in 1947 and returning in 1948, he had an offer to sign with the Tigers and an even more lucrative offer to sign with the Boston Red Sox. Once he had returned to school and mulled over his opportunity to sign a pro contract, he realized his greatest ambition was to play baseball, so he decided to sign with Detroit in January 1949.

His father, Arlie (short for Arlington—which is my middle name), was a big Tigers fan, and my dad also felt he had a better chance to advance as an infielder with the Tigers. So my dad drove to Detroit with his father to sign a pro contract on a Saturday. Arlie had to co-sign the contract, as my dad was a month short of being 21 years old. This was one of the happiest and proudest moments of my father's life. Father and son returned to Flint on Saturday night, then both his parents drove my dad back to Michigan State in East Lansing the following day.

Then tragedy struck.

His parents hit a patch of ice on their drive home Sunday night and were involved in a head-on crash. My father's dad was killed, and his mother, Irene, suffered severe injuries and was in a coma for weeks. My dad was an only child. He had lost his father a day after signing his professional baseball contract, and his mother was seriously injured. She survived and lived to be an amazing 95 years old, never remarried, and stayed sharp as a tack living in the same house until the day she passed away.

She was such a quiet and strong woman and never felt sorry for herself or complained. She would mail me a $10 bill every so often when I went to school at Bowling Green to help with expenses. One of my greatest regrets is that I didn't get to spend more time with her. Once my dad passed away and my hockey career took off, we were only able to see each other a few times a year.

My dad spent the next two years, 1949–50, playing minor league baseball in cities like Jamestown, New York, and Durham, North Carolina. We heard the stories and have many scrapbook box scores from these years, when he played against baseball greats like Hank Aaron and others who started in the minor leagues. In reading through newspaper articles from my dad's pro baseball days, he was described as "Paul Bunyan" and the "Michigan Skyscraper" because of his size and his power for hitting doubles, triples, and home runs.

He was on track to make the major leagues until, like so many athletes in those days, he was drafted into the army in January 1951. He spent the next two years stationed at Fort Sheridan, Illinois, just north of Chicago. At that time, military bases had sports teams, and the competition between bases was intense. As was the case, there were a lot of very good athletes and future major leaguers in all sports who were drafted into the service. It was high-level competition.

My dad was a star athlete in three sports at Fort Sheridan—baseball, basketball, and touch football. He was the leading scorer on the basketball team playing at center, the touch football team won the championship, and he was a star on the baseball team. Dad was described as being a natural on the baseball diamond, the football field, and the basketball court. Articles described him in such eloquent terms during his playing days. He was "the most graceful big man I've ever seen," according to Tigers scout Jack Tighe.

Other comments included that he "throws the ball like a pea" with his strong arm and that "although he wears a size 13 shoe, he's fast for his size and covers ground at his position like a cat."

Dad had a long and easy stride, but he was one of the fastest on the team. One of my dad's greatest feats was when he was playing in Jamestown. In the second game of a doubleheader where his team had amassed five home runs up to the eighth inning, Don Morrow drove the first pitch out of the ballpark and tied a 23-year-old league record for a team hitting six home runs in a game. He then came up to bat again in the ninth inning and slammed the first pitch out of the park to break the record!

He was called "one of the best major league prospects in the Tigers organization" by many people back in those days. One of my most cherished photos is my father in a Detroit Tigers uniform. We also have two Louisville Slugger bats with my dad's autograph stamped into the bat, just like Mickey Mantle. My brother made a trip to the Louisville Slugger bat factory many years ago and they still had our dad's signature stored away along with the mold used to stamp the bat!

Once his two-year Army stint ended, Dad was assigned to Buffalo with the Tigers organization to resume his climb toward the major leagues. As the story goes, he went to camp with Buffalo and outplayed the Tigers' top prospect at the time, but that player had a contract that stipulated he couldn't be sent down, so they sent my father down instead.

This discouraged him so much that he walked away and went home to Flint. According to my Uncle Cliff, my mom's brother who grew up playing baseball with my father and was a very good player himself, my dad was the best athlete to come out of Flint, and he should have played in the major leagues. Uncle Cliff said that when my dad lost his father in the car accident, he had nobody to instruct him and that his dad would not have allowed him to walk away from baseball.

So Dad returned home and started working in the auto factory. My mom, Loretta, had grown up near my dad's neighborhood and her brother Cliff and my dad grew up going to school and playing baseball together. He and my mom were married and us kids were born in 1955, 1956, and 1960. Now that he had a job and a family, Dad's sports playing was at the City League level both in baseball and basketball, which was still very good competition. He was chosen as an All-City player in both sports for several years. All of this led to my dad somehow taking an interest in hockey and getting my brother and me to start skating at a young age in our backyard. I owe my hockey career to my father and my family.

To me, my father's sports life is a story of what might have been. He excelled at every level in which he played, and if not for circumstances beyond his control in losing his dad and his decision to walk away, I believe he would have played major league baseball.

My father fell ill quickly and was diagnosed with brain cancer in the summer of 1975. It was very difficult for me to leave for my freshman year at Bowling Green that September, but he wanted me to go. My brother started his college hockey career at Ohio State a few months later and with the help of good friends, my dad, despite being very sick, was able to make a trip to Bowling Green to see my brother and me play against each other in February 1976.

He had started my brother and me playing hockey and coached us and now he got to see us both play in college, and I am forever thankful for that. Dad passed away just a month later in March 1976, never having seen the Olympics or the Stanley Cups.

Although I only knew my father for 19 years before he passed at age 48, he showed me that a person could be both quiet and strong, something that always has and always will stay with me.

In hockey, most players are superstitious, and everyone has their traditions and routines. After my father passed, when I stood on the blue line or on the bench for every national anthem before every game in college, the Olympics, and the NHL, I would look up at the flag and think about my dad and thank him for all he had done.

My father was with me for every game I played.

CHAPTER 3

BOWLING GREEN

BEFORE I ATTENDED BOWLING GREEN, I played one year with the Detroit Junior Red Wings, one of the few junior A teams in the United States at that time. They played at the old Olympia, where the Red Wings played before moving to Joe Louis Arena in 1979.

I skated with the junior Red Wings, who played in the Southern Ontario Hockey League, which was a tier II junior A league that was scouted by college coaches. I ended up with a handful of offers to play college hockey and narrowed it down to Bowling Green, which is in Ohio about 15 miles south of Toledo, and Michigan State in East Lansing.

Michigan State was an hour's drive west from where I lived in Flint, while Bowling Green was a two-hour drive to the south in Ohio. I visited both schools and made my decision to go to Bowling Green, mostly because of the smaller size. Michigan State was a little too big for me, while Bowling Green had about 16,000 students. I liked the feel of the place and the presence of Ron Mason, the head coach who recruited me.

I graduated from Davison High School in 1974 and took a year off between high school and college, spending that year playing in Detroit. I made the drive every day from Flint for practices and games, or to hop on a bus to travel to away games in Canada.

The fall of 1975, I started my freshman year on scholarship, which gave me my only chance to go to college.

I felt good about my decision to attend Bowling Green and play for Coach Mason. He was early into his own college coaching career and ended up coaching another 30 years, then became athletic director at Michigan State. He later coached players like Joe Murphy and Duncan Keith and many other future NHL players and stars.

I would wear No. 3 in college. As a freshman at Bowling Green, I was quite naïve. Everything was so new to me. Being from Flint, growing up in a factory town and then having an opportunity to go to college and play hockey truly opened my eyes and broadened my world.

Most of the people back home were destined to work in the auto factories. Hockey opened a huge door for me, which led to many bigger opportunities. I knew I had to work hard every step of the way to take advantage of those. My mindset was to put in the necessary effort to excel at every level.

Greg had also played with the Detroit Junior Red Wings before we began playing against one another in college. Bowling Green versus Ohio State was a huge rivalry. We were in the same conference in those days with schools such as Western Michigan, St. Louis University, and Lake Superior State. We had some real battles against these teams.

The CCHA (Central Collegiate Hockey Association) has changed in recent years, with Bowling Green in the same conference as Michigan Tech, Minnesota State, Lake Superior State, and Northern Michigan University, among others.

My brother was a Phil Esposito–style centerman, a big and strong net-front presence. Greg was 6'2" and had a thicker frame than me. Greg's strength was standing on top of the crease, battling for tips and knocking in rebounds.

Bowling Green played more of a physical/pro style of college hockey under Coach Mason. At the University of Minnesota—coached by Herb Brooks—they played more of a freewheeling skating and speed and skill game suited for their Olympic-sized ice rink. I would learn much more about that later.

Bowling Green had a pipeline for recruiting players from the Toronto area, so we had many Canadians who had played junior hockey up there, mixing in with Michigan guys like myself who played that same style of hockey.

There was a distinct difference between the CCHA and those established teams from Minnesota and out west and the Boston area.

My Bowling Green teammates included goaltender Mike Liut, who went on to star in the NHL for the St. Louis Blues, and he also played in Hartford and Washington. Forwards George McPhee and Brian MacLellan came in as freshmen when I was a senior.

You knew right away both George and Brian were good hockey players. They brought an energetic and physical presence to the team along with some big-time college scoring.

George was an intense competitor who could score. He notched 40 goals in 1978–79 and had 21, 25, and 28 goals in his next three college seasons. As a senior he won the Hobey Baker Award—given to the best player in college hockey—in 1982.

In the NHL, Brian had a good long career as a power winger providing size and toughness and scoring. George played for the New York Rangers for five seasons, so we played against each other in our regular season and playoff battles during those years in the early 80s. He played like the Tasmanian Devil, great energy and hustle and tough as nails. George was the ultimate competitor.

MacLellan had 34 goals in his freshman year, the same 1978–79 season I was a senior. He had 30-plus-goal seasons in the NHL with Los Angeles and Minnesota and scored 172 goals over his 10-year career.

George and Brian grew up together in Guelph, Ontario, and were recruited together to Bowling Green. Later in the pros they both played for the Rangers and worked together for the Washington Capitals in management positions. George became general manager of the Capitals in 1997 and Brian was promoted to the general manager position in

2014 and eventually became president of hockey operations for the Capitals.

George was named the original general manager of the Vegas Golden Knights in 2016 and has since moved to president of hockey operations for the 2023 Stanley Cup champions.

To this day, George is a good friend and he still calls me by my nickname, Bobo. Whenever he sees me, it's "Hello, Bobo, how are you?"

That takes me right back to Bowling Green.

GEORGE McPHEE
NHL executive, Bowling Green teammate

Ken was an elite defensive defenseman. Very mobile, tall with a long stick. You couldn't beat him with speed or smarts. He angled and rubbed players out of the play. Played the game honest and clean. As a teammate he was quiet, a first-class person all the way. A gentleman.

George is one of my favorite former teammates and just a great person. He has had so much success off the ice, and he was a handful on the ice. I remember a fight he had against Bob Nystrom at Nassau Coliseum and he gave Bob all he could handle. Nystrom was as tough a fighter as there was in the NHL. George was a terrific teammate and college star and a good pro as well.

With players like Liut and McPhee and McClellan and others, Bowling Green hockey grew into a power and continued to thrive following my time there, as players who came after me included longtime NHL defensemen Rob Blake, Kevin Bieksa, Dave Ellett, and Garry Galley along with forwards Nelson Emerson and Paul Ysebaert and Gino Cavallini.

GEORGE McPHEE

Bowling Green was one of the top five or six programs in college hockey those days. The team was performing very well on the ice, and there were players graduating each year and turning pro in the NHL.

No question I had special teammates at Bowling Green from the outset, and those four years definitely prepared me for what was ahead.

I came in as a raw, tall, and thin offensive defenseman who liked to rush the puck. As a senior, I had a college-career-best 52 points, including 15 goals.

But even more importantly, over my time under Ron Mason, I developed my defensive game. My size, reach, and shot-blocking became more valuable when the Islanders and others like Herb Brooks and his staff noticed my development and overall ability.

It's ironic because when I played with the Olympic team, I was paired with Mike Ramsey, who liked to take off up the ice when the chance was there. The funny thing is that Mike eventually turned into a defensive defenseman himself during his lengthy NHL career.

Mike and I were good partners on the ice. He was the offensive guy and I stayed back, and that worked well for us.

After joining the Islanders, it was the same when I was paired with Denis Potvin. He was an offensive star, and I liked being the guy to go out there and kill penalties and play defense. My game evolved from being more of an offensive guy in college to shutting things down as a defensive defenseman in the Olympics and with the Islanders.

Mark Wells, my Olympic teammate, was also my teammate on the Junior Red Wings and through all four years at Bowling Green. We were recruited together, we were roommates in college, and we won gold together in Lake Placid. Mark was my lifelong friend. He sadly passed at age 66 in May 2024, becoming the third player we have lost from our gold-medal-winning team. Mark Pavelich passed at 63 in March 2021 and Bob Suter at 57 in 2014.

During my four years of college, I never had a thought about leaving school early. I was going to finish my four years at Bowling Green.

Little did I know a scouting mission would occur during my freshman season that would prove to have a huge impact on my career. After my freshman season, I was drafted by the Islanders in the fourth round in 1976.

JIMMY DEVELLANO
Former New York Islanders chief scout
Back in late 1975, I was the head scout for the Islanders and working in Toronto. It so happened one night that Bowling Green was playing the Toronto Varsity Blues right here under my nose. I went to the game and I'm looking at younger players that might be eligible for the draft. On Bowling Green I see this big gangly kid about 6'3", 6'4", a right-handed shooting defenseman. I look and it's Ken Morrow from Flint, Michigan. He caught my eye. He was pretty good defensively, and he handled the puck very well. He had size and range. He was a freshman, about 19 years old. And I said, "You know, he's a bit of a prospect, a good prospect. He's got to go on the list, right?" And so I put him on the list.

Now comes the 1976 draft and I select Ken for the New York Islanders in the fourth round, the 68th player chosen in that draft. That means 67 guys went ahead of him. We took him as a kid whom we hoped with his size and strength would improve in college. And how do you do that? You leave him right where he is right at Bowling Green and hope each year he gets better. Sure enough, he did.

I didn't even know I was drafted that day. I don't remember getting a call. I received a letter from the Islanders a few days after the draft that made it official. It was very different that draft day than in today's NHL, where nowadays it is a celebration and media spectacle and every player picked is announced on social media within seconds of being selected.

I never had any pressure from the Islanders as far as "We want you to sign with us now" or anything like that. They supported my decision. They knew that the 1979–80 season with the Olympic team would be a great experience for me and for my development as a player. In fact, I didn't find out I would be coming to Long Island until I was in Lake Placid.

During the Winter Games, I bumped into Bill Torrey one day in the arena. "We're thinking of bringing you to Long Island once you sign with us after the Olympics," he said to me.

That was the first time I had heard of their plans. I didn't know whether I would be going to their minor league team in Indianapolis or to the big club.

I am so glad of the timing and that everything worked out that way so I was able to have the full college and Olympic experience.

My major was liberal arts, kind of a catch-all education. My interests going into college were math and science, and I took classes such as chemistry and biology my freshman year but found I didn't have the needed chemistry background from high school with the classes I took. I liked science, but once I got into the actual hardcore subject matter, I decided it was not for me.

So I changed to liberal arts, which gave me the chance to study a bit of everything as opposed to zeroing in on one thing. I had no clue what I wanted to do at that time. It all ended up working out well for me and my interests.

After playing 10 seasons in the NHL and having been around physical therapists and working with trainers, I think physical therapy might have been a profession I would have liked. I became an expert in that area, having now gone through eight knee surgeries and recoveries.

On the ice, in my four years at Bowling Green we had success right from the start and grew better with each season. We had a very good recruiting class in 1975 and Ron Mason was in the process of building what turned out to be a powerhouse program. We won our league three of my four years there and in my junior season we earned our first play-in game to the Final Four, now known as the Frozen Four.

At that time the Final Four consisted of two teams from the WCHA (Western Collegiate Hockey Association) and two teams from out east. We met Colorado College in the play-in game at home on March 18, 1978. We won 5–3 to advance to the Final Four in Providence, Rhode Island.

That game was especially memorable for me. The excitement on campus was off the charts—plus, this was an incredibly historic moment for Bowling Green and the CCHA. It was the school's first time in an NCAA game of this magnitude—with the opportunity to either end our season or have a chance to win a national championship.

I'm not sure a lot of people knew in those days what a great hockey school Bowling Green was becoming. It didn't have the hockey history that many of the other established programs had, but the success we were enjoying every year during my time there made our campus a hockey hotbed.

I have clear memories of walking across campus on game days and the excitement that followed the team. The school and the town were caught up in the winning and the hockey team. It was a great time for Falcon hockey!

We played in an arena that held about 3,000 people, and there were long lines standing outside the arena for hours in the dead of winter waiting for the doors to open. Every game was sold out and the students were crazy loud and really into the games, doing all the chants and antics college fans will do.

The fact that our team was winning and becoming more dominant in each of my four years made it all the more fun.

In 1978 at the Final Four, we lost 6–2 to Boston College in the first game, then played Wisconsin—and my future Olympic teammates

Mark Johnson and Bob Suter—in the consolation game. We beat the Badgers 4–3 to take third place in the NCAA championship tournament.

My senior year we also had a powerhouse team and had a dominant season, going 37–6–2 and earning another play-in game in 1979.

RALPH COX
U.S. national team teammate, University of New Hampshire player
I played against him in the 1978–79 season. UNH played Bowling Green in a weekend series. That's when I first got crushed by him.

This time for the play-in game we had to travel to Minnesota and meet Herb Brooks' team with eight guys who would later be my teammates in Lake Placid. The Minnesota guys told me years later that in the days leading up to that game Herb kept building me up as this great player, that nobody could stop me. He did this all week until they said by the time the game came they were so sick of hearing how good I was that they all wanted to run me through the boards! It was a typical psychological ploy by Herb Brooks. He was a master of mind games, as I would later learn.

We lost 6–3 and the Golden Gophers went on to win the NCAA Championship at the Olympia in Detroit, beating New Hampshire and North Dakota. It was Herb's third NCAA title of the 1970s with the University of Minnesota.

My college experience was everything I hoped it would be and more. Playing in those high-level and high-pressure games before packed crowds helped me become a better player and going to college helped me become a better person.

Of course, Coach Mason was such a key part of it all. He always talked about being mentally strong and was very much like Al Arbour in that he was tough but fair. He coached a pro style of hockey, which

29

is what I grew up playing in Michigan. I believe that's why so many of his college players had success in the NHL.

There was something special about Ron, just a tremendous coach. I definitely made the right choice.

My senior year was Ron's last season at Bowling Green. He went on to Michigan State the following year and coached the Spartans for 23 years until 2001–02, including winning the national championship in 1986. He had been at Bowling Green for six years after the first seven seasons of his college coaching career at Lake Superior State in Sault Ste. Marie, Michigan. Ron was the all-time wins leader in college hockey when he retired with 924 victories.

That mark was surpassed on December 29, 2012, by Jerry York, who replaced Ron at Bowling Green in 1979–80, then coached Boston College from 1994 to 2022.

Ron is the career wins leader at Michigan State with 635 and is Bowling Green's winningest coach by percentage. He had 33 winning seasons overall and his teams reached the NCAA tournament 22 times, six times as the top seed.

A legendary career for sure!

The other highlight for me at Bowling Green also came in 1978 after my junior season, the year I was named to the All-America team. That was historic, as I became the first CCHA player and first Bowling Green player named to an All-America team.

It was groundbreaking at the time and made my induction into the Bowling Green Hall of Fame in 1984 that much more special.

On top of that, the Falcons won the national championship that year, beating Minnesota-Duluth in quadruple overtime in the title game, which was held in Lake Placid.

The spring of 1978 is also when I got my first, and only, taste of international hockey before 1980. I received a phone call out of the blue in April from the manager of Team USA for the World Championships being held in Prague. I hadn't been skating for over a month, but was asked to join the team in Prague the next day. A spot had opened up because of an injury and they wanted me to fly over to Czechoslovakia as soon as I could get there. I quickly gathered my equipment and flew to New York, where I could get a passport the same day, then hopped on a flight overseas and landed the following day at noon. Team USA just happened to be playing the Russian national team that evening, which was unthinkable after all that had transpired the past two days. I hadn't been on skates in over a month, had never been to New York City or overseas, and was about to be playing the best team in the world that night. We ended up being tied 4–4 in the third period but lost 9–5. What an experience playing in that game and World Championship!

For Coach Mason and myself, the story came full circle in early 2016.

Shawn Walsh, who won two NCAA championships as head coach at the University of Maine, started out as a graduate assistant at Bowling Green in 1978–79 and was an assistant coach at Michigan State for five years before coaching Maine from 1984–85 until 2001. Walsh tragically passed away at the age of 46 in September 2001. Walsh had married Ron's daughter, and their son Travis was a defenseman at Michigan State in 2016.

Ron surprised me with a call one day telling me about Travis graduating from Michigan State and looking for a place to play next. He had come to play with the Missouri Mavericks of the ECHL (formerly known as the East Coast Hockey League) in Independence, a suburb of Kansas City. That team happened to be an Islanders affiliate that season.

Ron came to town to see his grandson play in Kansas City and stayed with Barb and myself at our home. It was the first time I had seen Ron in many years. We reconnected and it was really unexpected and incredible having him visit with us.

As luck would have it, Travis was called up to the Chicago Wolves in the AHL (American Hockey League), and I happened to be going to Chicago the next day. I was going to fly to see the Wolves play, but I said to Ron, "I'll just rent a car and we'll drive there together." So we shared the eight-hour drive the next day and it was wonderful. We talked about everything, as I hadn't ever shared time like that with Coach Mason.

Ron was living in Florida then, loving his life. He was deep-sea fishing and was the picture of health. If you looked at him, you would have thought he was 20 years younger. He always had a full head of hair, he was tan from the Florida sunshine, and he had plenty of energy as usual.

We got to Chicago and Ron saw his grandson play, then I continued on with my scouting trip.

Two months later, Ron was at his daughter's house in Michigan, where he woke up one morning and was struck with a sudden heart attack. He was gone at 76. It was shocking to hear the news.

I am so fortunate to have had that special day with Coach Mason.

CHAPTER 4

1979–80: 61 GAMES BEFORE LAKE PLACID

Just because you become captain doesn't mean you have to change. Sometimes people make the mistake of trying to change. But the reason you were chosen is the person you are. Be yourself. Be a leader. Make decisions that are best as a team, not as an individual. You have issues, come together as a team and talk about them. Don't become a dictator. Become a leader, a teammate, and a friend.

—Mike Eruzione,
1980 U.S. Olympic Hockey Team captain

MY COLLEGE CAREER ENDED IN MARCH 1979 with the 6–3 loss to Herb Brooks' Minnesota Gophers in a one-game play-in for a trip to the Final Four. Little did I know that eight of these Gophers players would soon be my teammates on the 1980 Olympic ice.

In the summer of 1978, I took part in the first-ever National Sports Festival in Colorado Springs at the Air Force Academy. Now that my college games were done, I knew the next step for me would be the Olympic team tryouts being held at the 1979 Sports Festival at the Broadmoor World Arena in Colorado Springs. This is where Colorado College played their games and where many of the U.S. figure skating stars trained.

The tryouts were being held in July, and since my college season had ended in March, I needed to keep skating and find a way to stay in shape until then. In those days we didn't have personal trainers like most athletes do today. On my list of things to do was finish my senior year at Bowling Green and get on the ice and skate as much as possible to get ready for the July tryouts at the National Sports Festival. There were 80 players who were invited to the tryouts. Most were college guys, plus a handful of players who were out of college and had kept their amateur status.

We were split into four teams of 20 players and the teams were named by regions—East, West, North, and Great Lakes. The tryouts were not practices and skills competitions like you might see today. These tryouts were held as a four-team round-robin tournament with a bronze medal and gold medal game at the end, and actual medals were given out. Herb and Craig Patrick and their staff all watched the games from above.

Considering everything that was at stake and given the fierce regional rivalries that were a big part of college hockey at that time, this was a highly competitive tournament. The Great Lakes team that I played on won the gold medal game by a score of 4–2, and I was fortunate enough to score two goals in that game.

I was an offensive defenseman in college and had 52 points in 45 games my senior year. Once I got to the Olympic team and then with the Islanders, I found there were guys who did the offensive thing much better than I did, so I evolved into more of a defensive defenseman.

Once the tournament ended, all 80 players were called into a conference room in the Olympic Training Center in Colorado Springs. It was here that Herb announced the names of the 26 players who made the first cut.

We would carry one extra goalie, three extra defensemen, and two extra forwards through our 61-game pre-Olympic season. We all knew Coach Brooks would have to make more roster cuts to get down to 20 players before leaving for Lake Placid in early February.

These would be hard cuts—six guys would not be going to the Olympics. The most notable became Ralph Cox, who was the last player cut—just as Herb himself had been in 1960 before the U.S. team won America's first hockey gold medal at Squaw Valley, California.

After the 26-player team was named, we were given several days to go home and gather our belongings and then make the trek to Minnesota, which is where our home base would be until February. We lived in an apartment building in Burnsville, a suburb just south of the Twin Cities. Our locker room was in the St. Paul Civic Center, which is where we held some practices and played a few games. We also played a couple of games at the Met Center in Bloomington, which is where the North Stars played.

We were truly "America's team" as we traveled the country and played the rest of our 61 games on the road.

If there wasn't enough happening in my life that summer, another unforgettable moment was about to happen in August—getting married to my wife, Barb. We had met at Bowling Green and planned a late-summer wedding. Herb let me stay behind for a few days while the team left on its first trip to Europe to play a series of games in Holland, Finland, and Norway.

The team started with two wins over Team Holland 8–1 and 11–4. I joined the team in Finland for the start of six games against squads from the Finnish league. We won four of those contests.

Then it was on to Oslo for the final two games of our European tour. This is when the famous "skating in the dark" incident happened in Norway. Throughout the course of the season and through the Olympic games there were several of what I would call "defining moments" we faced as a team. Remember that we had only been together for a couple of weeks. The "skate in the dark" was our first test as a team with Coach Brooks. These defining moments would eventually mold us into the team we became in February that was able to make the impossible come true.

We were in the capital to play two games against the Norwegian national team. The first game was a lackluster effort by us that ended in a 3–3 tie against a team we should have beaten.

Herb was not happy.

My memory of the event was that as we skated off the ice, Herb stopped us, then told us to line up at both ends of the ice with half the team at one end and half the team at the other.

He then pulled out his whistle and said, "If you aren't going to skate in the game, then we're going to skate now!"

We started doing our "Herbies," which were conditioning/punishment drills we did throughout the year. The guys who played for Herb at Minnesota knew them all too well.

The "Herbie" drill started at the goal line. You would skate to the near blue line and back, to the red line and back, to the far blue line and back, then all the way down and back, coming to a stop at each line.

Doing three or four of these at the end of a practice was common, but doing the amount we were about to complete after a full game was incredibly grueling. We kept doing "Herbies" for what seemed like 30 minutes, if not longer.

As fans were filing out of the building, many saw us skating and decided to stay and watch what was going on. Eventually, they got bored and left. The rink manager then came out onto the ice and told Herb he had to close up and go home, but Coach Brooks said, "Leave me the keys."

We kept on skating and skating so the rink manager went over and shut off the lights, thinking that would end things.

But we kept doing our Herbies in the dark, for what seemed like close to another half hour. We were given a few short breaks to skate around slowly to catch our breath and to give our legs a rest before going back to the drills.

What ended our session after what felt like an hour? Mark Johnson, our best player and a quiet leader, slamming and breaking his stick over the top of the glass during one of our breaks.

At that point, I believe Herb knew he had gotten his point across, and he called an end to the skate.

This "skate in the dark" brought our team closer together—a shared sacrifice where you push each other to get through it.

Herb said in interviews many years later that he simply wanted to send the message that our effort in that game was unacceptable, that we needed to respect the game of hockey and come ready to work and get better every day. He wasn't going to allow us not to do that.

That was one of many defining moments and lessons that stayed with us for our entire time together.

JOHN HARRINGTON
1980 U.S. Olympic Hockey Team forward

Herb was a hard-driving coach. I think he knew what kind of people we had on our team. He had done enough background on each player when he was putting the team together, knowing what his players were like and how they would respond to something like that.

Nine of our players skated for Herb at the University of Minnesota, and all these years later they still say that we got the soft version of Herb, that he was much harder on them at Minnesota than he was on the Olympic team.

In Herb's master plan, we were going to be the best-conditioned team in Lake Placid.

Being more physically fit in the third periods of games against elite opponents would be the difference-maker in Herb's mind. He had success with the same methods at Minnesota, where his teams won national championships in 1974, 1976, and 1979. His collegiate record was 175–101–20.

Herb was tough on the team and hard on certain individuals, but the result was that he pushed you beyond your limits and always got the best out of a player and a team. The Minnesota guys helped to smooth things over for all of us from the Norway incident onward.

Herb was a master at pushing the right buttons, and he was a brilliant tactician. He knew we would have to elevate practices and game plans and that he would have to be innovative in changing our style of play for Lake Placid. In Herb's mind, the same old way of doing things was not going to work. He set high standards from the start of tryouts until the end of our last game at the Olympics.

One story about Herb that I didn't find out until many years later was when he was asked about my beard. I was the only player on the Olympic team who had a beard. Ron Mason had let me keep my beard for my senior season at Bowling Green on condition that I kept it neat and trimmed. I also had my beard at the Olympic team tryouts. Herb had never said a word to me about my beard through the whole year with the Olympic team. Hearing Herb answer the question years later when asked why I was allowed to have a beard when he had a no-beard rule, he said, "I knew Kenny wanted the beard, and I didn't want the other players growing one, so my rule became whoever had a beard at tryouts could keep it." So I was the only one who was able to have a beard that year—though looking back at photos I didn't do a very good job keeping it neat.

Going back to the skate-in-the-dark incident in Norway, he certainly got his point across, as we demolished the Norwegians 9–0 one night later.

We returned from our European trip in late September and next up were four exhibition games versus NHL teams—the Minnesota North Stars, St. Louis Blues, Atlanta Flames, and Washington Capitals. We lost all four by a combined 24–8 margin, including a 9–1 loss to the Blues in Des Moines, Iowa, and a 6–1 defeat to the Flames in Grand Forks, North Dakota.

The first game against the North Stars at the Met Center in Bloomington was in front of a huge crowd, and we lost that one 4–2. For almost all of us, this was the first time we'd been on the ice with NHL players. There were more nerves than usual, and we knew there was a lot of pride involved for those NHL teams.

They were eye-opening games for us. This was a big deal, as in my case I was property of the New York Islanders since I had been drafted by them in the fourth round in 1976, but I hadn't signed yet.

This was another important part of our learning experience as a team, and after those four defeats we went on a 10-game winning streak, twice beating the Canadian Olympic team and routing college squads including Colorado College (10–1), the University of Minnesota (8–2), and Minnesota-Duluth (4–0) in Eveleth, hometown of one of our best players, Mark Pavelich.

The streak also featured a return to my hometown of Flint, Michigan—where we beat the Generals, who played in the International Hockey League, by a score of 15–0 on October 30, 1979. The game was a homecoming for me and to win by that score didn't seem right, as I had grown up going to Flint Generals games as a kid. The funny thing was when we were leading 15–0 after two periods, Herb came into the locker room and said, "Alright, no more shots on goal. We're just going to work on our weaving and regroupings." In the third period, I don't think we had a shot on goal. Every time we would come down, we would stop, throw the puck back, and just circle back. One of Herb's favorite sayings was, "Weave, weave, weave, but don't just weave for the sake of weaving.'" That was the only time we weaved for the sake of weaving!

We played such a vast combination of opponents that it couldn't help but make us more prepared and better as a team. Coach Brooks scheduled experiences against a variety of teams and that made us ready for any brand of competition that would come our way.

The game against the Generals was just an exhibition game for this minor league team, so we didn't get their best effort. To combat this, part of Herb's master plan was that he worked out a schedule of 18 games against the Central Hockey League clubs, and those games would count in their standings.

The CHL was one of the top minor leagues at that time along with the AHL and the IHL. We played against each CHL club. That list included the Salt Lake City Golden Eagles, Indianapolis Checkers, Fort Worth Texans, Birmingham Bulls, Tulsa Ice Oilers, Houston Apollos, Oklahoma City Stars, Dallas Black Hawks, and Cincinnati Stingers.

Our record was 14–3–1 in those 18 games, and we did get their best effort and many of the games turned very physical. Here were professionals playing against a bunch of college kids, so it got rough. Intimidation was a big part of hockey at that time and these games certainly toughened us up.

41

Toss in a few AHL opponents such as the Maine Mariners and Adirondack Red Wings, more college teams (Harvard, Yale, RPI, and Wisconsin), plus four games in various U.S. venues against Gorky Torpedo from Russia, and we had played against just about every style of hockey that existed in 1979–80.

In talking to certain people "in the know" many years later, Herb created our schedule with the intention of playing a variety of styles. There would be college and international teams that could skate and pro teams that would be tougher and more physical, and there would be breaks where we would work on our conditioning and training. We didn't know it at the time, but there was a method to his madness.

My uncle Cliff, my mom's brother, met Herb and was amazed at this list of games with the opponents Herb produced to show him. Literally everything was mapped out from day one!

We did these banquets all year long since most of our games were played on the road. They would normally do a banquet honoring the team, and we would play a game later that evening. It was part of a fundraising effort to help pay the expenses of the Olympic team. Being together for six months like we were had never been done before, so they had to cover the expenses.

My Uncle Cliff was part of the group representing Flint at the banquet. Because he was my uncle and also an executive with General Motors, he sat on the dais and was next to Herb.

Herb was outspoken and could talk your ear off on the state of hockey and things he was trying to do. My uncle many years later told me the story that would always stick with him—sitting next to Herb Brooks for a couple of hours. Uncle Cliff said that Herb shared his plans for the team. He remembered Herb saying, "Here's our schedule. We're playing a skating team on this date. Here we are playing a physical team. The guys are going to need some rest here." He had the whole thing mapped out before our season even started.

We were playing for our country—with the USA across the front of the jersey—and were getting to see a lot of the country during our travels.

We got a monthly stipend for housing and for food, enough to pay rent and put food in the fridge and gas in the car—that was it. Since we were based near Minneapolis, some of the Minnesota guys may have lived at home while the rest of us lived in an apartment complex.

BILL BAKER
1980 U.S. Olympic Hockey Team defenseman

Lake Placid and our 61 games before the Olympics was the most fun that I had playing hockey. We were college kids. Nobody was making any money. We were having a good time, having fun without the stress of college. It would be very hard to implement that again. I didn't think about the getting hurt part.... I would love to go back to 1980 for 15 minutes to take it all in and remember everything better. I should have been taking notes.

There is also a funny story that Mike Eruzione tells that demonstrates just how we became close off the ice in those first weeks together.

MIKE ERUZIONE

During the pre-Olympic months when we were based in Minnesota, I was living with Ralph Cox, and we didn't have a car. So, we bought Kenny's brother's car, a green 1972 Camaro, just to get around. We paid them $400 and used the car to mostly go to practice and back. Before we left for Lake Placid, Kenny gave us the $400 back and we returned the car.

I remember that vintage green car and how it got me through my college years, and then Mike and Ralph drove it to practice and back.

43

It was an example of how everyone helped each other and how we were in this together.

The entire situation was unique, as I believe ours was the first Olympic team to spend a whole season together, to live and grow as a team both on and off the ice.

MIKE ERUZIONE

We learned to play as a team long before the Olympics. It wasn't only two weeks in Lake Placid. It was a process that started way before that. It started when we were eight or nine years old, when we started playing hockey. It was an incredible group of guys who had incredible values. Every day we came to practice, rolled up our sleeves, and went to work. Our coach, Herb Brooks, called us a lunch-pail, hard-hat group of guys. That's what we were along with some talented players. It was commitment plus respect and pride that we had as a hockey team in ourselves and each other.

It was a great time in my life. I had just finished my four years at Bowling Green, then went directly to the Olympic team. The timing couldn't have been better. My sights were set on working hard and playing on the Olympic team. There were no thoughts yet of turning pro. I just wanted to play the game at the highest level.

MIKE ERUZIONE

I never saw anybody beat Kenny Morrow one-on-one, even in practice all year. If you had a choice, you'd go down the other side instead of his side. He made the game so simple. He just kind of keeps to himself and does his job.

JOHN HARRINGTON

When you talk about what happens on the offensive end of the rink, it must start somewhere. Kenny had an ability to move the puck, to make the right play and to make an accurate play. He was that guy, somebody from whom you knew exactly what to expect. That's how he was going to play.

It was known there were NHL teams interested in signing several players who had been drafted. Herb and the Olympic Committee had to navigate the possibility that some guys could turn pro and therefore would not be eligible to play for the Olympic team.

Joe Mullen was one player who decided to sign a professional contract with the St. Louis Blues. He went on to a great 16-year NHL career, playing more than 1,000 games, scoring 502 goals, and winning three Stanley Cups (with Calgary in 1989 and Pittsburgh in 1991 and 1992) plus multiple awards.

Playing for the Olympic team was an incredible honor and a once-in-a-lifetime opportunity. There was always the chance of getting hurt, but it was a risk none of us gave a second thought about.

There wasn't anything that Herb did that was by accident. He planned and prepared everything and made sure we became a team, not a group of individuals.

JACK O'CALLAHAN

1980 U.S. Olympic Hockey Team defenseman

Herb did not negotiate accountability for anyone. He set the bar very high, and the closer we got to it the further away he moved it. That kept us grinding and pushing and made us all better players in the end.

The way Herb would later describe it, ours was a team he would have loved to get close to and have a beer with, but he had to stay distant. Craig Patrick handled the task of staying closer to the players and being a buffer between the team and our coach.

In our five-month season leading up to the Olympic Games, we finished with a 41–17–3 record, which included those four losses to those NHL teams in September and winning only three of seven games against Team Canada despite outscoring them 28–22. In those 18 CHL contests, we outscored them 85–57 overall.

In December 1979 in Lake Placid, we won a gold medal at the pre-Olympic tournament, which was a dry run for the Olympics. We were undefeated in four games, outscoring the teams by a 15–6 margin. These were the international B teams for Russia, Sweden, Canada, and Czechoslovakia, featuring some players who would be in Lake Placid in February.

This is also where we held our team Christmas party, in the small cafeteria upstairs in the Lake Placid arena where we would later win gold again. We each drew a name and anonymously bought a gag gift for that person. Herb received a whip and an oversized toy whistle. This was the only time all season where Herb let his guard down and had a beer with the guys. The gift I received was a beard trimmer.

The long "grind" before the Olympics reached its climax on February 9 at Madison Square Garden in New York, three days before we were scheduled to open at Lake Placid against Sweden. That final contest before the Winter Games was to be played against the Russian national team, who would be overwhelming favorites to win their fifth straight Olympic gold at Lake Placid.

We got our butts handed to us, losing 10–3, and as Al Michaels later described it, "10–3 made it sound closer than it was."

According to an account of the game in the *Washington Post*, "There were no visible protests to the Soviets' appearance in Madison Square Garden, although attendance was only 11,243. Those who came cheered loudly at every opportunity, be it American goal or solid American check. For a patriot, there were insufficient opportunities to celebrate either."

The *Washington Post* story went on:

"Banners were prohibited, but one enterprising group raised one for a few minutes before it was detected. It read somewhat futilely, as it turned out, 'Russians are Red, Violets are Blue, Gold Is for U.S., Nothing for U.'

"The Soviet team is so certain of winning the gold medal at Lake Placid that U.S. Coach Herb Brooks said, 'I am not worried about the Russians…. We have to be worried about the Swedes and Czechs.'

"Viktor Tikhonov, the Soviet coach, suggested that Brooks had been playing possum and said through an interpreter that, 'I had the feeling they had a lot in reserve.' He also declined to evaluate his team's performance, because to 'show the real strength of a team you have to play against a really strong opponent. Only then can you make a judgment.'"

Two things came out of that Madison Square Garden rout. First, it got us on the ice with this vaunted "Big Red Machine" and got our nerves out, and secondly, it made them overconfident that any potential future game against us would not be a challenge.

Herb and the Olympic Committee deserve immense credit for realizing the importance of playing a 61-game season leading up to the Olympics. (I played in 58 of those 61 games.)

Our team had learned a new coaching style, implemented new systems, and survived relentless training and demanding conditioning regimens. All of these elements would play a huge part in what would follow less than two weeks later about 285 miles north of Manhattan in a tiny village not far from the Canadian border.

FIVE GAMES AT LAKE PLACID

We played together for six months before the Games.
And we were a lot better than people realized.

—Mike Eruzione,
1980 U.S. Olympic Hockey Team captain

THAT STATEMENT FROM OUR CAPTAIN WAS TRUE. We had become a much better team heading into our arrival in Lake Placid than before we started our 61-game grind back in September. We now had to put aside what happened at Madison Square Garden and prepare to play our best hockey.

The feeling coming into that opening game against Sweden can best be described as "nervous excitement." Everything we did from the tryouts in July through our exhibition season was geared toward that February 12 game against a strong Swedish team. We had played our last pre-Olympic game against the Russians at Madison Square Garden on February 9, then bussed to Lake Placid afterward, up in the mountains in northern New York less than 100 miles from the Canadian border.

This was the real deal, something we had been preparing for all year. We were finally in the Olympic Village, and our families were making their way to Lake Placid. It just so happened that our first two games against Sweden and Czechoslovakia were vitally important—they would be our toughest opponents in our division, and only two teams from our group would reach the medal round. The Czechs were considered the second-best team in the world and Sweden was considered a medal contender; both were seeded ahead of us.

I don't recall what Herb said to us before that first game, but I can guess he told us that we were prepared for this moment and to "play your game," something he kept reminding us of throughout the year and the Olympic tournament.

This opening game against Sweden had a strange feel to it because it was the day before the Opening Ceremony and the building was only about half-full, with probably around 4,000 fans. Hard to believe looking back that such an important game was played under these circumstances.

Our opponent featured mostly Swedish Elite League players, the NHL equivalent in Sweden, with men of various ages, none of whom had yet played in the NHL.

Seven of their 20 players—including speedy forward Mats Näslund, goaltender Pelle Lindbergh, and my future Islanders teammate on defense, Tomas Jonsson—would go on to have successful and notable careers in the NHL.

As expected, Sweden was a very good team then and they continue to be a hockey power today. We suddenly had to face this challenge of real Olympic competition.

After finishing on the wrong end of that 10–3 rout by the Russians at the Garden in our last pre-Olympic game, our mindset had to be "in the moment," as now the games counted.

The Winter Games had started, but they hadn't officially opened yet, and we were already facing our first big test.

The tournament was structured with 12 teams split into two divisions of six teams each. A team had to finish in the top two in its division to make it into the medal round. We were going to know very quickly where our team stood after our first two games. Without pulling off an upset, we most likely would have been out of the tournament after five games.

We didn't have the luxury of easing in and getting up to speed in those first games. We came out tentative and flat in the first period against Sweden, possibly the result of too much anticipation and so much riding on this opening game.

Sweden's Sture Andersson scored at 11:04 of the first period, redirecting a centering pass from Lars Molin—who later played for the Vancouver Canucks—past Jim Craig. That was the only goal of the opening 20 minutes.

I did have a breakaway in the first period, when the game was still scoreless—a great chance to score the opening goal of the game and the Olympics. It was a break-in down the middle of the ice where I came in and fired a low shot on the fly while there was an opponent racing back behind me. Lindbergh made the initial save and slid out of the net while doing so, with the puck ending up behind the goal. My momentum carried me past the net, and I circled behind, picking up the loose puck with a clear path for a wraparound at the other side into a wide-open net.

I had this golden opportunity to score the first goal of the Olympics for us, but just as I went to stuff it in at the post with no goalie in the net, the defenseman who had come racing back stuck his stick out and stopped it on the goal line.

No goal for me and no lead for our team.

I can still see that wide-open net vividly in my mind. I can't believe I didn't score!

We came into the locker room after our first 20 minutes of Olympic play, and that is when we got to see the full force of a Herb Brooks wake-up call. Rob McClanahan, who was one of the nine players on this 1980 Olympic team who played for Brooks at Minnesota, went nose to nose with Herb, who had come charging in through the locker-room door looking to confront him.

Robbie had taken a hard hit into the boards in the opening period and had suffered a deep thigh bruise that he tried to play through. Apparently, the trainer and Rob had come to a decision that he wouldn't be able to continue playing, and Rob had started to take his equipment off.

This confrontation may not have been a shock to the guys who played for Herb, but I sat there in disbelief watching this unfold, as they yelled and screamed at each other face to face. I was thinking, *This can't be happening; 20 minutes into our first game and we are falling apart!*

In hindsight all these years later, it is much clearer to see why Herb did what he did in the locker room at that moment. He knew Robbie could handle it—he knew our team was strong enough to handle it—and it was an opportunity to jolt us after a lackluster first period.

It was a stunning tactic at the time, but it shocked us into realizing this was not just another game in our long season. A couple of players jumped up and separated Herb and McClanahan, and Robbie did return to the ice in that game, skating with a limp, and ended up scoring some huge goals for us the rest of the tournament.

The incident proved to be another one of those defining moments for the team, like the dark arena skate in Norway. These were dramatic moments that brought the team closer together. We needed a wake-up call, and Herb gave us one.

After going through most of the second period without scoring, Dave Silk finally notched our first goal and tied the game with 28 seconds left—with assists by Mike Ramsey and Mark Johnson.

Sweden then took the lead again at 4:45 of the third on a goal by defenseman Thomas Eriksson, who later played 208 games for the Philadelphia Flyers, where he was Lindbergh's teammate.

And then we played the rest of a tense third period pushing to get that tying goal.

The game was fast-paced and up and down the ice with both teams having good chances, but Craig and Lindbergh stopped everything. Give Sweden credit; they were a medal favorite and they frustrated us. It came down to the final minute, and we were behind by a goal. Herb made the decision to pull Jim Craig for an extra attacker with 41 seconds remaining and a face-off in the left corner of Sweden's end.

As I have said many times over the years when asked about our "miracle" gold medal win, a lot of things had to go right along the way, and this was one of those moments.

On the ice for the face-off were Schneider and Silk, with Pavelich taking the draw. Mike Ramsey and Bill Baker were on the points and Mark Johnson was on as the extra attacker. The face-off went back to Ramsey, who took a shot from the left point that was blocked. He collected the loose puck and sent it over to Baker at the other point, who rimmed it behind the net to Schneider, who then bumped it further along the boards to Pavelich.

Pav then made a brilliant pass into the middle of the ice to Baker sliding down from the point and he ripped a slap shot all in one motion. Pav was a magician with the puck and always seemed to make the dazzling play look easy; this was another example of his wizardry.

Baker had a great shot, and he most definitely showed it as he rifled the puck past Lindbergh!

BILL BAKER
1980 U.S. Olympic Hockey Team defenseman
It was like in slow motion. I shot, but I couldn't really see where the puck went from there.

Baker's shot slammed into the netting behind Lindbergh, who never had a chance, with 27 seconds left. What an exhilarating burst of excitement, going from sitting on the bench seconds away from a loss to a huge tie. We couldn't afford to lose our first game—it would have been demoralizing and it would have put us behind in our quest to make the medal round.

We still joke with Mike Eruzione about Billy's goal being the biggest one of the tournament.

There was no overtime in these Olympic Games, so it was key to get this tie and in such unlikely fashion—it felt like we won. A huge boost!

55

Baker firing home that tying goal was amazing, especially coming against a very good young goalie like Lindbergh. I saw a quote years later from Herb saying that if he knew we would have to play against the superb Lindbergh, he wished the Flyers would have signed Pelle when they drafted him in 1979 so he wouldn't have faced us in Lake Placid.

I would play against Pelle and the Flyers many more times in the years ahead. He had his best season in 1984–85, going 40–17–7, winning the Vezina Trophy, and leading Philadelphia to the Stanley Cup Final, where the Flyers lost in five games to Edmonton.

Lindbergh was a formidable opponent that day in Lake Placid and later, in the NHL, on the ice at Nassau Coliseum and at the Spectrum. Tragically, Pelle died when he was just 26 years old in a November 1985 car accident near the Flyers' training facility in New Jersey, a very sad day for hockey.

The day after the Sweden game was the Opening Ceremony, which was held on a cold February day at the fairgrounds a couple of miles outside of town. It was surreal taking part in a ceremony I had grown up watching on TV, and here I was marching into the stadium in front of our home crowd.

The relay route of the Olympic torch retraced the American Revolution Bicentennial Trail, passing through Washington, D.C.; New York; and Philadelphia. On February 6, 1980, the flame reached Albany, where the relay split in two, with one route going through the Adirondacks and the other up the Champlain Valley. Two days later, the double flames were reunited at Lake Placid.

The torch lighting was done by a non-athlete that year. Dr. Charles Morgan Kerr, a psychiatrist at the University of Arizona, was the last of 52 torchbearers in the United States.

It was of course thrilling to be part of the Olympic Opening Ceremony as the host country, walking in wearing our cowboy jackets and hats and seeing athletes from all the other countries in one place.

A downside of that day was the bus system collapse. Many in the crowd, including our families, had to wait hours in the cold, and some took to walking a couple of miles back downtown in the freezing cold. There weren't enough buses available in Lake Placid to handle all the people in town for the Olympics and get them to events, and the roads weren't able to handle the extra traffic. This made major headlines until organizers finally added more buses and got the transportation straightened out several days later.

On February 14, the day after the Opening Ceremony, we faced Czechoslovakia in our second critical contest in a row, and we played what I would describe as our best game of the tournament. There was a buzz in the arena, and it was end-to-end and hard-hitting action right from the drop of the puck, with a lot of goals being scored as we were skating and generating offense. It was the style Herb built our team to play.

Remember that the Czechs were considered the second-best team in the world and the only team many believed had a chance to beat the Soviet Union. Their roster was loaded, starting with the three Šťastný brothers from Slovakia—Peter, Anton, and Marian—who would all later defect to play for the Quebec Nordiques in the NHL.

The fans were loud and energetic throughout, with sustained cheers and chants of "USA, USA" echoing in the arena.

I injured my shoulder on the first shift of the game. Seconds after the opening face-off, the puck went over to the boards near their bench and I leveled Marion Šťastný with a hit that caught him by surprise. The play continued on for a few more seconds as he got back to his feet and the puck eventually was dumped into my corner.

I went back for the puck, and he came charging in behind me and quickly got his revenge for my hit on him by running me into the end boards. He hit me hard and I felt my shoulder crunch, and I knew that wasn't good. That hit separated my shoulder, but it was mild enough that it wouldn't keep me from playing.

All hockey players play through injuries, and this was no different. The good thing is that first shift set the tone for the rest of the game. With all that was at stake, both teams let it be known that this was going to be a rugged battle right from the start.

The Czechs scored first on a goal by Jaroslav Pouzar—who later won three Stanley Cups with Edmonton—at 2:23 of the opening period before Eruzione tied it at 4:39.

A minute later, the relentless Schneider-Pavelich-Harrington line—known as "the Coneheads"—combined on a Pavelich goal to put us up 2–1 at 5:45.

Marian Šťastný then tied it 2–2 at 12:07.

We kept skating and pressing and hitting, and that pressure started to pay dividends. Schneider put us up 3–2 at 4:33 of the second on another setup by Pavelich, then Johnson scored at 15:28 to give us a 4–2 lead.

The crowd and the atmosphere in the building were electric. Phil Verchota and Buzz Schneider then widened our stunning lead to 6–2 in the third period, and we finished off the onslaught with a goal by Rob McClanahan at 10:54.

It was a 7–3 final score, and despite being outshot 31–27, we took the play to them with our speed and tenacity and spirit. This was an effort and a team that America could be proud of with the collective relentless determination we brought to the ice that day. This had to be what Coach Brooks had envisioned for our team, the reason he trained and pushed us so hard for all these prior months—for a game and result like this against a hockey power like Czechoslovakia.

BUZZ SCHNEIDER
1980 U.S. Olympic Hockey Team forward
Herb was tough but fair, and his word was golden. I believed in him, that's for sure. I loved playing for him. We won the NCAAs playing for Minnesota in 1974 when I was a sophomore. It was the first one ever for the Gophers…. Herb was the perfect coach for our team heading for Lake Placid. He picked the guys who could skate.

The win over the Czechs was a springboard for us and was paced by the Conehead line.

JOHN HARRINGTON
1980 U.S. Olympic Hockey Team forward
We were just three guys who buzzed all over the place and Pav had the eye. Herb kept us in check, though, knowing we would have theoretically easier opponents in the next three games of the round-robin. He wanted to make sure we stayed on an even keel.

The next two games against Norway and Romania were ones we were supposed to win. The Norway game was played in the old 1932 rink that was attached to the new arena; each team had to play a game there. Norway was a physically big team that skated well, and they presented a challenge for us in the early going. In front of 1,500 people, we fell behind 1–0 on a goal by Geir Myhre 4:19 into the game. Their goalie, Jim Marthinsen, stopped all 16 shots in the first period.

It was a very sluggish and sloppy first period for us, probably a bit of a hangover from the big win two nights earlier. In the locker room between periods, Herb read us the riot act. A team like ours had to win the games we were supposed to win and then upset some of the teams we weren't supposed to beat.

Conditioning was huge for us, and we kept learning that lesson as we fell behind in six out of the seven games during the Olympic tournament.

We played our best in the third periods. That punishing conditioning we were put through during the previous six months made us that much stronger than the other teams. This is what the Russians would do to other teams, and Herb wasn't going to let that happen to us. We would be able to skate with them and play with them in the third period. The result is we simply outworked and outskated other teams late in games, which was the biggest reason we won the gold medal.

Norway was the same opponent we had a 3–3 tie against back in September in the first of two games in Norway. That game forced the infamous postgame skating punishment in the dark.

Norway took a penalty almost immediately at the beginning of the second period, and Eruzione quickly tied it at the 41-second mark. Johnson scored four minutes later before Silk made it 3–1 at 13:31.

We came out of the locker room and got a spark with that quick Eruzione goal and then asserted ourselves to take the lead and not look back.

My Bowling Green teammate and roommate Mark Wells scored at 4:28 of the third period, and then I scored my only goal of the Olympics at 11:29 with a low shot from the right point that found its way through traffic and past Marthinsen.

After narrowly missing my chance against Sweden four days prior, at least I could say I scored a goal at the Olympics.

Once we got going after that sluggish opening period, we dominated the game overall, winning 5–1 with a 43–22 shots advantage. We should have had a few more goals, but their goalie played well. We overcame some adversity and fought through to take a game we were supposed to win and now were 2–0–1 along with Sweden at the top of our group.

Next came Romania on February 18, a relatively easy 7–2 win with a 51–21 shots advantage in our favor. It ended up being the only game at Lake Placid in which we didn't trail.

All four lines contributed in this game, the only one in which we scored first, with Schneider finishing off yet another Coneheads passing display to open the scoring.

Winger Eric Strobel made it 2–0 at 15:52 of the first before Wells scored at 9:34 of the second to make it 3–0.

Romania's Doru Tureanu broke through at 13:40 of the second before Schneider and Steve Christoff scored to increase our lead to 5–1 early in the third. Alexandru Hălăucă managed another goal for Romania before Neal Broten and Rob McClanahan finished the scoring for the 7–2 final.

Next up to finish off our preliminary round was a game against West Germany on February 20.

West Germany was historically a tough opponent for the USA, playing a physical North American brand of hockey. The West Germans also had kept the Americans from winning a bronze medal at the 1976 Winter Olympics and beat the Brooks-coached national teams twice in the 1979 World Championships.

We knew this grudge match was going to be a tough test for us.

Like clockwork, we fell behind, but this time by two goals as they scored 1:50 into the game and again on the power play 15 seconds before the end of the first period.

But we fought through another early-game deficit and we found our legs in our fifth game in nine days. We scored four straight goals, two each in the second and third periods, for a 4–2 final.

It was a good win and a good sign for our team. We finished 4–0–1 in the preliminary round and were heading into the medal round. Facing adversity and coming from behind in four of our first five games, we were showing perseverance and building character with our young team. We were a team with an identity, there was a relentless determination to our play, and we were getting stronger and dominating third periods.

As Herb Brooks described us at one time, "We were a hard-hat and lunch-pail team that came to work every day." We were a team that embodied those great American traits, and I believe that is a big reason why so many Americans remember 1980 so well.

"We're so proud of them," Bev Baker, mother of Bill Baker, was quoted as saying after the win over West Germany. Mrs. Baker was wearing a red, white, and blue sweater with stars and stripes woven into it. She said it belonged to Mark Johnson's mother, adding, "We all have taken turns wearing it to each game."

In our rally against West Germany, two of the goals came from McClanahan, who was one of our best players after his opening-game injury. Both goals were assisted by defenseman Dave Christian and forward Mark Johnson.

One of Herb's most brilliant maneuvers with our team was when he moved Dave Christian from his normal forward position back to defense. This happened at some point during our pre-Olympic season. Dave was highly skilled and had the hockey IQ to be able to make the switch—not many players could do that. He came from a family of U.S. hockey royalty—his father, Bill, and his uncle, Roger, won the USA's first hockey gold in 1960. Dave's nephew Brock Nelson is a current star for the New York Islanders.

Dave brought a dynamic element to our defense, and he was involved in so many big moments for us in Lake Placid. He could skate the puck up ice and generate offense almost as a fourth forward.

With 1:29 left in the second, Eruzione dug the puck out of the corner and fed Strobel in front; Strobel's shot rebounded back to Neal Broten, and he rifled home a low shot.

Early in the third period, Christian again sent McClanahan in on goaltender Sigmund Suttner, and McClanahan snapped home a wrister from the right side. Phil Verchota's deflection of a Christian slap shot completed the scoring, giving Christian three assists.

I saw Coach Brooks as a great "bench boss," a coach who was in command behind the bench during games.

BILL BAKER

Herb would change forwards and defense and was in control of the whole bench. He had a tremendous ability to know what was going on during a game.

My defense partner was 19-year-old Mike Ramsey, our youngest player and the first American to be taken in the first round of the NHL draft. Mike was selected 11th overall by the Buffalo Sabres in 1979. He was super talented. He was big and could skate; he would rush the puck up ice for a scoring chance at one end and deliver a big body check at the other end of the ice. He went on to a long and very successful NHL career. We complemented each other well with our styles of play.

Thanks to Herb's approach to picking this Olympic team and having us live and play together for six months and 61 games, facing pro, college, and international teams who all played different styles of hockey, we were able to grow together both on and off the ice to become a team.

With the intense conditioning, playing a system of puck control that was new to us, and innovative training methods, Herb had prepared us, and it paid off as we were undefeated through our first five games.

As Herb would say, "I wanted to take the Europeans' game and throw it right back at them."

Dumping and chasing wasn't going to work. We spent those six months together working every day at practice and every game on those very things.

Another one of Herb's great quotes was "Plan your work, then work your plan."

Part of Herb's plan was to keep distractions to a minimum, so he kept us away from press conferences and other stuff going on around us.

As the schedule dictated, we just didn't have a lot of free time to get out and see other events. We were staying a couple miles outside of town, so we would have to find transportation and then fight the crowds and everything else. It was hard to get out and see other events because everything was so spread out. Skiing was up in the mountains; speed skating was at the Oval in town, and other events like bobsledding and ski jumping were outside of town. I didn't get to see any of the figure skating, but I did get to see Eric Heiden win one of his five gold medals in a speed skating event.

Otherwise, we were practicing on off days and trying to rest and eat right and maybe see our families in between games every other day.

After beating West Germany, we now had a medal round battle looming against the Russians, and we had less than 48 hours to prepare.

CHAPTER 6

THE LONGEST 10 MINUTES

LOOKING BACK ON THE HOURS LEADING UP to facing the Soviets on February 22, 1980, what is remarkable is how Coach Brooks was able to keep us isolated throughout the Olympics, which allowed us to keep to our routine and stay away from distractions.

It was play a game one day then practice the next throughout the entire Games, and I recall our mindset wasn't much different before this game compared with all previous games. I am sure there was some nervous anticipation in the room, but there was the same routine and preparation we were accustomed to. We were a young team—with an average age of just 22—and I don't know that we were feeling a whole lot of pressure.

The anticipation of the game being USA against Russia during such a turbulent time made it David versus Goliath on ice. Al Michaels described it as "the Cold War being played out on a sheet of ice in Lake Placid." The odds were stacked against us, and all this was happening on an Olympic and international stage.

We had been building momentum, getting better and coming from behind in almost every game. We were improving and gaining confidence as the tournament went along. Because we were huge underdogs—having lost to the Russians 10–3 in our final pre-Olympic game less than two weeks before—there was less pressure on us. We could just go out there and play, as we were expected to lose—and to lose big.

Our team was simply conditioned to play the way we had played for the entire tournament, and we kept getting stronger each period. Looking back, it was all part of Herb's master plan. That drubbing at Madison Square Garden on February 9 turned into a game, and ultimately a loss, that proved beneficial to us.

Ironically, the Soviets' rout of us in the game at Madison Square Garden did them more harm than good. The score was 6–1 Russia after two periods, which featured some highlight-reel goals, including a 360-degree spin-o-rama goal on the fly by Sergei Makarov. We were amazed and disheartened at the same time. It was the men against the boys that night.

Once the Olympic games started in Lake Placid a few days later, we were playing good hockey and building momentum through the first five games, while the Soviets had a couple of games that were closer than expected. Canada had them tied in the third period, and in typical Russian fashion, they scored two late goals to win the game.

"These guys are human, and they aren't unbeatable" was the perpetual message from Herb.

There was no guarantee we would even play the Soviets in the Olympics. We had to finish in the top two teams in our division to make it to the medal round, which was our goal from the start. And we did play our way into the medal round along with Sweden, Finland, and the Soviets.

The Russians were considered the best team in the world and had four dangerous lines. Their fourth line would have been a first line on most teams. They had a handful of young stars, but they were also a seasoned championship team that had won world championships and every Olympic gold medal since 1960.

They had Makarov, a 21-year-old superstar, and Vladimir Krutov, a 19-year-old new-wave Soviet player known as the "Russian Tank." They had brothers Alexander and Vladimir Golikov plus Helmut Balderis, Alexei Kasatonov, 35-year-old legend Boris Mikhailov, 32-year-old Vladimir Petrov, and 21-year-old star defenseman Viacheslav Fetisov, plus the scoring machines Alexander Maltsev and Valeri Kharlamov and all-world goaltender Vladislav Tretiak in net.

We weren't particularly focusing on specific players on their star-studded roster. It was instead a conscious approach to play our game and not let the Soviets play theirs.

"Play your game! Play your game!" Herb emphasized to us constantly as he stood behind the bench. He didn't want us to get caught up in the moment. I remember him reinforcing this, especially in the third period as we were holding on to a one-goal lead.

After the team was selected and from the start of our season, Herb was intent on doing things differently. Our training, conditioning, and style of play were going to be unlike what any other USA hockey team had prepared for.

That's also when we were introduced to many of his favorite sayings:

"Weave, weave, weave, but don't just weave for the sake of weaving."

"The legs feed the wolf."

"You're playing worse every day, and right now you're playing like it's the middle of next month!"

"You don't have enough talent to win on talent alone."

And the one that left everybody scratching their heads, "You look like a monkey screwing a football out there."

That last one is a classic! The guys embraced it, even though we are still trying to figure out what it truly means.

The bottom line is that Herb got his points across. He let us play to our talent and it worked.

Herb essentially said throughout the months before Lake Placid, "I'm going to give you guys a lot of freedom offensively," but he also told us, "When you don't have the puck, I will demand you guys are structured and play a sound defensive game."

If you asked all of us players before the Miracle game what our goal was, it was to keep the game close. This was in line with Herb's defensive philosophy back to his college teams.

STEVE JANASZAK
University of Minnesota and 1980 U.S. Olympic Hockey Team goaltender; 1979 NCAA national champion
Coach Brooks built his teams from the defensive side. In the five years I played for the guy, we *always* had excellent defensemen. The objective was to win the 1–0 game; make no mistakes and capitalize on at least one of the mistakes your opponent made.

Herb's speech to us before the game will forever be remembered as one of the greatest motivational speeches ever given.

Imagine 20 young hockey players packed into a small locker room, minutes from stepping onto the ice to play in the game of their lives. Herb walked in, looked around the quiet room, then said, "You were born to be a player. You were meant to be here. This is your moment!"

When the game started, we knew the Russians could explode at any time and put a game out of reach early. We were guarding against that from the beginning. The big thing we wanted to avoid was giving up three or four goals in five minutes. We knew they were capable of that and could take over a game with their offensive firepower. With Jimmy Craig playing so well, plus the resilience and confidence we had developed through the Olympic tournament, we were able to keep it close.

Krutov started the scoring for Russia at 9:12 of the first with an assist to Kasatonov. Then Buzz Schneider—who scored a hat trick against Tretiak at the 1975 World Championships in West Germany—tied the game with another goal against the star Soviet goalie at 14:03 on a set up by Mark Pavelich.

Buzz told me, "For some reason, I have his number."

BUZZ SCHNEIDER
1980 U.S. Olympic Hockey Team forward
That goal was special. I played against the Soviets maybe a dozen times in all those world tournaments going back to 1975. And I was one of three players to ever score a hat trick against Tretiak.

Makarov put Russia ahead 2–1 at 17:34 of the first before arguably our most important goal of the tournament, when Mark Johnson scored with one second left in the period.

This goal developed from something we practiced throughout the year. If a defenseman had the puck and didn't have a play, rather than dump it in, we would circle a forward behind, drop the puck back, and that player would pick up speed and attack. On this play I dropped it back to Dave Christian, who fired the puck at the Soviet net, where Tretiak was forced to make a save.

Then Tretiak somehow left a careless rebound with only a couple of seconds remaining in the period. Since it was a play we had rehearsed, the instinct was there, and Johnson didn't quit on the play. He split the Soviet defense and tucked the rebound past Tretiak with one second remaining to stun them. We went into the locker room tied at 2–2, and that gave us a big boost.

When the second period started, you could see the Russians' determination to score three or four or five goals and put the game out of reach.

We knew they could score at will. They outshot us 12–2 in the second period, but Jimmy made big saves and we hung in there even as Russia scored the only goal of the middle period. That came from Maltsev at 2:18. Still, we had minimized the damage. We were only down a goal heading into the third, which had proven to be our best period throughout the Olympics.

After the second period, there was a unique energy in our room. We had the home crowd, and we were only down one goal. Al Michaels was quoted many years later saying that before the game he and Ken Dryden "were only hoping that the game would stay close."

We were feeling pretty good at that point—there were not a lot of nerves. If we had been tied or maybe up a goal heading into that final period, maybe we would have been tighter. Looking back, the best scenario was the one we were in: down 3–2 and in a position where we could open up and go for it rather than sit back.

It happens all the time in sports where protecting a lead with a "prevent defense" leads to sitting back and preventing a win.

JOHN HARRINGTON
1980 U.S. Olympic Hockey Team forward
We knew we could skate faster than them, and it was just our mental conditioning as well as physical conditioning. That was such a big part of our success.

Backup goaltender Vladimir Myshkin had come in for the second period, and we only had two shots on him during those 20 minutes.

A lot has been made of the Soviet team pulling Tretiak after the last-second Mark Johnson goal. The Russian players look back at it and say it was a huge mistake.

At the time, I don't remember us even talking about it in our locker room. It wasn't like we went in and said, "Tretiak has been pulled, we've got them now."

We had scored two goals on Tretiak in the first period. And there's no saying we wouldn't have scored two more. The fact that he had been pulled wasn't a factor for us at all. It didn't affect anything with how we approached the rest of the game. We just kept playing our game, as Herb preached.

The third period was unique for many reasons. In looking back, the final 20 minutes were broken down into three segments.

The tension and anticipation in the arena were palpable. The play was sluggish through the first seven minutes. There were a lot of whistles, and we just couldn't get anything going. Still, it remained only a one-goal margin for the Russians.

Also, I had been butting heads all game long with Krutov. He wasn't tall or exceptionally huge, but he was thick and he played a North American–style game.

He and I had collided several times, and there was one point during the second period where he was digging away at the puck in our crease and I cross-checked him into Jim Craig, who stayed down on the ice for a couple of minutes.

There was a pile-up at the crease. I got a penalty and the Russians got a penalty.

Later in the game, there were a few more times when Krutov and I ran into each other. On this particular play in the third period, I hit him at our blue line, and the puck went back into the corner. Neal Broten grabbed the puck and skated behind our net. I was standing in front and Krutov skated by and high-sticked me up around my ear, then slashed at Neal's stick.

Looking back at the game on video, Ken Dryden said on the broadcast, "They got him for a slash on Neal Broten," but the penalty really was a high-stick on me. That call was at the 6:47 mark of the third, two minutes for high-sticking on Krutov. The penalty was a result of Krutov and me going at each other all game. One thing led to another and then a penalty got called because of the battle within the game between Krutov and myself.

Not much was happening for us on the ensuing power play until the final rush, when Dave Silk made a play at their blue line as he was absorbing a hip check. He threw the puck toward the net, and it took a fortunate bounce off a Soviet defenseman's skate before Johnson swept it in to tie the game 3–3 at 8:39. It was Johnson's second goal of the game, and what a big one it was! His goals were definitely timely and big.

Right after that goal, the next shift the Russians kept the pressure on and had a good scoring chance and another soon after. They hit the outside of the post on one and missed another chance at the post. Again, we were resilient. Jimmy made the saves, and we didn't sit back.

At the exact 10:00 mark, our miracle moment arrived as the puck found Mike Eruzione's stick in the high slot.

As he skated down the middle of the ice, Mike snapped a shot off his back foot using a defenseman as a screen and the puck found its way past Myshkin. That seeing-eye shot—with Harrington on one side of Myshkin and Baker on the other as the shot flies past the goaltender—has been watched and rewatched millions of times.

BILL BAKER
1980 U.S. Olympic Hockey Team defenseman

Pav was in the corner with the puck, and they were late on the line change, so I jumped up into the play. I was going to the net and I thought he was passing it to me, but there's no way Pav would have missed that badly. The pass was behind me but Rizzo was right there. I put my stick down, and I don't know if Myshkin thought I might tip it but the shot went in just as I was going by the net. And the photo of the moment has me with my stick in the air.

That's when we jam-piled onto the ice, something we did all tournament from the first game to the last. When we scored a goal, our whole bench emptied. It was allowed, we did it, and it was part of who we were, a group of excited young kids playing for our country.

I remember I was on the outside of the pile, and I looked up at the clock and there was exactly 10 minutes to go. I distinctly remember saying to myself, "This is going to be the longest 10 minutes of my life, trying to hold a one-goal lead against this team."

That is when the period moved into its third segment. Following those quiet initial seven minutes, then scoring two goals in less than 90 seconds, we had this endless final 10 minutes of trying to hold off this legendary Soviet team that could seemingly score at will.

The clock was slowly winding down until we had a minute and a half left and a face-off in their end. We had Johnson, McClanahan, and Silk up front and Ramsey and myself on defense.

You couldn't script any of this ending; it just happened.

People have often asked what it was like being out there for the last minute of that epic game. My answer: the only thing on my mind was getting the puck out over the blue line! *Don't spend any time in your own end,* I kept telling myself. My only mission was to try and keep the puck out of our end at all costs.

CRAIG PATRICK
Assistant general manager and assistant coach at Lake Placid
Quite frankly, I think we were in better condition than the Russians. I got to know some of them. They believe we outskated them.

The Russians kept attacking, but we somehow managed to hold them off. Petrov had a chance in the final minute with a backhand shot in close that missed the net. Near the very end, the puck was in the other corner and there was a huge collision along the boards between Ramsey and a Soviet defenseman with about 15 seconds to go, then Johnson knocked the puck behind the net to my side with 10 seconds left.

I went into the corner knowing there wasn't much time remaining, and I didn't want to move it up the boards because Soviet skaters had that covered. I fired the puck up the ice away from the boards, knowing it was open. Normally I wouldn't take that chance throwing the puck up the middle but, in this circumstance, it was the best play. The puck hit Silk out by the blue line; otherwise it would have gone down the ice and time would have run out.

It hit Dave and bounced down by his feet and then was knocked over to the boards and that's how the "Miracle" game ended. Time just ran out on the Soviets and their gold medal dominance.

Thankfully, I get to hear my name in the famous Al Michaels call, which still gives me chills when I hear it all these years later: *Morrow is back there, now Johnson, 19 seconds. Johnson over to Ramsey. Bilyaletdinov gets checked by Ramsey. McClanahan is there. The puck is still loose…. 11 seconds, you've got 10 seconds. The countdown is going on right now. Morrow, up to Silk. Five seconds left in the game. Do you believe in MIRACLES? YES!!*

(With Dryden's "unbelievable!" for added effect.)

When I knew it was over, I threw my arms up in the air and circled back toward our net, and that's the famous photo of the team celebrating in our end that made the cover of *Sports Illustrated*. No words were needed.

DAN BROOKS
Herb Brooks' son

It was a magical and emotional moment. It was much more than a sports story. It was an American story.

I hadn't remembered what I did in those seconds after the buzzer sounded and the game ended. In the well-known photo, I am standing behind the pile of players with my head turned to the side. I wasn't quite sure what my reaction was when the buzzer sounded until I watched replays many years later from a different angle and realized Mark Johnson

THE LONGEST 10 MINUTES

and I had grabbed each other, then I ended up behind the pile of white jerseys near our net.

Words can't adequately describe the moment.

For me it was, *Did this really just happen?*

For the Soviet players who rarely got to show their emotions, it had to be shock and disbelief.

BILL BAKER

We win and we were celebrating while the camera panned to them. They had a few smirks going, almost like they were saying, "Wow, that looks like fun." Like, "Maybe we should try that sometime."

Herb kept saying to us all year, "Look at these guys; they are not playing very well. These guys can be beat."

As only Herb could do, he kept trying to bring them down to our level—that the Russians were human.

The way the tournament was set up, Herb knew there was a chance we would not play them, but he prepared us all year as if we would. Our goal at the start from when the team had our first practice was to make the medal round. That meant we would be playing the Soviets.

BILL BAKER

Lake Placid taught us how important it was to be in shape in the third periods. We carried that throughout the slate of games before the Olympics and during the Games. We were motivated, and with the emotion we played with, we always had a chance. We had a shot against the Russians, and we beat them.

When you look back, it's almost like Herb knew that we would get our chance and pull something off. It was all part of Herb's master plan.

DAN BROOKS

My dad was young, just 42 years old in 1980. I saw how hard he was on his players, but he was committed and driven. He was so prepared, so focused, and those players knew that. They must have had confidence he was standing behind the bench, and I think they took on the identity of their coach.

Out of respect for all-time-great player Boris Mikhailov, Herb even found a way to get across his message with humor. Boris closely resembled Stan Laurel, the comic actor who was part of the legendary Laurel and Hardy duo with Oliver Hardy.

Herb would say, "Stan Laurel? You guys can't beat Stan Laurel?"

Knowing what I know now, it was all part of his psychological plan of getting our team in the right mindset.

It continues to be a memorable and iconic moment in American sports history. It is remarkable what Herb was able to orchestrate and pull off and what our team was able to accomplish.

CHAPTER 7

THE AFTERMATH

We used to say we would have liked to stay together as a team and see how we would have done in the pros. Food for thought.

—Rob McClanahan,
1980 U.S. Olympic Hockey Team forward

AFTER THE UPSET WIN AGAINST RUSSIA, we were obviously on cloud nine, but it wasn't as if we were spraying champagne like we had just won the championship of the world.

We had been coming from behind all through the Olympic tournament, and holding on to upset the Soviets was a monumental win for our young team.

But we needed to temper our emotions, as we still had another game to play against a very good Finland team that was seeded ahead of us.

The win against Russia was on Friday evening. We had a practice Saturday morning before our Sunday morning game against Finland, and Herb came in and put us through our hardest practice of the entire tournament. It was almost like he was angry.

We were looking at each other, wondering, *What is he so mad about?*

He felt he had to bring us back to earth very quickly after that euphoric win over the Soviets the night before. Normally a team would do a light skate with such a short turnaround between games, but Herb wasn't going to let us bask in the glory of what had happened Friday.

Maybe no other coach but Herb Brooks would have done what he did on that day between the two biggest games of our lives.

Herb had also prepared *himself* for this pivotal moment, which makes what followed all the more remarkable.

We had to "forget" Friday night's epic win because we had one more tough opponent to overcome in order to secure the gold medal. If we didn't beat Finland, we would lose the gold, and there may not even have been a silver medal or any medal at all for us because of the strange math at work in the medal round. There was a chance that if we had lost by a certain number of goals, we could have ended up with nothing.

Not likely, but possible, and that was a shocking thought!

So that extra reminder—that one last driving practice—was necessary, and Herb had prepared us all year long with our training to be able to handle it.

That Saturday morning, I remember seeing more New York State Troopers around our practice. They were stationed everywhere in Lake Placid for security. Some of them were asking for autographs—that is probably when I signed my very first one.

We knew that facing Finland would be a sobering test, because they were very good, an experienced team that played more of a North American style of hockey. What was in our favor was that we were completely into a groove and on a roll by that time. We were playing well and were prepared both mentally and physically for this last challenge.

Herb was intent on keeping us isolated and away from the press throughout the tournament, especially after the Russian game. As players we weren't doing formal or daily interviews with the media, and I am sure there were a lot of requests by that point. We had been kept in a bubble and that continued to work in our favor—no distractions.

MIKE ERUZIONE
1980 U.S. Olympic Hockey Team captain

We didn't know what was going on around the world, around the country. We were just playing. We had no clue the country was watching the way they were. That's what was great about it. We weren't allowed to talk to the media. We were in a cocoon. There was no Twitter, no Facebook, no

ESPN! Cable television wasn't really around yet. Imagine if it happened today? Wow!

Herb knew what we were there for and that we still had to show up and beat this team on Sunday with the whole country and the world watching. He did a masterful job of deflecting everything. He and Craig Patrick protected us. We were a group of young men and keeping our feet on the ground was crucial.

I laughingly say that I missed out on joining with people dancing in the streets after we beat the Soviets that Friday evening. I never realized until years later—when watching some of the videos on YouTube showing a few of our players with their parents among the throngs of people on Main Street—what I had actually missed. I stayed behind at the arena after the win because I had to ice down my injured shoulder after the game. I took my time and once I finished, I went out a side door and hopped into a van back to the Olympic Village, which was outside of town. The driver took the back streets to avoid the wild celebrations and people jamming Main Street downtown. I never really knew or saw the craziness that was going on in Lake Placid—I missed all of it!

I went back to my trailer, where we didn't even have a TV set. We did have a small transistor radio, and I was able to come across a few AM channels. Every radio station I tuned into up in the mountains of upstate New York was talking about the game. That was my first realization that all of this was bigger than we thought.

We knew the people in Lake Placid were thrilled, but I had no idea people outside of Lake Placid were talking about the dramatic upset win over the Soviets. I remember listening to one station where callers were chiming in and this one guy said, "They [the U.S. team] could be playing the Montreal Canadiens on Sunday and they would beat them!"

That was amazing to hear.

If someone had told me on February 23, 1980, about the level of impact this stunning victory over the Soviet team would continue to have more than 40 years later, I wouldn't have believed them. The unique bond we developed as a team certainly helped us get through those magical 48 hours, even if it has taken all these years to fully absorb and appreciate the scope of what we accomplished.

BUZZ SCHNEIDER
1980 U.S. Olympic Hockey Team forward

It was fun to go through it with the guys, and probably no one understands it like us 20 guys, a special group. Everybody belonged on that team. Herb picked the right players. All the guys could skate, and it worked out well. It is one of those phenomenal things that is hard to explain.

Our 10-year reunion at Lake Placid was the first time we were together again since winning the gold. At that time, we were saying to ourselves, *Wow, I can't believe they are bringing us back 10 years later.*

We were surprised people were still talking about it after a decade, let alone 44 years later! The running question every time we get together is, "Can you believe we are still doing this?" And we are getting more requests now 40-plus years later than we were back then.

Why? It's a great question!

Beating the Soviets wasn't just a hockey game for most Americans, many of whom likely had never followed or watched hockey before. It was the USA versus Russia during the Cold War—it was everything that was happening in the world. Russian troops had invaded Afghanistan; American hostages were being held in Iran.

Our economy was in rough shape. Inflation and interest rates were high—there were lines at gas stations. Americans needed something to grab onto and feel good about—a jolt of positive energy. The surge of patriotism, the thrill of watching college kids upset a Russian hockey superpower team—reigning Olympic and world champions at that particular moment in time—swept us into history forever.

I have people come up to me all these years later with tears in their eyes when they talk about it. That's the effect that victory had, and it continues to amaze and humble us as a team.

Time—you could say this about the pace of life—is moving faster and faster, and people want to hold on to a feel-good moment like that. It has been one of the great joys of my life, people approaching me and wanting to tell their story of where they were and who they were with when they watched us win.

And every story I hear tells of the impact it had on people. For some, it was the first time they ever saw their father cry. Others found themselves hugging total strangers. For many, it was the first time they watched a hockey game, and then they went on to become a lifelong fan or player. I have heard many miltary people who were in the service at that time tell of how proud they were for our country. Stories from some service members in the Navy and Air Force who were following Russian ships and planes and signaling back and forth to them that we had beaten their Soviet hockey team. I have heard thousands of great stories.

Even if people were too young to remember it or hadn't been born yet, they tell me they wish they were alive to see it and talk about the *Miracle* movie or documentaries, which brought it to life for them.

Over the years, I never had the chance to talk to any of the Russian players. It wasn't until the late '80s that some of them were able to come over to North America. I did get the chance to meet Vladislav Tretiak once in Chicago when he was goaltending coach for the Blackhawks in the mid-2000s. I cautiously walked over to him in the press box at the United Center and started to introduce myself. "I know who you are," he said with a smile.

I have seen documentaries in recent years from the Soviet side, with some of their players being interviewed. Those have been interesting to watch. I have learned things I never knew, stuff that was going on in their locker room and on the bench and with their coach.

They were always so stoic and robotic—all they did was dominate and win. Nothing seemed to faze them. But watching these interviews about what was going on—with Tretiak being pulled and what they were thinking as the clock was winding down—it brought a new perspective and appreciation listening to them talk about it.

Dr. George Nagobads—who passed in March 2023 at age 101—was our team doctor. He was from Latvia. He had this thick Eastern European accent. He had been to the Olympics back in the 1950s and '60s, so he had been around for a long time and he knew a lot of the Russian players because he grew up in that area. He talked to some of the Russian players after the game and their reaction was they were surprised we came out so strong right from the start.

You never could see any emotions from them on their bench. They were so methodical with everything they did. To hear them tell the stories in those documentaries was eye opening. It was mentioned how the Soviet players were coming back to the bench as the clock was winding down and they were saying, "Somebody's got to score a goal." They were like, "We're trying, we're trying." It gave a sense of something you never saw from that team, that there was a little bit of panic or worry, I guess, that they never showed.

There's a great extra story about Doc Nagobads that he told recently at one of our fantasy camps for the 1980 team at Lake Placid.

He was taking questions from campers and telling stories I had never heard before. He was asked why, when television cameras showed Herb during the game, Doc was standing with his arms folded next to Herb and looking at a stopwatch. With his thick accent, Doc Nagobads said, "I didn't see any of the game. All I was doing was saying, '30 seconds, 35 seconds.' All I was doing was staring at my watch!"

What Herb had him doing was standing there through the game, looking at his stopwatch and calling out time for the shifts.

There was a reason behind everything Herb did. He wanted the shifts to be a certain amount of time. He figured you would have to be at your fastest to keep up with the Russian team.

It all adds up. It's not just the head coach and the players. You have trainers and doctors and people who become important. Doc Nagobads was important to our team like Craig Patrick was. He had a wealth of knowledge, being from Latvia and knowing the international game. I'm sure he was a big help to Herb as well. He was an incredible man.

The Soviets' speed and dazzling skill and their play together as a group of five on the ice is what stands out the most. One of their top star forwards—Valeri Kharlamov—was fast. There was a specific play earlier in the game where he came flying through the middle of the ice. I used to like to try and catch guys off guard and make a stand before our blue line, and I caught him by surprise at the red line as he was motoring through. He went up in the air, his legs went out from under him, and he came crashing down on his backside. It turned out to be a pretty good hit—he wasn't expecting someone catching him like that. He was such a legendary Soviet player with his speed and scoring.

He tragically passed away in a car accident at just 33 years old in August 1981.

I didn't get to play against any of the Soviet players who eventually reached the NHL by the end of the 1980s. Fetisov and Kasatonov joined the New Jersey Devils in 1989–90, the year after I finished my playing career with the Islanders. Makarov joined the Calgary Flames that same season.

With the victory over the USSR behind us, the final game against Finland started at 11:00 AM on Sunday, February 24. It was a different feeling going into that game because we weren't huge underdogs anymore.

After Herb's memorable speech before the Soviet Union game, the guys remember his speech during the Finland game ending with, "If you lose this game, you will take it to your f—ing graves."

BUZZ SCHNEIDER

"I remember Herb saying that. What stands out to me knowing Herb was that he was not a swearing man. I never heard him say the F-word before that speech. Caught my attention."

With all that was at stake, there was immense pressure on us to win, and for the first two periods not much was going well for us. We just couldn't get anything going. We had a few chances but their goaltender, Jorma Valtonen, made some key saves and kept us frustrated.

The Finns played a style familiar to North American hockey, and we weren't able to break through this sluggish game through 40 minutes of play. Finland had scored early on a goal by Jukka Porvari at 9:20 of the first period. Steve Christoff tied it on a big goal for us at 4:39 of the second period, then Finland went ahead 2–1 on a goal at 6:30 by Mikko Leinonen—who later would play for Herb Brooks with the New York Rangers, where he set an NHL record for most assists in a playoff game, with six, against the Flyers in April 1982. (Wayne Gretzky tied this record in 1987.)

MIKKO LEINONEN
1980 Finland Olympic Hockey Team forward; New York Rangers 1981–84
It was a huge game for both teams. Finland was fighting to win its first Olympic medal ever. And the USA had a chance to win gold. The game at Lake Placid was very intense.

The tension was mounting as we were so close to something we had worked so hard for and what was previously unthinkable—a gold medal. Remembering that the third period had been our best throughout the tournament, we knew we would have to get after them in that final period.

The great story, which I heard for the first time recently, that assistant coach Craig Patrick has told is that Herb came up to him out in the hallway after the second period and said, "Craig, you've got to go in there and say something to them; they just aren't listening to me."

Craig is a quiet and reserved guy and was our steadying voice throughout the year. Craig said he opened the door and started to walk into the room to say something to us. He said everyone was up on their feet, and Jack O'Callahan and a couple of other players were standing there. Jack was a fiery leader and brought so much passion on the ice and in the locker room.

Craig stepped into the room and before he could get a word out, Jack said, "Craig, get out of here.... No f—ing way we are going to lose to a bunch of Finns."

Then everybody started jumping up and down as Craig turned around and walked back out.

CRAIG PATRICK

That's exactly the way it happened.... Herb asked me how it went, and I said, "We're in good shape."

When the third period started, as O'Callahan would later say, "As soon as they dropped the puck, we steamrolled them."

We probably should have scored five goals in that third period, but we did score three. Dave Christian made a great rush and pass to get things started for us leading to Phil Verchota scoring the tying goal. After that, you could see we were not going to be denied.

I have said this all along and for all these years since—that third period against Finland was our proudest moment as a team. With the whole world watching and with the gold medal there for the taking, we played our best period of hockey.

Not long after the tying goal, we were pressuring and Mark Johnson, as he so often did, made a great play and got the puck to Rob McClanahan at the post, who stuffed it past Valtonen to put us ahead 3–2 at 6:05.

Then, we faced adversity as we were called for three penalties within the next 10 minutes, including a couple of back-to-back penalties, which put our penalty killing to the test. The last penalty call came with just over four minutes remaining and us protecting a one-goal lead. This is when the determination and resiliency we had built as a team over the past six months came through for us.

Our final goal happened as a result of Steve Christoff forcing the play and digging the puck out from behind their net and Mark Johnson scoring a brilliant shorthanded goal driving to the net and burying his own rebound. It was a goal no one will ever forget at 16:25 to make it 4–2 and essentially clinch the gold medal.

If Finland had somehow tied the game on any of those power plays, we could have been right back into the position of potentially going home with no medal at all.

Hockey is a game of inches and key moments, and we made the most of those throughout these Olympic games.

We were now up 4–2, with the crowd going crazy and growing louder and louder. Then we hit the post, then the crossbar, then shot another puck over the net in the closing minute.

We finished the final period of our last game as a team that was an unstoppable force.

What a great way to end it!

STEVE JANASZAK
University of Minnesota and 1980 U.S. Olympic Hockey Team goaltender; 1979 NCAA national champion

We outscored our opponents 16–3 in third periods in Lake Placid, including a margin of 5–0 in the third periods of the last two [medal-round] games against two of the best teams in the world. When you combine that conditioning with a group of guys who hated to lose as much as we did—both collectively and individually—the results are amazing. And somehow, Herb was able to break down individual egos so, by the end, winning was all that mattered.

That final period was the true definition of a team effort. It personified and highlighted, on a world stage, what we had become since coming together in the late summer of 1979. As the clock was winding down, on the bench you could see the excitement building and the realization of what we were on the verge of accomplishing.

It was our proudest moment—down a goal against a team that was considered better than us, with three penalties called against us, and we still outscored them 3–0 in the third period. Another dominant late-game effort thanks to the relentless training and conditioning Herb had put us through from that first practice six months ago.

We were a bunch of young guys who would not be denied.

Who were they a week and a half ago? Al Michaels said in his call of the game. *Morrow, Ramsey, Baker, Silk, Broten, McClanahan, O'Callahan. We all know now.... 12 seconds to the gold medal. The whistle stopping the clock at seven seconds.... The crowd is going INSANE at the moment. Bedlam in here. Five seconds to the gold medal. Four to the gold medal, this impossible dream...COMES TRUE!*

And then we celebrated at the same end of the rink that we had after beating the Russians less than 48 hours earlier.

That's when you're thinking of your family and all of those who have sacrificed and helped you along the way. I was looking up into the stands for my wife and my mom. A few of our team's family members even made it onto the ice along with several fans who draped a flag around Jimmy Craig, who was looking for his father in the stands.

At that point, it was the purest kind of joy a person can have. We were all trying to absorb what had just happened.

During the medal ceremony, with the gold medals around our necks, we stood at the red line and sang our national anthem and watched the Stars and Stripes rise. It was a moment you can only dream about and yet it was real.

As always, I thought of my dad and all the sacrifices he and my family made to help me get to this moment.

When the anthem ended, nobody had told us what to do; that's when our captain started pointing and waving for us to join him on that small podium where he stood.

It was perfectly improvised.

And that might have been *the* greatest miracle of all—20 guys up on that tiny podium!

DAVE SILK
1980 U.S. Olympic Hockey Team forward

It's getting up on the podium that I look back on as my favorite moment. It was all about the team.

Al Michaels said it was symbolic of how close we had become that we all fit up there with arms raised and our No. 1 fingers in the air.

MIKE ERUZIONE

It was just a reaction, and it was the right reaction. It was a sports moment that truly brought people together. And of all sports, ice hockey.

After we stepped down from the podium, we walked a lap around the rink. They had taken the glass down from the boards for fans to better see the medal ceremony and people were handing us these small American flags to wave.

It was not scripted; it was all about this team of exuberant young guys immersed in the moment, proud to be an American and proud to represent our great country.

MIKE ERUZIONE

This moment was special to a lot of people for a lot of reasons, not just hockey reasons. I understand it and I get it. This was greater than a sporting event. I said it many times. If you believe in something and you're willing to work hard, you can accomplish it. And I think our team epitomized that.

I would say it ended perfectly for us.

BARB MORROW
Ken's wife

My mom told me she was in church on that Sunday and the priest said, "No sermon; have to watch the hockey game," and let them out early! We heard from friends that cars were stopped on the side of the road beeping and honking after the win.

And with our team, the celebration is still going strong more than 40 years later.

That's the best part of all!

CHAPTER 8

HERB BROOKS

THERE'S NO QUESTION HERB BROOKS was a complex figure. One of a kind.

He had a degree in psychology and a supreme confidence, so much so that he successfully lobbied the United States Olympic Committee on his own behalf to coach Team USA at the Lake Placid Olympics. And then, once hired, he insisted on picking his own players.

Herb had led the Minnesota Golden Gophers to three NCAA championships, so his request held provenance, but the idea of a coach preselecting a team was unheard of at that time.

Whether Herb succeeded or the USOC capitulated, Herb's wish was granted and he set out to put his team together. He wanted coachable players, not necessarily the best 20 players. You have to remember, this was at the height of the Cold War, and Herb was fully aware there would be a ton of high-pressure situations ahead both on and off the ice. A player needs to respect a coach and trust in his system, and Herb had that with our group of players.

Many of the players did have history with Herb prior to the Olympics, and it was great to have their perspective.

BILL BAKER
1980 U.S. Olympic Hockey Team defenseman
He never let his guard down. I had him four years at the University of Minnesota, then Lake Placid, then one season with the Rangers in 1982–83. He often wouldn't give you the time of day; sometimes he wouldn't even talk to you. He never wanted to relax in front of us.

But Herb was also a brilliant hockey mind and an innovator. He'd be seen jotting down plays as they popped into his head, even scrawling them on a napkin during a meal. He also wanted to get to know his players, see what made them "tick." I appreciate that he took the time to learn what motivated each of us individually so he could successfully motivate the team as a whole.

JACK O'CALLAHAN
1980 U.S. Olympic Hockey Team defenseman
I really like the way Herb took time to get to know each player. He gave us those psychological tests, and that gave him insight into how to motivate each player individually. He never treated people the same. He treated people as the individuals they were, and he took time to understand how to motivate each person. Some people responded better to being yelled at and cajoled. Others, like me, it worked better when you spoke to me and respected me and got me to buy in to your ideas.

Herb knew exactly what buttons to push. He was a master motivator. He pushed and pulled this diverse group of college kids in order to get them out of their comfort zone. He was demanding of his players but also gave encouragement when the time was right. Those moments didn't come easily, but it's also part of what made him a brilliant coach.

JOE MICHELETTI
University of Minnesota 1974 and 1976 NCAA champion
Herb is the greatest coach I ever played for. He had a remarkable ability to read people, what made them tick. It was obvious in what he did with the Olympic team. No one else could have done this but Herb.

One thing a couple of players on our 1980 Olympic squad did was to compile a list of "Herbies," quotes from Coach Brooks that struck a chord or made us chuckle. Teammate John Harrington even had a notebook where he wrote down all the sayings.

JOHN HARRINGTON
1980 U.S. Olympic Hockey Team forward
If Herb said something different—one of those quixotic quotes—guys would kind of look across the locker room and give a raised eyebrow like, *Hey, don't forget that one.* Some things were funny, some were serious.

It was devastating to hear of Herb's passing in August 2003. He was just 66, far too young. Even then, his passion for the game of hockey was just as strong; he had attended a U.S. Hockey Hall of Fame celebrity golf event and was headed to the airport early in the morning when the accident happened.

As a testament to how respected he was, more than 2,500 people, including our 1980 team, attended the memorial service in Minnesota.

I am sincerely grateful to have been coached by and to have known Herb. He was intent on getting the best out of you. He was a coach and a man whose impact and legacy will remain forever.

I wanted to share a few thoughts from Herb's family and additional teammates and NHL players.

KELLY BROOKS PARADISE
Herb's daughter

Nobody truly understood at the time the impact the win over Russia had on the world. We were in such a bubble there. I can still almost hear and feel that building. It was shaking with "USA, USA" chants. When we saw my dad there, his mind wasn't with us. He scribbled everything on napkins at restaurants. He was always writing down lines and plays. He's the first coach to receive an Olympic gold medal and I am eternally proud and grateful for that.

PATTI BROOKS
Herb's wife

Thinking about Lake Placid, it has been so long and so much has happened since then. But some of it does seem like yesterday. I refer to it as my other life. I went there more or less as a mother with Dan, who was 12, and Kelly, just eight. We'd go out to dinner and Herb would be juggling lines and writing notes. We only met up with him once in Lake Placid, and he was so distracted. As he should be. Kelly still tells me that she remembers watching Dave Christian's mom waving a giant American flag. That memory stays with me. And to this day, when I watch repeats of the Russia game, it's almost like they are not going to make it. We didn't really realize the true impact of that game until we were handed shopping bags with telegrams. I found myself reading hundreds and hundreds of them. I even found one from somebody I knew back home in Minnesota. It was all incredible. I am happy the movie *Miracle* brought it back around so young people could learn the story. It was so singular. It won't and can't happen again.

Before I met Herb in 1964, I had never seen a hockey game in my life. Since then, I have seen more than most human beings. Herb liked the underdog. And he talked to everybody. Our UPS guy once stopped at my door to tell me, "Herb always came out to talk to me about the grass and the trees." When he was coaching the Rangers and I would pick him up after practice in Rye, he would be the last one out and come out of the rink with his arm around the janitor. He had an amazing way about him, that's for sure.

CRAIG PATRICK

Herb and I got along forever. We had a good relationship. We played together as far back as 1969–70 with the U.S. national team. I had to let him go with the Rangers, but I hired him back in Pittsburgh.

BILL BAKER

From a coaching standpoint, how could I thank him enough? I won two NCAAs and a gold medal. I have only praise for him as a coach and mentor. He was so prepared all the time, and he taught me so much about myself. You have to have respect for the man and what he did for you.

JOHN HARRINGTON

I saw somebody who was coaching his players. He didn't want to look like he was friends with anybody or that he was playing favorites. But years later, when I was in coaching, I always appreciated how open he was about his thoughts and how helpful he was. He would always say, "John, you're having success as a coach. It's up to you to have convictions for what you're doing."

When he was scouting in later years and I would meet him at the rink, he'd always kind of remind you that you were the player, and he was the coach. But I saw a different Herb. He became a mentor to me as a coach, and that's certainly helped me when I got going in a coaching career.

STEVE JANASZAK
University of Minnesota and 1980 U.S. Olympic Hockey Team goaltender; 1979 NCAA national champion

My memory of Herb Brooks was when we sat down and he offered me the opportunity to go to Lake Placid and let me know that, likely, I would not play. He said he would "most likely go with Jimmy throughout the tournament," and if I didn't want to go, he would understand and would take Bruce Horsch.

He told me that if I went, my job would be "to be ready, work hard, and not complain." After I said that of course, I would go, we stood up, shook hands, and his last words to me as a player were, "Don't screw it up."

RALPH COX
Final cut from the 1980 U.S. Olympic Hockey Team

I always had dreamed about being an Olympian, not a pro. But stuff happens. I never blamed Herb. I had a good relationship with him. I had broken my ankle, and I couldn't quite recover. It is what it is. I am honored because I had a great time with those guys and I had an amazing hockey career in my life, including nine unbelievable months with that team.

Herb was a good guy and good coach. He just had a decision to make. I was reading a story in *Sports Illustrated* some years ago and the question was put to Herb: "When the 4–3–2–1 countdown was happening for the gold medal, what was on your mind?" And he goes, "Ralph Cox." That was a "wow" moment for me! That's how I knew how painful it was in 1960 for him. He knew. Only Herb would know that pain.

RON DUGUAY
Played for the Brooks-coached New York Rangers for two seasons, including a 40-goal campaign in 1981–82

I think Herb had an awareness of who I was and he knew how he was going to use me. He gave me Mark Pavelich as a linemate, whose stay-in-motion style was very suitable to mine, and that elevated my game. We clicked right away. With Herb, you always felt prepared. There was teaching and we were well-conditioned.

BOB BROOKE
Joined Brooks-coached New York Rangers after 1984 Winter Olympics

I learned a lot from my brief time playing under Herb. He was an intellectual in a locker-room setting and used his training to get players to believe in his game plans. He also had ways of uniting his team under a common drive, sometimes at risk of his own peril. We lost him way too soon. I am certain he had much more to contribute to the growth and success of hockey everywhere.

MIKKO LEINONEN
1980 Finland Olympic Team forward; New York Rangers 1981–84

Herb was a good teacher, telling us players what kind of game he wanted us to play. For me, he was honest and told me what he expected me to do on the ice. He also used my strengths in all possible positions as center, wing, and D-man on a power play.

I had good chemistry with both Herb and Craig [Patrick] because they knew that we European players had some knowledge and skills. Both liked the European style of hockey combined with Canadian and American styles. Herb understood that already in the early '80s.

DAVE MALONEY
New York Rangers captain 1978–80; played for Brooks-coached Rangers 1981–84

Herb was so revolutionary as to how the game would be played. The game was so linear back then. His style fit into my skill set. And if you fast forward to today, it wasn't that much different than the game is now. He would set up drills on the ice and we would go from there. It was a dramatically different way to play the game.

I was so excited when I first met him. I knew the Olympic story, of course, and we eventually had four 1980 U.S. Olympians [Pavelich, Baker, Silk, McClanahan] on the Rangers. He was very innovative, and he demanded you be the best player you could be. And once you became acclimated, it really was fun.

I had the three best years of my career playing for Herb.

We just couldn't beat the Islanders. And nobody else could beat the Islanders either. So we weren't alone in that.

DON MALONEY
New York Rangers forward who played for Brooks 1981–85

I got along very well with Herb. Basically, what he said to do, I did. He was so revolutionary in his vision of the game and his idea of how games should be played, focusing on puck possession.

The success of the Olympic team gave him the platform to go to the NHL and implement his beliefs in how to play and have success. He was very innovative—not only his game-planning strategy and the type of players he liked but the way he planned practices and how hard you practiced.

I remember our first Rangers training camp with him in Finland in 1981. I thought we'd get off the plane and go to bed because that's what you did. Nope. We went right to the rink, and he started with these crazy practices, holding the puck, swinging back, making plays off face-offs. So creative.

You have to be my age or older to remember what the NHL was like in the late 1970s and early 1980s. Basically, it was up and down your wing, dump it in forecheck, and chase it the other way.

His thoughts and ideas were way ahead of time. The game is being played today the way he envisioned more than 40 years ago.

FRANK BROWN
Covered Lake Placid for The Associated Press and the Rangers for the *New York Daily News*

I covered the pre-Olympic tournament. I had met Herb and developed a connection. He was incredibly outgoing, except for when he put on his coach hat, and he didn't take it off a lot.

You have to remember that Lake Placid was before any social media. The priority on being at an event was very high. There was no watching on a laptop or a phone. If you weren't there, you couldn't watch it live. Newspaper coverage was as "real time" as it got.

Herb made certain there wasn't a whole lot of information getting to his players. He knew it would take everything to even have a chance against any of the opponents, much less the Russians or Czechs. The Czechs weren't as intimidating as the Soviet team but they sure were No. 2.

Sweden, being Sweden, was as formidable as any of them. Baker scored to tie it and it was like, "Hey, this was the upset of the tournament." I was treating a 2–2 tie like it was an upset. That point was a factor; you're talking about goal differential. You didn't want a deficit at any time.

Herb was eternally trying to modernize the game, focused on bringing the hybrid style—mixing North American and European styles—to the forefront. He would have had a lot to say about the way the game is played today if he were alive. He would have really appreciated the emphasis on skill over size, speed and power over brawn. This is what he preached from the minute I met him.

MIKE RICHTER
New York Rangers 1994 Stanley Cup–winning goaltender; played for Brooks at the 2002 Winter Olympics in Salt Lake City
He had these pro guys on that team and had to form totally different relationships and ways to relate. He was able to bridge a different environment and get plenty out of grizzled NHL veterans—just as he did with college guys 22 years earlier. It was amazing and a total privilege to be on his team. He was all about focus and compete.

CHAPTER 9

FROM LAKE PLACID TO LONG ISLAND: 1980 STANLEY CUP PLAYOFFS

A LOT WAS HAPPENING IN MY LIFE in a short period of time—from winning an Olympic gold medal on Sunday, February 24, then flying to the White House early Monday morning and meeting President Carter, then flying to Pittsburgh later that afternoon to spend a couple of days at my wife's parents' house in Ohio.

I was really looking forward to some time to regroup and to take in what had just happened and quickly transition to the next chapter in my life.

While many of my Olympic teammates were having parades and celebrations in their hometowns, I was traveling to Long Island on Thursday to meet with Islanders general manager Bill Torrey to sign my first NHL contract for $50,000 and take part in my first practice.

I can't say enough good things about how welcome the Islanders players made me feel, especially remembering I was joining the team late in the season and possibly taking somebody's job.

I practiced Thursday and Friday and then played in my first NHL game on Saturday afternoon, March 1, at Nassau Coliseum against the Detroit Red Wings, just six days after winning the gold medal. I was thrown into the fire right away, as the Islanders needed to see if this new kid could play in the NHL because the trade deadline was just two weeks away.

It was a whirlwind, but looking back it was a good thing that I didn't have a lot of time to think about everything that had happened. I had to put Lake Placid behind me and concentrate on winning a job with the Islanders and earning a paycheck. Along with the challenge of life in the NHL—being on the ice every day, practicing and playing games and traveling—there was now a new pressure to play well and to win. Thankfully I was joining a New York Islanders team that had quickly gone from expansion team in 1972 to a rising power in the late '70s.

Joining the team and going right into the lineup was surreal. All of a sudden here I was playing on a team that was the best in the NHL the previous season but had suffered a couple of recent playoff losses as favorites. The first was a tough loss to Toronto in Game 7 in 1978 and then there was a crushing loss to the rival Rangers in 1979.

I had followed the Islanders on TV and in the newspapers whenever I could after they drafted me in 1976. Now here I was playing NHL hockey just a week after winning gold at Lake Placid.

It was a blur for me and for Barb, as we had to suddenly shift from the Olympics to NHL life within days after the White House visit.

There were also constant reminders of what we had just accomplished in Lake Placid.

BARB MORROW
Ken's wife

I don't think I ever realized the impact of the games until I left Lake Placid. I was not a happy camper, as I had to bus to Albany with my luggage and some of Ken's to catch a flight to Pittsburgh (near my hometown) after the Olympics. When I arrived in Pittsburgh, Ken had arrived earlier from Washington, D.C., and when I walked off the plane, there were cameras on me with Ken greeting me. Somehow the news stations found out he had arrived and were there to interview him. It was all overwhelming to me then.

I will always be grateful for the treatment we received from Bill Torrey and Al Arbour and the Islanders organization.

Everything that I experienced in my first days as an Islander spoke volumes about the class of the organization and the character of the players in that locker room.

Mr. Torrey had told me at Lake Placid that his plans were to bring me straight to Long Island right after the Olympic Games.

After my first home game against the Detroit Red Wings on Saturday afternoon, we played in Pittsburgh the next day. My first road roommate was Billy Harris—who was the expansion Islanders' first-ever draft pick at No. 1 overall in the 1972 NHL Amateur Draft. He quickly became a big part of the Islanders' rise in the standings in the '70s. Less than two weeks after I played my first game, Billy was part of a blockbuster trade-deadline deal as he was moved along with rugged defenseman Dave Lewis to the Los Angeles Kings for center Butch Goring.

JIMMY DEVELLANO
Former New York Islanders chief scout

Bill Torrey and I determined that we thought Ken could come in and play on our defense. We needed to get a second line behind the Trottier line. Teams were shutting down Trottier's line with Bossy and Gillies in the playoffs. We needed another center so we could form a big second line so opponents couldn't always concentrate on just stopping that first line.

We traded Dave Lewis and Billy Harris to the Los Angeles Kings. Both were popular Islanders. They were both guys that me and Bill and Al liked. It wasn't easy to make that trade because when you like somebody, it's hard to trade them.

But we had been upset the two previous years when we should have taken longer runs. Butch Goring became available, and we felt that he would be the perfect guy behind Trottier, so we made the deal.

111

> We do not make that deal if Ken Morrow is not ready. I can tell you unequivocally that Bill and I both felt Kenny could step in and replace Dave Lewis, which he did. And of course, the rest is history.

I played in 18 games to finish out the regular season, and we got hot down the stretch after the Butch Goring trade, going undefeated in our last 12 games before the playoffs started.

Looking back at my first game in Islanders colors that Saturday afternoon at Nassau Coliseum, the big news was that Denis Potvin was returning after missing half the season with a thumb injury.

My introduction to the NHL included taking my first penalty just 7:12 into the first period for tripping, and Detroit's Dan Labraaten scored on the ensuing power play. The Red Wings led 3–1 after the opening period.

We had goals from Duane Sutter, Garry Howatt, and Bryan Trottier, but Detroit held on to win 4–3, with Mike Bossy scoring the potential tying goal just one second after the final buzzer.

Playing at the Coliseum on Long Island, with the Islanders logo at center ice, was a dream come true for me.

STAN FISCHLER
The Hockey Maven
Al [Arbour] saw a lot of himself in Ken and wasted no time throwing Morrow into a starting position once the 1980 Olympics were over. To Al's credit, the manner in which he helped Morrow was another reason for the club's success. Kenny became a quiet NHL star overnight.

Duane Sutter and Anders Kallur were young newcomers to the lineup during the 1979–80 season. With the addition of Duane and Anders,

Gordie Lane and Butch, and myself, the team had a different look from previous years heading into the playoffs.

DUANE SUTTER
Four-time Stanley Cup winner with the New York Islanders
Obviously the Islanders had a huge 1978–79 regular season and a disappointing '79 playoffs. The '79 off-season beginning with my draft was probably extremely important to the organization. And then adding Gordie's physical game, the team's physical confidence grew. The late-season additions of Butch and Kenny solidified our depth from the top of the roster to the bottom.

The acquisition of Goring proved to be a tremendous boost to the lineup. The talk at that time was that the Islanders needed a second-line center to play behind Trottier, and Butch turned out to be the perfect fit.

With his energetic hustle and all-purpose style of play, he made an impact on a game in all facets: scoring, checking, and on the power play and penalty kill.

He had played his entire 11-year NHL career with the Kings, and he brought a fresh perspective into the locker room, saying, "You guys don't know how good you are."

He was an outside voice and a former opponent who knew how good this Islanders team could be, and he felt the guys needed to hear that.

BUTCH GORING
Four-time Stanley Cup winner with the New York Islanders
I knew they were a good team when I arrived. The whole league knew they were good. There was an attitude of what expectations were. It was,

We're supposed to win. That's it. You could feel that right away. That air of expectation was there from my opening time as an Islander.

We went unbeaten in our stretch of the final 12 regular season games, going 8–0–4 heading into the playoffs. It started with a 4–1 win over the Colorado Rockies. Next, we routed St. Louis 6–2, Chicago 6–1, and Atlanta 6–3.

We were winning games and building momentum that would carry into the playoffs.

The playoff setup was different back then, based strictly on points with the top 16 of 21 teams making it into the first round of the Stanley Cup playoffs. Divisions and geography did not matter at that point, so the No. 1 seed played No. 16 and the No. 2 seed played the No. 15 seed and right on down the line.

Also, 1979–80 was the season the NHL expanded from 17 to 21 teams with the addition of four cities from the folded World Hockey Association: Edmonton, Hartford, Quebec, and Winnipeg.

We finished as the fifth seed with 91 points, while Philadelphia (116), Buffalo (110), four-time defending Stanley Cup champion Montreal (107), and Boston (105) were the top four seeds.

We found ourselves in a first-round best-of-five series against the 12th-seeded Kings, who had the famed high-scoring Triple Crown line of Marcel Dionne, Charlie Simmer, and Dave Taylor. In a shorter best-of-five series, the margin of error is slimmer, as one bad game can affect the outcome.

The first game was an 8–1 blowout win at home with Trottier scoring a hat trick before the end of the second period. Billy Smith lost his shutout with just 40 seconds left, but we had the first win of the series, and the fans went home happy.

Game 2 was the complete opposite, as the Kings scored the first six goals of the game—including two by Taylor—and they rolled to a 6–3 win to tie the series at 1–1 before it shifted out west to the Forum in Los Angeles.

The Kings were a dangerous team, and we knew an offense like theirs could be hard to shut down once it got going.

And that is exactly what happened early in Game 3 as Kings defenseman Mark Hardy scored unassisted just 1:31 into the contest and Simmer—who had 56 goals during the regular season—scored twice. The Kings held a 3–1 advantage heading into the third period.

If we let this one slip away from us, we would be facing elimination on Kings ice in the next game!

Upsets are more likely to occur in a best-of-five series. Who knows what would have happened if the Kings had held that two-goal lead and eventually won the series? Would the Islanders' fortunes—and roster—have changed after a third straight playoff loss as the favorite?

Thankfully we weren't going to find out, as goals from Clark Gillies at 3:22 and Goring, the former King, at 6:34 of the third period tied the game.

That sent this crucial contest into overtime—the first of the Islanders' many overtime heroics that became routine over the next five springs.

For a guy who didn't score many goals, just under seven minutes into the overtime period I slid down from the right point and fired a good shot off a pass from Wayne Merrick that tested Kings goaltender Mario Lessard, and he made the save.

After the ensuing face-off and about 15 seconds later, the puck found me again just inside the middle of the blue line.

I let go with my patented half-slap shot along the ice and toward the net, and with the hockey gods smiling on me again, it deflected off a defenseman's skate and went past Lessard for the overtime winner!

It was my first NHL goal, and what a memorable one it was. I remember being mobbed in the celebration. What a huge come-from-behind win for our team—just a great feeling and such a relief. Now we would go into Game 4 with a chance to end the series rather than facing an elimination game, which is how slim the margin can be in the playoffs.

Looking back at that moment, I was so happy we won I didn't even realize it was my first NHL goal.

As we came to find out over the next five playoff seasons, overtime became our time and it propelled us to many series wins.

In our locker room during the break before overtime was starting, it had become an Islanders tradition to ask the question out loud, "Who's going to be the hero?"

I found it to be a great shot of confidence knowing that one of us was going to be that guy—that we weren't going to sit back and hope something good might happen; we were going to make it happen!

We carried the momentum from that overtime win into Game 4 and beat the Kings convincingly 6–0 to end the series in four games and avoid a Game 5 at home. Billy Smith made 20 saves and Alex McKendry came up huge, scoring twice for us—the only two goals he would score in his brief Islanders career, but they were big ones.

Garry Howatt, Bob Bourne, John Tonelli, and Butch Goring also scored for us.

Next up would be the rugged Boston Bruins. They were the fourth seed and featured tough guys Terry O'Reilly, Stan Jonathan, John Wensink, Wayne Cashman, and others along with scorers that included Rick Middleton, Peter McNab, and Jean Ratelle and young future stars Ray Bourque, Al Secord, Brad McCrimmon, and Craig MacTavish. They also had legends Gerry Cheevers in net and Brad Park on defense.

We were the underdog going into this series against the Bruins, and the first two games of this best-of-seven started in Boston Garden.

Every shift was going to be a physical battle, especially in the Garden, where the ice was small and the corners were tight and the fans were right on top of you. This series became a "welcome to the NHL" experience for me.

The opening game was tight checking and hard hitting all the way through. It was a scoreless battle into the third period before McNab scored for Boston 51 seconds in, but Howatt answered back three minutes later, tying the game and eventually sending it into the extra session.

Overtime magic struck again as Gillies ended it just 62 seconds in on a great top corner shot on a rush down the wing.

Once the puck dropped for Game 2 you could see that the Big, Bad Bruins were going to try to take us off our game after we jumped to a 1–0 lead and the rough stuff was going to heat up. Intimidation was a big part of the NHL in the '70s and '80s.

This game ended up setting a penalty-minutes record for the playoffs at that time. The fighting started with heavyweights Gillies and O'Reilly going at the 2:46 mark in their first of two fights, then heavyweights Bob Nystrom and Wensink at 15:31 and Gillies and O'Reilly again at 19:53, just before the end of the first period.

Then the infamous bench-clearing brawl followed a few seconds later as the period ended. There were fights breaking out all over the ice. Looking back, this game became a galvanizing moment for our Islanders team.

For us, Duane Sutter, Howatt, Bob Lorimer, and Gord Lane were gone with game misconducts, which also took Secord, Cashman, Mike Milbury, and Jonathan out of the Boston lineup. Once things settled down and both teams were back to playing hockey, the score was 3–3 heading into the third period. Bob Miller put Boston ahead at 10:51 only to have Nystrom score 15 seconds later to tie it 4–4.

It was about halfway through this third period that I suffered an injury to my right knee after getting tangled with Don Marcotte in the corner. After we tangled, we both fell backward to the ice and I felt a pop in my knee. Once I got back to the bench, I let our trainer know and then tried to skate on it during the next stop in play, but I wasn't going to be able to continue for the rest of the game. At that point we were down to three defensemen, after losing Lane and Lorimer from the brawl and myself to injury, leaving only Denis Potvin, Stefan Persson, and Dave Langevin.

Although I did not play, I stayed on the bench, and of course the game ended up going into overtime for the third time in four games. *Again* we scored another quick goal, this one from Bourne just 1:24 into the extra session as he rifled a slap shot past Cheevers from the blue line. What an incredible goal! This was a statement win for us with guys standing up and sacrificing for each other and for the team and coming away with two overtime wins in tough Boston Garden.

The Bruins were stunned, having lost both games at home and now having to go to Nassau Coliseum for the next two.

The next morning I was in Manhattan at NYU getting an arthroscopy done. While I was still awake and watching on a TV monitor, Dr. Minkoff was snipping and pulling a piece of torn cartilage about the size of a quarter out of my knee. After wrapping it up I was able to walk out of the room and was lightly pedaling on a stationary bike that evening.

I had never heard of an arthroscopy before that day, as I believe it was a fairly new procedure. I injured my knee on Tuesday, had surgery Wednesday morning, and missed Game 3 at home on Thursday, which we won 5–3 thanks to a couple of markers from Trottier plus goals from Tonelli, Bourne, and Nystrom.

By Friday, I tried skating at practice, and it was decided I would return for Game 4 at Nassau Coliseum on Saturday, April 21—just three days after my arthroscopy—where the Bruins tied the game late and then won in overtime 4–3 on a goal by O'Reilly at 17:13 to send the series back to Boston for Game 5 the next night.

Here we were back in Boston Garden the day after the Boston Marathon—the one Rosie Ruiz faked her way to winning. Amazing that many playoff games were played on consecutive days, but that's how it was in the NHL at that time.

We fell behind 2–0 fairly early in the game and things could have started slipping away for us—but we had another defining moment in this series and in that playoff year.

We fought our way back from a two-goal deficit, just as we had done against the Kings in the previous round.

It started with a late-second-period goal by Stefan Persson. Then we tied it and went ahead early in the third on goals by Duane Sutter and Gillies—two goals assisted by our late-season acquisition Goring. Denis Potvin iced the win scoring at 14:27 of the third period.

Talk about a character builder! Winning three games against this tough Bruins team in that building was unthinkable going into the series.

My long season that started at the Olympic tryouts in July was being extended again. We were becoming a team to be reckoned with and who had quickly been built into a contender. We had a great mix of veteran players and leaders and young stars who had been drafted through the mid-'70s and acquisitions like Goring and Lane who were making a difference.

The Islanders had been through those devastating playoff losses in '78 and '79, and it was a driving force that they didn't want to go through again.

Lane was my defense partner through most of that first Islanders season. What a perfect pairing for me. He was a guy no opponent wanted to mess with on the ice, and for me coming into the league, guys were going to test you. To have Gordie on the other side of the ice was a great help for me. We still laugh about our "direct passes around the boards" to our wingers, meaning we rimmed the puck around the boards and blamed the wingers if they didn't get it out.

Lane was a left shot; I was a right shot. We were both more defensive than offensive; it was a good partnership. Al Arbour had three distinct pairings, with Denis and Bobby Lorimer as the first pairing, Persson and Langevin as the second, and Lane and myself as the third. With an offensive and defensive guy in the top two pairings, we had three real solid duos.

JIM FOX
Los Angeles Kings defenseman for nine seasons starting in 1980–81
Ken was like a grapevine. You try to get somewhere, and he would scoop you up. Getting around him was very tough. He controlled an area. We knew where he came from with the Olympic team. There was a lot of respect for Kenny.

Gordie and I just took care of our own end, and if we happened to score a goal that was icing on the cake.

To this day, he's a guy I have stayed close to. We speak regularly; he's not one to reminisce about the old days and has many interests beyond hockey. What a good person and good friend he has been; we have many laughs together when we talk.

BILLY SMITH
Four-time Stanley Cup–winning goaltender with the New York Islanders
Gordie Lane brought the same thing that I brought—a little bit of, if you're not keeping your head up, you're going to be in trouble.

Coming from the college game and the Olympics, neither of which allow fighting, I didn't grow up having had to fight my way to the NHL. I took the body and my wife called me the "king of cross-checking" when I played with the Islanders, but I was big enough at 6'4" and 205 pounds that I could stand up for myself when needed.

My first fight in the NHL was in my second season and happened to be against Brian Sutter in St. Louis. Like all the Sutter brothers, Brian was a buzzsaw who played with competitive and physical intensity every shift of every game.

Against Boston, when the benches cleared during that brawl, I got grabbed by Dallas Smith, a veteran defensive guy who played an honest game and was physically strong. He basically grabbed hold of me and said, "You aren't going anywhere, kid," and I couldn't break loose from his grip.

It was another "welcome to the NHL" moment!

In that first fight of mine against Brian Sutter, I was coming up the ice after we had run into each other behind the net. He was tugging at me like he wanted to fight. We dropped our gloves, and I just started throwing punches.

Trottier and I still laugh about this as he has told me over and over, "You just beat the crap out of his stomach," realizing that I was just throwing body shots.

I might have had four or five fights in my 10-year NHL career. They were certainly not classic fights. I would describe myself as having played a hard, honest, physical game, and I was big enough that most guys weren't going to try to take advantage of me.

I ended up playing with two of the six Sutter brothers who played in the NHL, Duane and Brent. What an amazing accomplishment for that family. They are Canadian hockey royalty!

They all brought a fierce competitive spirit and a lot of talent. I heard about their stories growing up on the farm and going to battle against each other, as brothers will do. They also had the occasional NHL scrap when they faced off against each other in a game, after having spent the night before at dinner together.

Funny that my first NHL fight was against a Sutter.

DUANE SUTTER

Kenny had an immediate presence with his stellar defensive game. He instantly became a solid partner for Denis. And in years later, he found a knack to score a handful of critical playoff goals.

In that Boston game with the big brawl, the Nystrom–Wensink fight was the most intense fight I had ever seen. In those days players were able to huddle around a fight that was going on. I happened to be standing about three or four feet away from these two feared fighters who were going toe to toe. Bobby got the better of Wensink that day. In my mind, I'm thinking, *This is the NHL, this isn't college.*

At the end of the fight, they still had a hold of each other's collars and the linesman had come in to break it up. Nystrom still had his fist up with the jersey clenched under Wensink's chin. As I was standing there, I saw Wensink bite down on Bob's finger, and that was an, *Oh my god, wow!* moment—anything goes!

Nystrom was the most intense competitor I ever played with.

BOB NYSTROM
Four-time Stanley Cup winner with the New York Islanders

Kenny was a great find for us. We knew about him—with his reach, he could reach right across the rink, for godsakes. He was a pain in the rear end for forwards. He blocked shots. He just covered the whole ice, it seemed.

There was another memorable moment for me in that Boston brawl game when I had a flashback to my college days as a rushing defenseman.

Right after the Nystrom–Wensink fight in the first period of the scoreless game, I made a rush up ice with the puck and luckily made a move with the puck past young Ray Bourque and came out the other side for a shot on goal as I was falling to the ice. Trottier was there to put home a rebound into a wide-open net for a 1–0 lead.

After we survived the Boston series, next up was a semifinal opponent who played an opposite style of game than the Bruins. The second-seeded Buffalo Sabres, coached by the great Scotty Bowman, were a speed and finesse team led by the famous French Connection line of Gilbert Perreault, Rick Martin, and Rene Robert.

They had stars up and down the lineup, which also included Danny Gare and André Savard and big Jim Schoenfeld on the blue line.

This was such a different opponent than the "rock 'em, sock 'em" style we had to play against Boston. Buffalo played more of a Montreal Canadiens style—they could skate and they could score.

One common thread I have heard from former opponents of ours all these years later is that those Islanders teams of the early '80s could play any style of game that was required—rough and tumble if needed or simply outscoring teams.

Again, we opened with two games on the road, and again there was another key overtime goal in Game 2 by Nystrom in double OT for a sweep of both games in Buffalo.

At that stage, we were really on a roll in the playoffs.

We were trying to keep this dangerous Sabres team from breaking loose offensively—they were an early version of the Edmonton Oilers, and it was quite the challenge containing them.

It was a clean series, as that was their style. After a 7–4 home ice win in Game 3 at Nassau Coliseum and a 3–0 series lead, we were one game away from a first-ever Stanley Cup Final. What you come to find out is that the fourth win is always the most difficult, and this Buffalo team made sure of that.

In this series I was also playing against my fellow Olympic gold medal teammates Mike Ramsey and Rob McClanahan. Suddenly here they were on the other side of the ice with the Sabres and the Cup Final on the line. The bond we shared in Lake Placid will be lifelong, but at that moment we were playing in the NHL and making a living and competing for the ultimate goal—a Stanley Cup.

Mike ended up as one of the youngest and best U.S.-born players in the NHL. He had a long, All-Star career and is one of the all-time great Buffalo Sabres. Robbie scored some huge goals during our gold medal run, including the third-period game-winner against Finland that won us gold. He also ended up playing for coach Herb Brooks again with the Rangers, which was Robbie's third stint under Herb after playing for him in college and in the Olympics.

Winning in overtime against the Kings, then those first two overtime games in Boston, then another one in Buffalo, we were making our own fate.

With a 3–0 series lead and a Stanley Cup Final berth for us on the line, the Sabres took Game 4 by a 7–4 score at Nassau Coliseum, then won 2–0 in Game 5 on their home ice to force the series back to Long Island for Game 6.

We quickly found ourselves down 2–0 after two goals by the great Gilbert Perreault. Then another one of those defining moments happened for us—one we were familiar with again in these playoffs as we were behind by two goals. The good thing is that there was a lot of time left in the game and we were on home ice.

The comeback started with a quick answer by Tonelli at 8:08 of the first period soon after Perreault's second goal. Then a power-play goal just 31 seconds into the third period by the great Mike Bossy tied the game, and the go-ahead goal by Bob Lorimer halfway through the game gave us a 3–2 lead.

Bob was a defensive defenseman like myself who didn't score a lot, but he had assisted on Nystrom's double overtime winner in Game 2 and he now scored the biggest goal of his career in this crucial game.

A third-period goal by Duane Sutter and an empty-net goal by Bourne made it a 5–2 final score.

We were going to the Stanley Cup Final!

CHAPTER 10

1980 STANLEY CUP FINAL

AFTER GETTING PAST THE HIGHER-SEEDED Boston Bruins (fourth) and Buffalo Sabres (second), we were headed to the Stanley Cup Final to face the top-seeded Philadelphia Flyers. We had won as the underdog in the previous two rounds, and we would be the underdog again in the Cup Final. I had come to the Islanders from the Olympics, where we had played the underdog role well, and now we were doing the same in these Cup playoffs.

In the 1979–80 NHL regular season, the Flyers had a historic 35-game unbeaten streak, the longest in American professional sports, which still stands today. They had 25 wins and 10 ties without losing a game. There was no overtime during the regular season back then. Many of the players on that team had won the Cup in 1974 and 1975; legends like Bobby Clarke, Bill Barber, Rick MacLeish, Bob Kelly, and 50-goal scorer Reggie Leach were part of this record-setting team.

Philadelphia finished first in the NHL with 116 points and had rolled past the Edmonton Oilers, the New York Rangers, and the Minnesota North Stars to reach the Final under coach Pat Quinn.

Their 35-game streak went from October 14 to January 6, mostly with 22-year-old Pete Peeters in goal. He finished that season with a 29–5–5 record.

The Flyers dominated the young Gretzky-Messier–led Oilers in three straight games, overpowered the Rangers in five games, and defeated the North Stars in five to reach the Final. The Flyers were the favorites going into the 1980 Cup Final as they attempted to win their third Stanley Cup in seven years.

This was the Islanders' first Cup Final, which came after a couple of disappointing playoff losses in 1978 and 1979. I had joined the team on March 1, played in 18 games to finish the regular season, and had been through three rounds of the playoffs. Now here I was, getting ready to play in a Stanley Cup Final.

Truly incredible!

Game 1 was played at the Spectrum in Philadelphia, which was a very tough building on visiting teams. Mel Bridgman and Mike Bossy traded goals in the first period and Denis Potvin and Bobby Clarke did the same in the second period. After MacLeish gave the Flyers a 3–2 lead with less than seven minutes left in the third, Stefan Persson scored a critical goal for us on the power play at 16:18 on a great pass from Bossy.

This was a big moment where a couple of guys, Bossy and Persson, stepped up and changed our fortunes for the game and possibly the series. If we didn't tie the game and send it into overtime, the series may have swung the other way after the opening game.

All through these playoffs, different guys were coming through with clutch plays that changed the outcomes of games.

Regulation ended with the score tied at 3–3. Here was another overtime game and the chance for someone in our locker room to be the hero. This overtime didn't last very long, as a penalty call put us on the power play. Penalties were rare in OT back then, but it was an obvious one, as Tonelli was hauled down as he was skating past the Flyers defenseman. It was a penalty call that had to be made. Our power play struggled to get anything going through most of the man advantage. There was a face-off outside the Flyers' blue line with 34 seconds left in the penalty, and for some reason Al decided to put me out there with

Denis. I normally didn't get any power-play time. I used to joke that the only time Al would use me on the power play was if there were five seconds left and the face-off was in our end.

After the face-off, Philadelphia shot the puck down the ice. Once I retrieved the puck, I moved it to Denis for one final rush up the ice before the penalty ended. He pulled up inside the Flyers' blue line and passed it over to me; I quickly dumped it down into the corner, as I was being pressured. Bob Nystrom was there and battled the Flyers defenseman for the puck and it ended up sliding behind the net, where Tonelli grabbed it and made a quick pass to Potvin as he moved down from the point.

Denis snapped a quick shot on the move that beat Peeters and gave us the Game 1 overtime win, just four minutes and seven seconds into the extra session. It was the first overtime power-play goal in Stanley Cup Final history!

We had overtime magic working for us in these playoffs, and there would be more to come later in the series.

We didn't fear overtime. We were a confident team when it got to that stage because of all the success we were having. We believed someone in our locker room was going to make the big play or score the goal to win the game.

Having played in the pressure-packed Olympic Games three months earlier served me well for these playoff games. I had recent experience that I could draw from for these high-pressure situations.

We also had a core of guys on this Islanders team who had been through rough playoff defeats the past two years, and they were refusing to let that happen again.

I have always been thankful for my good timing, joining the Islanders at the right time after the team had learned the hard lessons and before they were about to go on this historic playoff run. I was getting swept up in a wave that was rolling.

Barb and I had been living in a Holiday Inn since we arrived in late February, and it was now the middle of May. Even when we had a home playoff game, I had to move from the Holiday Inn to the East Norwich Inn, as we had a team meal and curfew when staying there the night before a home game.

It was eat, sleep, and breathe hockey. There was definitely a playoff routine you would fall into, and this was the most important time of the year for a player.

Preparation and routine are what take over your life at that time of year.

We had taken the first game of the series. Now the Flyers wanted to assert themselves in Game 2 and they did, scoring three goals in each of the first two periods for a 6–2 lead in cruising to an 8–3 win.

We had split the first two games in Philadelphia, but we certainly didn't feel good after the 8–3 trouncing.

You have to have a short memory after a loss like that. We would have to play much better on home ice. One thing that was dominant for us was our power play. We had scored three power-play goals in the first two games and it had been on fire all through the playoffs. The Flyers had to be very aware not to rough it up too much, as they were known to do, or to take bad penalties.

Our power play was as responsible as anything else for our success in our 19 series wins over five seasons. If the Flyers were going to take penalties, our power play was going to make them pay.

Our top power-play unit was lethal, consisting of Trottier, Bossy, and Gillies with Potvin and Persson on the point. Then we had guys like Goring, Tonelli, Bourne, and Duane Sutter on our dangerous second unit.

Our power-play success had to make them hesitate to play their normal intimidating brand of hockey, which earned them the nickname the "Broad Street Bullies."

We came out onto home ice at Nassau Coliseum for Game 3, and the crowd was as loud as I had ever heard it. This was the first Stanley Cup Final game ever played on Long Island.

We fed off the energy and adrenaline and put the last game behind us quickly, scoring an early shorthanded goal by Lorne Henning, who was a great penalty killer. We then scored three power-play goals for a 4–0 lead after 20 minutes. Our power play was hot and added two more goals in the second period for a 6–0 lead. The game ended up 6–2 after we scored five power-play goals and a shorthanded goal—six goals that were scored by our special teams. All five of the power-play goals came from our big guns—Potvin (two), Gillies, Trottier, and Bossy. The Flyers were paying the price for the penalties they were taking.

Game 4 two nights later now became the pivotal game of the series. With a win, we'd have a 3–1 series lead and be one victory away. With a loss, we'd be even at 2–2 and Philadelphia would reclaim home-ice advantage.

Once the puck dropped for Game 4, our power play came through again, as Bossy opened the scoring seven minutes into the game. Then a Goring goal at the 13:06 mark gave us a 2–0 lead. It was another fast start for us, just like in the last game. After a Flyers goal in the second period cut into our lead, goals by Trottier, Nystrom, and Gillies in the third period offset a Ken Linesman goal and we ended with a 5–2 win and 3–1 series lead.

We were now one win away from something we could only dream about, but everyone knew the fourth win would be the toughest. When you are that close to something you desperately want and are up against a fierce opponent, you face the ultimate test of your will to win.

Our power play and overtime wins had been carrying us through the playoffs and this series. Billy Smith was building his reputation as a star playoff goaltender. He had made 34 saves in our Game 4 win. You don't win any championship in hockey without great goaltending. We had that in Lake Placid with Jim Craig on our 1980 Olympic team and Billy was providing that for this Islanders team.

Billy was one of the fiercest competitors I ever played with. He brought that to his crease every game, where he was highly protective of his territory, hence the nickname "Battlin' Billy." Throughout our Stanley Cup runs, he built his legend as the best "money goaltender" in playoff history. He came up the biggest in the biggest games. He also had such a one-of-a-kind personality. He was straightforward and he told it like it was.

On game days you didn't want to go anywhere near him. He had his routine; he would sit in his stall with his equipment stacked in front of him, and nobody came near him or dared say anything to him. This was how he prepared himself. Coach Al Arbour knew how to handle Billy and all of the other strong personalities on our team, which was a big reason for the Islanders' sustained success back then.

My style of playing defense meshed well with how Billy wanted a defenseman to play situations. I liked to stand up and force plays and keep shots to the outside. Playing defense is a game of angles and forcing opponents into low-percentage areas. Billy's approach was, *I'll handle the shot; you clear the rebound and bodies from the front of the net.*

BILLY SMITH

Four-time Stanley Cup–winning goaltender with the New York Islanders

Kenny was a great asset. He brought you a steadiness that was unbelievable. Nobody could get around him.

Chico Resch was the other star goaltender for the Islanders in the '70s. Chico was a great goaltender in his own right, as the Islanders were blessed with two top goalies. Chico was terrific in net and such a different personality than Billy. Chico was talkative and cheerful; Smitty was all business. Two great goalies and such a stark contrast with their personalities and approaches to the game.

CHICO RESCH
Stanley Cup–winning goaltender with the New York Islanders, 1979–80

I don't know if I played with a defenseman who was more reliable. You never worried about that guy. Kenny's personality is just the way he played. I don't remember a mistake he ever made. Kenny was as perfect a defenseman as I've ever seen. He came in from the Olympics and it wasn't a big adjustment.

Now we were heading back to Philadelphia with a 3–1 series lead. And the Flyers were facing elimination, which made them even more dangerous as a team. Going into that atmosphere on their home ice, with the crowd and with the Stanley Cup trophy in the building, we were overpowered 6–3 by a team making a statement. We did have a 1–0 lead after the first period, but they scored three goals in the second and three more goals in the third to push the series to a sixth game. We did score two more power-play goals in the game, both by Stefan Persson.

So here we go back to Long Island for Game 6, an afternoon game on Saturday, May 24, 1980. It happened to be an unusually hot day. Both teams were worn out and tired. You could see it on the players' faces. Combined with the heat and early start, it was going to be a tough one.

When people ask me about the Stanley Cup playoffs, I describe them as a war of attrition and survival of the fittest. It is a grueling test, fighting through fatigue and injuries for two months, games every other day and sometimes back-to-back practices and travel on the off days. That is why routine and preparation become so important. I remember the difficulty of walking up two flights of stairs in the Coliseum as the playoffs went along.

We would have to keep the shifts short, especially on a hot, humid day where you could feel it in the building. The exhaustion was evident for the players on both teams. You don't get this far without it taking a toll.

It was an eventful and dramatic first period, as Philadelphia was trying to assert themselves and intimidate from the start, but we had guys who answered the bell. There were early high-sticking penalties to Paul Holmgren and Gord Lane, and then one to André Dupont. A few minutes later there was a scuffle in front of the Flyers' bench, where Bob Kelly was mixing it up, and he turned around toward me looking to start something. Before I knew it, Nystrom jumped in, and they went toe to toe in a fight. We ended up with the extra penalty and then found ourselves two men short just 30 seconds later.

The Flyers now had a two-man-advantage power play, and they opened the scoring with a goal. I was on the ice and Bobby Clarke locked my stick under his arm as the pass was made to set up the goal. It was a veteran move by Clarke on a rookie like myself, and he got away with it. Denis Potvin tied it four minutes later on another power-play goal for us, then Duane Sutter and Brian Propp traded goals later in the period for a 2–2 tie after a hard-fought 20 minutes of play.

On the controversial Sutter goal, the play was clearly offside before the goal was scored. No doubt linesman Leon Stickle missed the call. Flyers fans still complain more than 40 years later about that missed call. My thoughts are that the missed offside call on the Sutter goal just evened the table for the missed penalty call on Clarke for holding my stick on the Flyers' first goal. They had a two-man advantage and he still got away with a penalty that essentially kept me from using my stick to defend the play. Let's call it even steven. I don't feel bad about the offside goal at all.

In the second period, Bossy scored on the power play at 7:34 to put us ahead 3–2, and then Nystrom scored a huge goal just 14 seconds before the end of the period to give us a 4–2 lead heading into the third.

We were 20 minutes away from hoisting the Cup.

Nystrom was dominant in the game up to that point, with a fight in the first period and what seemed like the biggest goal of the series at the end of the second period. He was a warrior. His title of Mr. Islander is well-earned and deserved. To this day, the Nystrom Award is given to the Islanders player who personifies "leadership, hustle, and dedication."

An original Islander since the team's first season in 1972–73, Bobby was a heart-and-soul competitor. He fought the toughest guys and he scored some of the biggest goals in Islanders history. He never wore another team's jersey. He played all of his 14 seasons, 900 regular season games, and 157 playoff games in Islanders Blue and Orange.

His goal at the end of the period was his eighth of the playoffs. Bob was the guy who took it upon himself to lead by the example of, *We're not going to be denied.*

At the start of the third period, the Flyers' desperation and their championship heart showed themselves. They scored a quick goal to make it 4–3, then another at the 6:02 mark to tie the game. In the blink of an eye, we had lost our two-goal lead and we were fighting for our playoff lives. Philadelphia had several players who had won Cups a few years earlier, and they had that experience to draw from. Even though we had veteran guys, this was all new to us.

We were on our heels and we had to get things settled down. Al was always stoic behind the bench, and as the period went along the pace was slowing down from the heat in the building and the ice conditions and the fatigue. It then becomes about not making a costly mistake and capitalizing when you do get the chance. Regulation time ran out and we were now faced with the biggest overtime of our lives. Nobody wanted to go back to Philadelphia for a winner-take-all Game 7.

CHICO RESCH

We were leading by two goals heading into the third period, so when they tied it and we entered OT, it was a bit uncertain how it would end. Fortunately, it was Game 6, so if we lost we would still get another chance to win it in Game 7. For Philly it really was sudden death. Not only in the game but the series.

Everyone on both sides was drained physically and mentally.

Al always preached, "If the chance is there, we're going to go for it." We got caught sitting back at the start of the third period. We weren't going to sit back in overtime. We were going to take the chance and go for it and try to win the game, not sit back and hope.

Who's it going to be tonight? was our mindset.

Duane Sutter was a vocal guy, and when leaders like Potvin, Gillies, Trottier, and Nystrom spoke, they had your attention.

You keep to your routine in these situations. Your practice habits, training, and routines are what keep you sane as an athlete.

Al would always walk into the room around the five-minute mark before the period was starting. The door would open and Al would come in and do his two-minute talk. "Here's what they are doing; here's what we need to do." He always exuded calm and confidence in everything he did as a coach.

The best thing for a player under these circumstances is to simplify. Don't get caught looking ahead and don't try to do too much. Take it shift by shift and make the simple play. I can't imagine the tension the fans were feeling in the stands. It is much harder to watch than to play.

It is usually the unexpected and dirty goal that gets scored in overtime, rarely a picture-perfect play. This Cup-winning overtime goal was the result of practice habits. Al drilled fundamentals and making sure guys did certain things well, both as forwards and as defensemen.

Our forwards always worked on crisscrossing behind each other when they attacked the offensive zone and the defensemen.

The play that led to the winning goal had been practiced over and over by our forwards. It was as much for the defensemen as it was for the forwards when we practiced it.

Nystrom and Tonelli will tell you they worked on that exact play a thousand times in practice.

Going back to the Olympics, it was the same as the goal Mark Johnson scored at the end of the first period in the Miracle on Ice game. That goal against the Russians that tied the game at 2–2 started from a play that we'd worked on time and again in practice with Herb Brooks.

Practicing paid off in both historic games.

CHICO RESCH

Watching the puck get turned over by Philly at center ice didn't necessarily appear like, *OK, this is going to turn into a monumental goal for the Islanders.* But Lorne Henning made a quick pass to Johnny Tonelli. And as John entered the zone, Bobby Nystrom, a right-handed winger, was driving the net from the left wing and could be in position to shoot the puck on a one-timer if John could pass it to the needed position for Bobby to do that. It would have to come where the puck was traveling to Nystrom's back skate. But John directed the puck a little in front of Nystrom's front skate.

So, watching, it wasn't like, *Great pass; Bobby's going to hammer this home.* The backhand deflection that Bobby made to get it up and over a sliding Pete Peeters was brilliant. But because it wasn't your typical goal-driving goal, there was a second or two delay for it to register that Nystrom had just executed a brilliant finish to the rush and we had won the Cup. Bobby would forever be known as "Mr. Islander." And then the excitement and relief just exploded in all of us.

When Nystrom redirected Tonelli's pass past Peeters at 7:11 of that epic overtime, hearing the roar of the crowd and jumping over the boards is what I will always remember.

LORNE HENNING
New York Islanders forward who passed the puck to Tonelli to start the sequence on the winning goal

It was so much relief to finally win in a world of questioning as to whether we were good enough. We had finally done it. It's just like a marathon, and I think it was just a relief to finally get to show everybody that we can do it. We did win and we obviously were so happy.

In overtime, my shifts were probably 20 to 30 seconds long, and then I would come back to the bench and gather the energy to go out for my next shift. I didn't see the winning goal when it happened; my head was down, and I was catching my breath as I was sitting on the bench.

JOHN TONELLI
Four-time Stanley Cup winner with the New York Islanders

I definitely saw it go in. I saw the open net and I saw that puck after Bobby deflected it, and it was a perfect deflection. He just caught it at the right spot. I could see that thing just floating toward the net. Pete Peeters was coming my way and the puck was going the other way. To end that game the way we did and to end that game on the winning side was the final step to achieving what our team had tried to achieve for so many years.

Then, it was mayhem!

BOB NYSTROM
Four-time Stanley Cup winner with the New York Islanders

My initial thought when that puck went in was, *Thank god this is over!* You're worn out, you're tired, you're sore. I just said, "Thank god."

The first thing that went through my mind was, *We don't have to practice tomorrow.* Then it was, *We don't have to go to Philadelphia!*

There's a great photo I have of me jumping into Trottier's arms after I jumped over the boards. I leaped over without touching the boards, which would normally be impossible.

BRYAN TROTTIER
Four-time Stanley Cup winner with the New York Islanders

I jumped over the boards and my foot somehow caught the top. So I didn't immediately make it into the pile down in the corner to celebrate with Bob. Then everyone was doing interviews and celebrating with the Cup, and when I finally saw Bob maybe an hour or so later, he goes, "Where have you been?"

After the feeling of relief, it was another celebration for me of disbelief and pure joy, the same as in Lake Placid three months earlier. I was again a part of something unimaginable.

BARB MORROW
Ken's wife

I don't think I realized the importance or significance of Ken being the first player to win a gold medal and a Stanley Cup in the same year until years later…. We had lived in the Holiday Inn for three months after we arrived, because they weren't even expected to go far, so they just told us to stay there. And I remember the parade—people were everywhere lining the streets.

Mr. Islander said it best.

BOB NYSTROM

The bottom line is that we were a true team, just a great mix. And once we won the Cup, we didn't want to give it up. It was ours, and we truly believed we were going to win every year. We weren't going to lose.

CHAPTER 11

1981 STANLEY CUP PLAYOFFS

Morrow family photo circa 1963; left to right: Dad, Don; brother, Greg; sister, Kathi; me; and Mom, Loretta. (Ken Morrow)

My 1976–77 season with the Bowling Green Falcons. (Ken Morrow)

My dad, Don Morrow, with the Jamestown Falcons in 1949. (Ken Morrow)

NEW YORK ISLANDERS, 1155 CONKLIN STREET
FARMINGDALE, NEW YORK 11735 (516) 694-5522
(N.A.E. INC. — General Partner)

NATIONAL HOCKEY LEAGUE
February 23rd, 1979

Mr. Ken Morrow
727 Chelsea Ct.
Davison, Michigan 48423

Dear Ken:

Just a short note to say I enjoyed watching you play and getting a chance to speak with you about your hockey future.

Enclosed please find a 1978-79 Islander Factbook, so you can read about our organization.

Best wishes to you and your team as you go to the NCAA's in Detroit. As I told you, we will get back to you early in the summer.

I am,

Most sincerely yours,

NEW YORK ISLANDERS

Jim

James Devellano
Director of Scouting

JD:jb
Enc.

Letter sent to me in February 1979 by Jimmy Devellano, the Islanders scout who discovered me back in December 1975. (Ken Morrow)

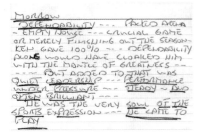

Herb Brooks' handwritten note card from 1978–79 with my attributes. (Kelly Brooks Paradise)

Family photo pre-Olympic game in Flint, Michigan, October 30, 1979; left to right: Herb Brooks; my mom, Loretta; me; my wife, Barb; my sister, Kathi; and Mark Wells. (Ken Morrow)

U.S. team photo taken in St. Paul Civic Center, January 1980, prior to final roster moves. (Ken Morrow via USA Hockey)

Team USA marching in for the Opening Ceremony at Lake Placid, February 13, 1980. (Barb Morrow)

Bill Torrey's ticket stub from 1980 Olympics gold medal game, February 24, 1980, signed by me, Mike Eruzione, and Jim Craig. (Rich Torrey)

Backside of my gold medal from 1980 in Lake Placid with original blue/white ribbon. (Ken Morrow)

Celebrating with goalie Jim Craig after defeating the Soviet Union in the "Miracle on Ice" at the Winter Olympics on February 22, 1980. (Focus on Sport/Getty Images)

Left to right, Dave Silk (No. 8), me (No. 3), Rob McClanahan (No. 24), and Mark Johnson (No. 10) in action against Valeri Kharlamov (No. 17) of the Soviet Union during the 1980 Winter Olympics. (Focus on Sport/Getty Images)

Celebrating after receiving my gold medal on the ice at Lake Placid Olympic Center on February 24, 1980, in Lake Placid. (Ken Morrow)

White House, February 25, 1980. I am standing directly behind Rosalynn Carter. Eric Heiden (who earned five gold medals in the 1980 Olympics) is standing to the right of President Carter. (Ken Morrow)

Left to right: Uncle Cliff Seder, me, Herb Brooks, Flint Mayor James W. Rutherford, and Gale Cronk on the tarmac at Flint Bishop Airport on October 29, 1979. (Ken Morrow)

Ticket stub from April 10, 1984—
Game 5 against Rangers at Nassau
Coliseum. (Peter Schwartz)

Game action in September 1981 at Nassau Coliseum.
(Bruce Bennett/Getty Images)

Me (second from left); my daughters, Brittany (left) and Krysten (right); and my wife, Barb
(second from right) at the *Miracle* premiere with Kurt Russell and Goldie Hawn, February 2004.
(Ken Morrow)

Madison Square Garden group photo in main arena, December 1999. I am in front of Kareem. (Ken Morrow)

Barb and me with our children and grandchildren in Islanders jerseys. (Ken Morrow)

Family Photo at Walt Disney World in Florida, 2004. (Ken Morrow)

Clark Gillies and me on Nassau Coliseum ice in the mid-1980s, when we co-owned Champion Limousine. (I was a guest driver one day for a wedding!) (Ken Morrow)

Barb and me on April 10, 2010, at our daughter Krysten's wedding. (Ken Morrow)

Revealing my plaque as I was inducted into the New York Islanders Hall of Fame prior to a game against the Edmonton Oilers on December 31, 2011. (Christopher Pasatieri/NHLI via Getty Images)

My Olympic gold medal and ring and my four Stanley Cup rings on display in Kansas City in February 2022. (Ken Morrow)

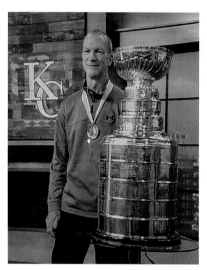

Posing with my gold medal and the Stanley Cup in Kansas City TV studio on February 27, 2019. (Ken Morrow)

Me (right) and my siblings, Greg (left) and Kathi (center), in the summer of 2024. (Ken Morrow)

Long Beach, New York, on June 9, 2023, following Allan's first Euchre lesson! Left to right: Allan Kreda, Barb Morrow, me. (Allan Kreda)

WE WERE A DOMINANT TEAM during the 1980–81 season, piling up 110 points to lead the league.

This was my first full season with the Islanders, and our team was now the defending Stanley Cup champions. With that came a new level of confidence and belief in ourselves, and there was also a responsibility to be at our best every night. The players who had been here through the rise in the '70s and the tough playoff losses in '78 and '79 had put that behind them, and now we were all at the top of the mountain.

The challenge going forward would become staying at the pinnacle—not being satisfied, staying hungry, and pushing ourselves to be better than the game before.

We had a lot of personalities but not a lot of egos, and once we stepped into the locker room and onto the ice, it was all about the team. I have always believed for a team to have success you need stability and strong leadership at the top and then it filters down throughout the organization. The Islanders had that with general manager Bill Torrey and coach Al Arbour, the perfect duo. The organization became a reflection of the GM and the team became a reflection of the coach.

The best way for me to describe Al Arbour is that he was tough but fair, like a stern father figure who would give you a kick in the pants when you needed it and a pat on the back when you needed that. He drilled and preached the fundamentals, and the Islanders were a team that did not beat themselves. We were also a team that could play any style of hockey needed to win a game. We could skate and score in a wide-open game against Montreal, we could play a tight-checking game against Boston, or we could have a physical battle against Philadelphia if needed, as we had the guys to do that.

We now had a new level of confidence, one that comes with winning a championship. It wasn't cockiness, but more a feeling that if we played our best, we were going to win most games. We had a great mix of superstars and role players, and now we were becoming this unstoppable force.

From the time I arrived on Long Island until the day we won the Cup, Barb and I had spent 13 weeks making the Holiday Inn our home. After the Cup celebrations, we were more than ready to look for a permanent place to live. We found a house in the picturesque town of Northport on the north shore of Long Island. It had been a 12-month journey for me since the start of my training for Olympic tryouts in June 1979 until that unthinkable moment of skating and holding the Stanley Cup over my head in late May 1980. I had played in more than 100 games, which included the pre-Olympic season and Lake Placid games and then finishing the NHL regular season and right into the Stanley Cup playoffs.

Many of these games were high-pressure Olympic and playoff games. The only thing on my mind was to take it easy and not think about hockey when the season finally ended. From gold medal to Stanley Cup was exactly three months, February 24 to May 24.

As we were about to find out, summers are absolutely amazing on Long Island. Training camp in September came too quickly, but there was a new excitement and a new challenge ahead.

In 1980–81, Mike Bossy scored 68 goals and we also had eight players with 20 or more goals. Mike set high expectations for himself; scoring 50 goals had become common for Boss, so he wanted to push himself to greater heights by publicly announcing he was chasing Rocket Richard's 50 goals in 50 games record.

Everyone on the team wanted that record for Mike almost as badly as he wanted it for himself. Who else but Mike would score two goals in dramatic fashion in the last five minutes of Game 50, against Quebec Nordiques goaltender Ron Grahame, to make history?

On his 50th goal, he was the only person in the world who could get off a shot like that.

In his autobiography, *Boss—The Mike Bossy Story*, the Islanders sniper recalled the moment he confessed his prediction to his brother-in-law.

"I told Bob that scoring 50 goals was a thrill," he said, "but it wasn't going to be enough. I needed a greater challenge. I'm going for 50 in 50. It hasn't been done in 36 years. I wanted it."

Bossy already had three seasons of 51 goals or more and he led the NHL in goal scoring. After scoring a hat trick against Chicago, Mike had a four-goal game against Minnesota, increasing his total to 19 goals in 16 games.

On December 2, 1980, we beat Colorado 5–1 as Mike scored the 200th goal of his career, which brought his tally to 27 goals in 27 games.

On December 21, after we routed the Blackhawks 9–0 in Chicago, Boss was up to 37 goals in 36 games.

"I know I need 13 in the next 14 games," he said in his book. "The team's going well; my linemates are going great and that makes it easier."

Bossy had another four-goal game against Pittsburgh, followed by a hat trick against Washington, for 48 goals in 47 games.

Then he didn't score a goal in the next two games, so the drama peaked on Saturday, January 24, 1981, in Game 50 against Quebec at the Nassau Coliseum.

It was 4–4 midway through the third period, with Mike being held scoreless.

Then, it happened.

At 13:56, we went on the power play, and Mike scored his 49th goal. He now had four minutes and ten seconds to match Maurice Richard's mark.

Arbour had Bryan Trottier out with Mike and John Tonelli. As he so often did with tenacity, Tonelli was pressuring the puck in the Nordiques' zone. He deflected a puck that ended up on Trottier's stick on the sideboards, and Bryan instinctively knew where Mike would be and put the perfect pass across the zone onto Mike's blade. As only Mike Bossy could do, he rifled a quick shot in one motion, and the goaltender had no time to react. It was a classic Bossy goal and a historic one, with only 1:29 left on the clock.

This is how Mike described the play in his book.

"I yelled and waved my arms. Trots always played as if he didn't notice such things, but he did notice. I busted in from the left side."

Trottier: "I saw Mike and all I did was try to get it to him."

The pass wasn't perfect, but it reached its destination intact.

"The puck bounced up as it hit my stick," said Bossy. "I just let it go as it came down and I shot it as quickly as I could. Grahame wasn't screened, but he didn't have his stick on the ice. My shot whipped under his stick, between his skates and—IN!"

Mike and Bryan had a sixth sense of knowing where each other was on the ice and making a pass to the right spot at the right time. I saw them do this time after time at practice because they worked hard at it. They were usually the last two to leave the ice after a practice, staying out to build on the chemistry they had together as linemates.

We went on to win the game 7–4, which made his feat that much more special.

What an incredible and memorable moment for Mike and the team.

Mike's heroics were symbolic of how our team was able to embrace the success of individual players with the overriding goal of team success. We were a team in our prime with a great mix of veterans and younger guys. Denis Potvin, Trottier, Bossy, Clark Gillies, Tonelli, and Nystrom were still in their twenties. Billy Smith and Butch Goring were 30 and 31, respectively, and playing at the top of their games.

We barreled through the season, finishing with a league-high 48 wins.

When it was time for the playoffs to start in April, we were more than ready to defend the title. We steamrolled Toronto in three straight games by scores of 9–2, 5–1, and 6–1, with Trottier and Bossy having 10 points each in the series win.

After two lopsided home wins, we led Game 3 in Toronto 5–0 while still in the first period and cruised to a series sweep.

Next up were the young and high-flying Edmonton Oilers, led by 20-year-olds Wayne Gretzky and Mark Messier.

They had served notice in their sweep of an aging Montreal Canadiens squad in their opening series—this was a changing of the NHL guard. Montreal had 103 points during the season, 29 more than the Oilers, but the veteran Canadians proved to be no match for these young Oilers, losing 6–3, 3–1, and 6–2.

The previous spring, the four-time defending Cup champion Canadiens had been ousted by the Minnesota North Stars on a late goal in Game 7 by Al MacAdam. That ended Montreal's reign through the late '70s.

You could see that this Edmonton team was going to become a force to be reckoned with in the near future. They were riding a wave after their upset win over Montreal, and we knew they were going to be tough to handle, especially going into Northlands Coliseum in Edmonton. The city and that building were going to be rocking.

We beat the inexperienced Oilers 8–2 in the series opener at Nassau Coliseum, then won again 6–3 in Game 2 behind Denis Potvin's hat trick and five-point night for a 2–0 series lead before heading to Edmonton.

The Oilers won Game 3 by a score of 5–2, which set up a pivotal Game 4 the following night.

Paul Coffey and Jari Kurri scored early in the game for Edmonton, so here we were facing another 2–0 deficit in a crucial game, much like what had happened against Boston and Buffalo in 1980.

Potvin and Nystrom scored to tie it at 2–2, and then Trottier put us ahead 3–2 before Messier tied it midway through the second period. Tonelli gave us a 4–3 lead three minutes later, and that lead held up until Brett Callighen tied it for the home team at the 7:00 mark of the third period on the power play.

The score remained 4–4, which set up yet another overtime in a game that would be pivotal in helping decide this series.

We rarely saw the Oilers during the regular season and didn't know a whole lot about them. You could tell they were a very good young team and on their way up—not yet a finished product, but the pieces were in place with Gretzky and Messier and Coffey—as well as Jari Kurri, Glenn Anderson, Kevin Lowe, and other young stars, making Edmonton a dangerous opponent.

Overtime went back and forth, with the home crowd desperate for their team to tie the series. This was only the Oilers' second NHL season, and if they scored in overtime the series would be tied 2–2. Visions of another playoff upset would be harder for us to overcome.

These Glen Sather–coached Oilers teams of the '80s weren't intimidated by anyone, and they played with a cocky edge, which can be a good thing if channeled in the right direction.

Just over five minutes into overtime, the Trottier, Bossy, and Gillies line was forechecking and pressuring in the Edmonton end, which resulted in two good chances for us. Denis Potvin and I were on the blue line. Denis fired a shot that Moog stopped, and Bossy had a quick rebound at the side with Moog making another big save.

The puck eventually ended up behind the net and got swept to the front into a crowd of players. In the ensuing scramble, an Edmonton player tried to clear the puck out of danger and up the middle. I was able to stop it inside the blue line and snap one of my patented seeing-eye half-slap shots through the crowd and past the goaltender at the 5:41 mark of overtime.

This was my second overtime goal, and I scored it in similar fashion to the one I had netted the previous year in Los Angeles against the Kings. Clark was in front setting a screen. Bryan and Mike were creating havoc around the net. Gillies threw his arms in the air after the puck found the back of the net and a big group celebration followed. This was a scene that would be repeated many times throughout our 19 straight playoff series wins.

Our team had found a way again when it counted the most and we now had a 3–1 series lead and were heading back home to Long Island.

The Oilers had a lot of fight left in them, and they extended the series by winning Game 5 at Nassau Coliseum 4–3, our only loss of those playoffs at home. Now we would have to hop on a plane and fly all the way back to Edmonton and try to close them out in their building and with their newfound momentum.

Back at Northlands Coliseum for Game 6, forward Hector Marini scored early for us at 4:54 from Gillies and Trottier.

After Anderson scored for Edmonton on the power play 39 seconds into the second period, our Swedish winger Anders "Killer" Kallur, who was another one of our valuable additions the year before and who had missed our 1980 playoff run with a shoulder injury, scored his first goal of the 1981 playoffs at 13:12.

Nystrom then scored at 15:45 of the second to put us up 3–1 with assists to Marini and defenseman Bob Lorimer.

Hector was a player who had worked his way up from the minors and made the most of his playoff chance with us in 1981. We loved his hard-nosed work ethic. He scored eight goals in 45 regular season games with the big club, then scored three times and added six assists in nine playoff games, another clutch performer for us that spring.

Messier cut the deficit to 3–2 at 5:31 of the third. Then tenacious Duane Sutter, who was playing in front of family and friends, as he was from Viking, Alberta, not far from Edmonton, scored a huge unassisted goal on a wraparound to give us some much-needed breathing room. His goal put us ahead 4–2 at 9:16 before Mike McEwen iced the game and the series with less than five minutes remaining on the power play to make it 5–2 with assists to Bossy and Billy Smith.

Relief! And no Game 7 on Long Island!

Next up in the semifinals would be our Manhattan rivals, the New York Rangers, who were coached that spring by Craig Patrick and had upset the heavily favored Los Angeles Kings and St. Louis Blues. Ron Duguay and Anders Hedberg were flying, and Steve Baker had become their hero goaltender in those series wins.

This series would have extra meaning for those Islanders players who had been on the ice for Game 6 back in 1979 and prove to have a completely different outcome. That Rangers semifinal showdown win in '79 shocked the NHL top seed Islanders and sent the Rangers to the Cup Final for the first time since 1972.

The Rangers lost to Montreal in five games, giving the Canadiens their fourth straight Stanley Cup and extending the Rangers' Cup drought. The Rangers hadn't won a Cup championship since 1940, something Islanders fans did not let them forget.

The battle of New York in the playoffs was something very special. To see hockey getting front-page sports coverage in the newspapers and be the lead sports story on television newscasts—it was great! Along with this came added pressure to beat our archrival.

This series would be the first of what would become a regular occurrence in the early 1980s. Rangers versus Islanders got the adrenaline pumping even more during those playoff years for both the players and the fans.

RON DUGUAY

Rangers forward who faced the Islanders in the playoffs four times as a Ranger

It was the most enjoyable hockey that I played. Playing the Flyers in the play-offs, there was constantly the feeling you had to fight. Against the Islanders it was just hard, tough hockey. Sure, it would be intense up in the stands at the Garden and the Coliseum. Our series against them were respectful, about skill, toughness, and perseverance. It was hockey at its finest.

Whenever I think of those hard-fought series today—and how the rivals haven't met in the playoffs since 1994—I think about what a great thing it would be for the current generation to experience.

By the time we met in May 1981, both teams were filled with confidence, and we were one step away from going back to the Final and defending our Cup.

We took the first two games at Nassau Coliseum by scores of 5–2 and 7–3, but we knew the next two games at Madison Square Garden were going to be much more difficult.

The key for us would be getting off to a good start, taking the crowd out of the equation early and not letting the Rangers build any momentum. Game 3 on May 2, 1981, was a raucous Saturday night at the Garden. The crowd was ready to erupt from the drop of the puck.

We spoiled that by smothering them from the outset and scoring twice on the power play in the first period. Bossy at 14:36 from Gillies and Potvin, then Bourne made it 2–0 at 18:33 from McEwen and Trottier.

After those two goals—despite the loud chants and cascading boos against us—we basically had that game in hand the rest of the way.

I scored the next goal at 15:31 of the second period with an assist from Nystrom before Bobby Ny scored himself with five seconds remaining in the middle frame with an assist from hardworking center Wayne Merrick, another underrated and valuable player during our Cup runs.

Peter Wallin scored the only goal for the Rangers at 5:13 of the third before Merrick—who was fifth on our squad in playoff scoring that spring with six goals and 12 assists—completed the scoring at 14:54.

Despite the 5–1 final score, the Rangers were never an easy team to play against.

"Forecheck—backcheck—and everybody hits" was one of our mantras in the locker room. We had scorers, we had checkers, we had toughness—everyone was contributing. That explains a guy like Merrick scoring

18 points in 18 playoff games that year—only Bossy (35), Trottier (29), Potvin (25), and Goring (20) had more.

To top it off we had Billy Smith in goal, one of the all-time great playoff performers.

Two nights later, we finished off the Rangers 5–2 at the Garden, turning the "world's most famous arena" silent with Bossy scoring twice including the game-winner to complete the semifinal sweep.

Although all four games looked like comfortable wins on the scoreboard, I never, ever felt comfortable in a series—in any series—until the final buzzer.

A playoff series can take dramatic turns at any point if you let your guard down.

We had a coach and a team who were not going to let that happen.

The Minnesota North Stars would be our opponent in the 1981 Stanley Cup Final. This was Minnesota's first appearance in the Final, a huge event in the "State of Hockey," which was the home of Herb Brooks.

We won the opening two games at home, both by identical 6–3 scores. We knew the North Stars would be extremely tough in their building as the next two games shifted to the Met Center in Minnesota.

The North Stars may have been a surprise finalist, but they were playing really good hockey through the playoffs. They had size with the likes of Steve Payne, Bobby Smith, and Brad Maxwell.

They also had scorers with Dino Ciccarelli, Bobby Smith, Steve Payne, MacAdam, and my Olympic teammate Steve Christoff. Steve set the NHL rookie playoff goal scoring record during these playoffs. Ciccarelli was a young goal scoring phenom for Minnesota. There were "Dino" dolls throughout the stands that looked like the old Sinclair Gas dinosaur. Dino was a tenacious and ratty competitor who could beat a goalie with his lethal shot or score a dirty goal digging at the crease.

The North Stars had dispatched Boston, Buffalo, and Calgary along the way, losing only three games in the three series. We had only lost two games in our three series, both to Edmonton.

In Game 3 at Minnesota on May 17, Christoff scored on the power play 3:25 into the contest, then Payne made it 2–0 just six minutes into the game to send the deafening crowd into a frenzy.

That game could have gone south for us very quickly, as the North Stars were surging, but Bossy scored one of his signature goals 38 seconds after Payne's goal to help settle things down for us.

He pulled up just inside the blue line and fired a quick laser that caught North Stars goaltender Gilles Meloche by surprise. All in one motion, Boss stopped and snapped off a hard low shot that didn't give Meloche time to react.

If Minnesota had scored next, that may have been too deep of a hole for us to dig out from.

The North Stars kept pressuring and took a 3–1 lead on a goal by Smith at 16:30. We headed into the first intermission down by two goals.

We had barely survived the storm of that first period of what became a hard-hitting and chippy physical game. Nystrom scored for us to make it 3–2 at 4:10 of the second and then Goring—relentless as always—scored a power-play goal at 7:16 and added another at 11:51 to put us ahead 4–3. We had scored three straight goals to put ourselves in control of a game where they had us on the ropes after the first period.

We were a team that never panicked. Our coach was stoic behind the bench and we reflected that on the ice. Al used to remind us that "the roof could be falling in, but we are going to keep playing the same way," simply that we would not let anything affect us, not adversity or a surge of energy from the other team. We were such a sound team fundamentally and we had difference-makers and great role players at all positions.

The decibel level in the Met Center was off the charts from beginning to end and the North Stars gave us everything they had in this game. Billy Smith made save after save.

Goring's second goal—another product of hard work and determination—happened with Butch batting the puck out of the air baseball-style and past Meloche.

We took that 4–3 lead into the third period, but Payne scored again for Minnesota at 1:11 to tie it at 4. It was a great goal by Payne, who finished off a passing play with Tim Young and Christoff before sliding the puck past Smith. But here came the amazing Bossy again, just 54 seconds later, rifling the puck past Meloche to give us back the lead at 5–4.

It was as if Mike was not going to let Payne surpass him. Boss was always challenging himself. That was Mike's 17th goal of the playoffs and it came on a play that developed very quickly, catching the defense and goalie by surprise. Payne finished with 17 postseason goals that year.

The North Stars felt they had a real chance to make it a series if they could win Game 3 in front of their home fans and they were unrelenting with their play.

Butch Goring finished his hat trick at 6:34 to make it 6–4 but of course, that lead didn't last either. The never-quit North Stars pulled within one when Ciccarelli scored on a wraparound—his 14th goal to set a rookie scoring record in the playoffs with six minutes and 25 seconds left. The inflatable Dino the Dinosaur dolls were out in full force being waved in the crowd after that goal.

With Meloche on the bench for an extra skater in the last minute, there went Bossy and Trottier up ice with the puck after we broke up the last North Stars attack in our end. Bossy—who could have finished off a hat trick of his own—instead passed to Trottier, who fired the puck into the empty net to seal a crazy 7–5 win.

This win reinforced the fact that our team could win any style of game—whether it was tight-checking or high-scoring—and we had a lot of different guys coming up big in big moments.

We now had a 3–0 series lead, but we had been pushed hard and tested in a game that was a battle all the way through.

Minnesota sent its delirious fans home happy after a 4–2 North Stars win in Game 4. That shifted the series back to Nassau Coliseum for Game 5 and another chance for us to clinch the Cup at home.

This is where that championship mindset took over, as we weren't going to let this opportunity slip away. We jumped to a 3–0 first-period lead on goals by Goring, Merrick, and Goring again. Butch had that old helmet and his scruffy playoff beard and a long scar across his chin. His was the look of a playoff warrior.

We added a goal in the last minute of the second period by Bourne and another goal in the third by Mike McEwen at 17:06, winning this Cup-clinching game 5–1 and setting off a second straight home-ice celebration with our fans.

Goring deservedly won the Conn Smythe Trophy as the Most Valuable Player of the postseason.

With our run to the first Stanley Cup, we had to overcome adversity and doubts and we had to take down the Nos. 4, 2, and 1 seeds in earning our way to the championship. On our run through the 1981 season and in capturing our second consecutive Stanley Cup, we established ourselves as a true championship powerhouse.

ANDERS KALLUR
Four-time Stanley Cup winner with the New York Islanders
After you win it the first time, you're so proud. We never wanted to give it up.

Once you have a taste of winning the Cup and you taste the champagne drinking from the Cup, you don't want to let it go.

Who knew what lay ahead for us, but we had a great thing going, and we were in our prime as a team.

There was one personal highlight for me in this Final series against the North Stars. I scored a goal in Game 2 on home ice—another one of my "50 mile-per-hour" shots that found its way through. It made the score 5–3 midway through the third period.

This one wasn't game ending, as my previous two overtime goals had been, but for a guy who hadn't scored a lot of goals in the regular season (17 goals in 550 games), I seemed to have a knack in the playoffs (11 goals in 127 games, including three overtime goals).

There is no explanation why. I like to say that the hockey gods were very good to me, or maybe it was just sheer luck.

Whatever the case, it sure was a lot of fun for a guy like me to be able to score the occasional big goal!

CHAPTER 12

1982 STANLEY CUP PLAYOFFS

WE WERE FIRING ON ALL CYLINDERS throughout the 1981–82 regular season, finishing with a league-best 54 wins and 118 points.

We were dominant at every position, from the goaltending on out. Up front, we had a feared offense, with Mike Bossy scoring 64 goals and 147 points and Bryan Trottier having a career-best 50 goals and 129 points. We had scoring up and down the lineup.

The highlight of the regular season had to be our NHL-record-breaking 15-game winning streak from January 21 until February 20, 1982. During that streak, we were beating our opponents by an average of four goals a game.

Tonelli turned out to be the perfect player to score the late game-winning goal to break the record. It came in dramatic fashion, similar to what Bossy had done the season before for his 50th in 50. Just like Bob Nystrom, John had a knack for scoring big goals in big moments. We were going for the record and were tied at 2–2 in the last minute of a game at Nassau Coliseum against the Colorado Rockies, facing our former Islanders teammate Chico Resch in net. These heroic moments seemed to be made for our team, a time when someone would step forward and be the guy. As had come to be expected, lightning struck when Trottier and Tonelli combined on a play that broke the 52-year-old NHL record for consecutive wins.

JOHN TONELLI
Four-time Stanley Cup winner with the New York Islanders
We're coming out of our end, less than a minute to go. We gained their blue line and Trots drops it. I had all the time in the world to fire one. I just wound up and it happened to be a perfect screen. Chico never saw it. And there it was!

Success in big moments became a recurring theme for our Islanders team.

Once the playoffs started, we found ourselves matched against the Pittsburgh Penguins in the first round. They had finished 43 points behind us in the Patrick Division.

We won the first two games with relative ease at home, 8–1 in the opener after getting two goals apiece from Gillies and Trottier and then a 7–2 rout in Game 2.

After outscoring them 15–3 in the first two games, no one could have anticipated what was going to happen next and where we shockingly found ourselves several nights later.

Pittsburgh buckled down defensively, and goaltender Michel Dion stood on his head, stopping 38 of 39 shots in Game 3 as the Penguins won in overtime. It was a 2–1 final with the sudden-death goal scored by Rick Kehoe at 4:14 of the extra session.

Then, former Islander André St. Laurent scored twice in Game 4 at the Pittsburgh Civic Center, with the Penguins rolling to a 5–2 win to tie the series.

After breezing through the first two games of the series, we were now facing a deciding final game of this best-of-five. In a shorter series like this, the momentum can shift quickly. They didn't have any pressure on them, as they weren't expected to win, and Dion was playing out of his mind. Throughout hockey history, there are many stories of a goalie stealing a playoff series, and now suddenly it had become a real possibility for this Penguins team.

One more game on April 13, 1982, at Nassau Coliseum to decide who would move on. Would our quest for a third consecutive Stanley Cup come to an abrupt end in the first round?

This was the first time we had faced an elimination game since we started our championship run in the 1980 playoffs. Nystrom opened the scoring at 10:18 with assists to Bourne and McEwen before Pittsburgh's Kevin McClelland tied the score at 11:01.

The second period was all Pittsburgh as they scored two late goals—Mike Bullard at 16:10 and Randy Carlyle at 18:31—and in the blink of an eye we were down 3–1 heading into the third period.

I was on the ice for their third goal, and it was my giveaway that cost us as I lost the puck to their forechecker, who then passed it out to the top of the circle for a quick shot by Carlyle. So here we were again, facing a two-goal deficit in a series-deciding playoff game.

We had faced this same adversity in 1980 and 1981 against Boston, Buffalo, and Edmonton and managed each time to pull out comeback wins that clinched each series. But this was different. There would be no tomorrow if we didn't find a way to win.

The frustration and the desperation continued to build through the first 14 minutes of the third period as time was running out. We needed to score that next goal to give us any chance at a comeback.

Then "the magic" happened again…a confluence of decisions and events and big-moment plays that changed the course of history for our team. Pittsburgh took a penalty and Al Arbour made a goalie switch, briefly replacing Smith with backup goaltender Roland Melanson. In doing this, he gave our power-play guys a breather, since the rules at that time allowed a team two minutes to warm up a replacement goalie.

It was pure genius by Al with less than six minutes left.

"I've never done anything like that before," Arbour would later say. "But I had been thinking about it. It let everybody settle down and stop rushing things. And it worked."

Following that rest, fellow defenseman McEwen scored a huge goal on the power play at 14:33 with assists to Bossy and Trottier.

Mike's goal gave us new life and enough time left to make an improbable comeback. Then the unexplained (call it lucky) bounce of a puck with less than three minutes remaining and us trailing 3–2 led to the Tonelli game-tying goal with 2:21 left in the period.

My defense partner Gordie Lane and I were on the ice. I had passed over to Gordie, who skated to the red line and fired the puck into the Penguins corner. It was a dump-in that happens many times throughout the course of a game, but this time the puck took an unexpected bounce over Carlyle's stick blade as he was retrieving it and Tonelli was right there to snap it past Dion to tie it at 3–3.

I can say it felt a whole lot better being on the ice for this goal than for Pittsburgh's third goal near the end of the second period.

We were going to need more than 60 minutes to decide who moved on and who went home. These overtime games were becoming all too familiar for us, but we had become a team that thrived in these big-moment situations. Then, who other than Tonelli would play the hero again as he scored the series winner 6:19 into overtime.

Moments before, Bullard had hit the outside of the post on a two-on-one break as I slid to take away the pass to his winger. Then, just before Tonelli skated up ice with the puck on his final rush, Dave (Bam Bam) Langevin and McEwen each blocked a shot in our end before McEwen pushed the puck ahead to Johnny after his block.

Tonelli was not going to be denied as he hustled into the Pittsburgh end with the puck on his stick and tangled with the Penguins defenseman as both fell to the ice. John quickly hopped to his feet, corralled the loose puck, and sent it in front to Nystrom, who then made a move before being checked. That created a loose puck at the side of the crease, which JT snapped high into the net for the winning goal.

BOB NYSTROM
Four-time Stanley Cup winner with the New York Islanders

Johnny T gets that goal and I was laying on my back, watching the puck go over me and into the net. I really wanted to score that one too! But seriously, we always said between periods, "Who is going to be the hero?" And all the guys would pipe in with, "I am. I am. I am." Every one of the guys on the team felt the same way—they knew they would score the goal. Even if they didn't, the attitude was so important.

McEwen not only scored our second goal to get us back into the game, he also blocked a shot and made the play with the puck that led to the winning overtime goal.

So many fortunate things going our way and so many things we made happen for ourselves—the bounces, the blocks, the sacrifices, and the big-moment heroics.

This series was a big wake-up call for us. We had escaped with our playoff lives, and we weren't going to let ourselves get into that position again.

After a dominant season, we had survived the first round.

"The Penguins scared us half to death," Tonelli told *The New York Times* after the game. "Down two goals with five and a half minutes left is not the best spot to be in. But we've experienced such situations, though all we could do was keep saying, 'Keep it going! Come on! All the way!' and things like that. You do this to overcome your true feelings of hopelessness, though we never gave up."

BRYAN TROTTIER
Four-time Stanley Cup winner with the New York Islanders

There's a marvel about it all. Hockey fans, especially Islander fans, can appreciate these proud moments. We were a special group at a special time in a special place like Long Island. I think that contributed to the uniqueness of it all.

Now the Rangers—the Herb Brooks–coached Rangers—would be next.

The 1982 Rangers were a dangerous team and their style was hard to play against. They had all kinds of offensive skill, paced by playmaker and scorer Mike Rogers, who led them with 103 points (38 goals); Ron Duguay (40 goals); and my Olympic teammate Mark Pavelich, who notched 33 goals and 76 points in his rookie NHL season.

They also had the Maloney brothers. Having big, strong defenseman Barry Beck as their leader and with tough guy Nick Fotiu adding muscle to their lineup, the Rangers had a good mix of skill and competitors. You had to be aware of who was on the ice every shift.

Also on this Rangers team were my other Olympic teammates Dave Silk and Rob McClanahan. Robbie could skate like the wind and score. Silk was a good two-way guy who could check and score. Don Maloney was one of the best corner men in the league, always digging along the boards and strong with the puck. His brother Dave was a good competitive all-purpose defenseman, and speedy Finnish defender Reijo Ruotsalainen fit perfectly on this Brooks-coached team. He was fast and he had a great shot, which made him a dangerous rushing and scoring threat for the Rangers.

DAVE SILK
1980 Winter Olympics teammate
I remember skating around in warm-ups before a Rangers–Islanders game, and I remember skating by Kenny one time and saying, "Hey, Mo." Kenny didn't answer. He didn't say anything. When I saw him later, he said, "Don't talk to me. We don't talk to the other team." I laughed and said, "Alright." There was no fraternization.

The series opener at Nassau Coliseum had a wild start, with both teams scoring three times in the first period, including a goal by McClanahan at 17:28.

The New York rivalry was in full force, and Islanders fans wanted nothing more than to deny the Rangers any chance at the Cup. The "1940" chant echoed through Nassau Coliseum—that was the last time the Rangers had won the Cup—and Rangers fans were desperate to put an end to our championship run.

This was going to be a much tougher battle for New York than the sweep the previous spring. I knew what playing against a Herb Brooks team was going to be like, and he would have them prepared for his first run through the Stanley Cup playoffs.

He may not have been able to push and drive a veteran NHL team the same way he did at the University of Minnesota or with the Olympic team, but he was a great coach and he would get the best out of this team. Herb did get his message across, as the Rangers had 92 points that season before disposing of the Flyers in the opening round in four games.

After that wild six-goal first period, crafty veteran Robbie Ftorek put the visitors ahead 4–3 at 14:56 with assists to both Maloney brothers, Dave and Don.

McClanahan and I tangled midway through the third, and he went careening into the boards behind Billy Smith. Duane Sutter fought Rangers goaltender Steve Weeks midway through the third period.

The 1982 version of the Battle of New York was just getting started.

Smith stopped Duguay point-blank on a setup from Rogers with about seven minutes left. Smitty did the same to Don Maloney a minute later. As always, Battlin' Billy was holding the fort under pressure.

Tonelli came through again with another big goal, tying the game with under five minutes remaining, converting a slick pass from Nystrom—and it looked as though this opening game was heading for a frantic finish or overtime. It was wide-open playoff hockey, which was exciting for the fans but not so much for a defenseman like myself.

Bossy had a late chance on a backhand, but he was denied by Weeks before Ruotsalainen—who was set up by Rogers—fired a slap shot from the point that made its way through a screen in front.

It was now 5–4 Rangers late in the game.

Tomas Jonsson—another unsung star for us every playoff year—nearly tied the game again in the closing seconds, but Weeks made the save and time ran out amid a scramble at the crease. Tomas was livid as time expired, complaining to referee Ron Wicks that a Ranger had closed his hand on the puck in the crease, but it was to no avail.

Game 1 went to the Rangers and we would have to even the series the next night at Nassau Coliseum, which we did with a drubbing of the Blueshirts. After a rare home-ice playoff loss the night before, we were determined to assert ourselves and take back any momentum they might have. Potvin, Billy Carroll, and Duane Sutter each scored in the first period, then Sutter and Bossy made it 5–0 in the second before Ftorek broke through for the Rangers.

We had a commanding lead, and we weren't going to let up.

Trottier and McEwen added goals in the third period before Mikko Leinonen scored at 17:41 on an assist from Silk to finish the scoring in a 7–2 Islanders win.

The series was now tied at 1–1 and Game 3 became even more critical for us, as it was in the Garden and the outcome could swing the series one way or the other. Here was another huge challenge for us—going into a hostile building and facing a fired-up crowd and Rangers team. The New York rivalry off the ice between Islanders and Rangers fans was just as intense as the rivalry on the ice. This game would test us, but we had become a championship team that had built confidence and character by overcoming adversity in big games and tough environments. We were a team that played our best hockey when the pressure was turned up and when it was needed the most.

For Game 3, Herb switched goaltenders and went with Eddie Mio on home ice. He played well, as he usually did against us.

Bossy and Ftorek traded goals in the first, then Bourne scored on the power play at 7:44 of the second frame to put us up 2–1.

Ruotsalainen scored 19 seconds into the third period and then Mike Allison, a hardworking forward for the Rangers, sent the Garden crowd into a frenzy with a go-ahead goal three minutes later. Bourne, who was another underrated star for us and who was also considered the fastest player in the NHL at that time, scored again to tie the game 3–3 at 8:26.

The score remained tied, and it was another overtime and another chance for someone to be the hero. Just under three minutes into the extra session, Nystrom fired a low hard shot coming down the wing that was labeled inside the far post, but Mio made a great save.

Trottier won the ensuing draw in the Rangers' end, and I got off a good quick shot from the top of the circle on which Mio had to make another save. The rebound went deep into the corner on the right wing. Bryan got to the loose puck and snapped a backhand toward the net from a sharp angle—in overtime it is never a bad play to put the puck at the net—and his backhand found a hole to slip past Mio and find the back of the net.

Yet another Islanders overtime goal!

167

After falling behind in the third period on Garden ice, we found a way to win another big game. As was always the case, we had guys step up to make the difference—tonight it was Bourne scoring two goals and Trottier winning the face-off and then burying the overtime winner.

Over the years, people have asked me what my favorite building to play in was. I had the good fortune of playing in so many famous and historic arenas—the Montreal Forum, Boston Garden, Chicago Stadium, Maple Leaf Gardens, the Spectrum in Philadelphia, and the L.A. Forum. But the top of the list has to be the most iconic arena in the world, Madison Square Garden. Playing in the middle of New York City—thinking of all the famous performers and events it has hosted—and being part of a Rangers–Islanders rivalry, just incredible!

The first time I had been in MSG was for the epic 10–3 loss to the Soviet team just before the Olympics.

It was surreal, stepping onto the Garden ice for the first time, then seeing that imposing Soviet Red Army team with the CCCP across their chests and all these Olympic champions skating on the same ice.

The "USA" chants were echoing in the Garden that night but we didn't give them much to cheer about.

In our Game 3 overtime win, MSG went from frenzy when the Rangers took the lead in the third period to silent as we had again found a way to turn a series in our favor.

We then swept both games on Rangers ice with a 5–3 win in Game 4 before the Rangers returned the favor taking Game 5 by a 4–2 score in our building. So after five games and a 3–2 Islanders lead in the series, there had only been one home-ice win.

It was back to Manhattan for Game 6, and we got another gigantic go-ahead goal late in the third period from an unlikely source, Dave Langevin. He was a big, strong defender who took care of his own end and was known for his thundering body checks. He would crush guys along the boards or with an open-ice hit. He definitely kept opponents wary and with their heads up when he was on the ice.

Dave used to joke that his stick was a "meteor launcher" when he shot the puck. Well he launched one off a face-off win in the Rangers' zone and scored with less than seven minutes remaining to break the 3–3 tie.

What we did so well in this game and in the series was dominate winning face-offs, which allows you to control play and spend more time in your opponent's end of the ice.

Over my 32 years and counting as a scout, I have seen just how important winning face-offs can be to a team's success. Our Islanders teams during those Cup runs had some strong face-off centermen—led by Trottier and Wayne Merrick, along with Goring and Lorne Henning, Brent Sutter, and Billy Carroll.

Al would smartly send out two centermen if there was a face-off in our end, so if one guy got thrown out of the face-off circle, the other center could step in. Those wins would give you control of the puck in your own end and give you extra time and scoring chances in the offensive zone, which led to Langevin's goal.

The importance of winning face-offs can't be overstated, and it helped win us the deciding game of this series.

And I have to emphasize that Bryan Trottier was the best two-way player in the NHL and the world back then—although I did manage to dominate him playing cards (Euchre), but more on that later.

Next up after knocking out the Rangers, we would be meeting the Quebec Nordiques in the semifinals. They were another dangerous team who had just won the seventh game of their series against the higher-seeded Boston Bruins.

The Nordiques were a team that could score, with the likes of Michel Goulet and Réal Cloutier, Marc Tardif, and the three Šťastný brothers—who played in the 1980 Olympics for Czechoslovakia and had defected to North America. This series featured Islanders playoff experience versus a talented but inexperienced Nordiques team that had never been this deep in the playoffs.

Our experience and playoff dominance came to the forefront as we won the first two games at home by scores of 4–1 and 5–2. Wayne Merrick scored in overtime in Game 3 in hockey-crazed Quebec City, and then we finished the series sweep with a 4–2 win in Game 4.

We were back in the Stanley Cup Final for a third straight year!

This time, we'd be facing the Vancouver Canucks, in their first time making the Final. They were an extremely hard-nosed and hardworking team with Stan Smyl and Tiger Williams, Ivan Boldirev and Curt Fraser, and Harold Snepsts, along with their leading scorer, Thomas Gradin, and Ivan Hlinka. They also had former Islanders goaltender Richard "the King" Brodeur in net, and he had been carrying his team through the playoffs. The Canucks played a physical and in-your-face brand of hockey.

The first two contests were at Nassau Coliseum, and they came right after us in Game 1, which turned into an uncharacteristic wide-open game for us.

We were in a battle and trailing 5–4 later in the third period until Bossy became our savior—scoring his second goal of the game to tie it with under five minutes remaining, then scoring the most important goal of the series with two seconds left in the first overtime period.

It was a classic Bossy goal, one that nobody else in the world could have scored, which described many of his goals. Just as it looked like we were heading to a double overtime, he intercepted a clearing attempt by Snepsts in Vancouver's end and, in one quick motion as time was expiring, snapped a laser off the crossbar and in before Brodeur had a chance to react.

There wasn't anyone who could get off a shot like that, so quick and accurate and lethal.

Harold Snepsts surely still wants that clearing try back, 40-plus years later.

Thank you, Mike Bossy!

Tiger Williams, who had 116 penalty minutes in 17 games during the 1982 playoffs, made it his mission in the series to run at Mike and try to intimidate and take him off his game. Others had tried, but that only made Mike more determined to score goals. It was highlighted by this overtime goal and another that was to follow later in this series.

In Game 2, we found ourselves behind 3–2 going into the third period, but a couple of quick tallies gave us the lead and then Trottier scored on the power play at 7:18 to put us up by one in what became a 6–4 victory.

We traveled cross-country to Vancouver for Games 3 and 4, which may have been the best back-to-back playoff games we played during our entire playoff run.

Although the Canucks were down 2–0 in the series, the city of Vancouver hailed its returning heroes at the airport. Everyone in the packed arena was waving the "terrible towels" that had become a wild sight to see during these playoffs at the Pacific Coliseum. It had started from an incident in an earlier playoff game in which coach Roger Nielsen waved a white towel surrendering to the refs, which the fans turned into a craze.

Game 3 turned into a textbook 3–0 win as we shut them down and took the crowd out of the game. This was also the game in which Bossy scored that other spectacular goal that I mentioned earlier.

He was about 15 feet from the net, in front and a bit to the side, when he had his feet pulled out from under him and remarkably got off a backhand shot while he was in the air parallel to the ice. No disrespect to legend Bobby Orr and his famous goal that ended the 1970 Cup Final, but Mike was actually in the air when he released his backhand. That was the most incredible goal I have ever witnessed—the absolute best!

During a longer break between Games 3 and 4, some of the guys decided to charter a fishing boat on an off day. Several of my teammates and I went fishing on one of the beautiful inlets near Vancouver, surrounded by mountains and leading out to the ocean. Several of the guys were avid fishermen, having grown up in Canada. I was not an avid fisherman and had never done any fishing on the ocean. We were on the boat for about two to three hours, and guess who was the only one who caught a fish? That would be me, the guy who didn't know what he was doing. I caught a salmon, more than two feet long. We had it boxed in dry ice and took it back to New York a couple of nights later. Gordie Lane, who was an outdoorsman, had a delicious salmon dinner from Vancouver once we got back to Long Island.

Three nights after our Game 3 win came our chance to clinch the Cup, a game where we weathered the storm early and took the lead on a Goring goal midway through the opening period. Stan Smyl scored what turned out to be the Canucks' only goal of these two games in Vancouver, a late first-period tally that evened the score at one apiece.

Two Bossy power-play goals in the second cemented the game for us and the Conn Smythe trophy for himself as playoff MVP. We were playing at the top of our game, and Smitty was unbeatable in net.

We had swept the semifinals and Cup Final and won nine straight playoff games in the process.

We were dominant!

Our third Cup in a row and it turned out to be the only one we would win on the road. The plane ride home was memorable—a charter flight from coast to coast that landed around 6:00 AM at LaGuardia. There were a couple of thousand die-hard fans to greet us at the airport—players who had no sleep, red eyes and all.

Funny story—the Mannix family lived in a house behind us and had become our second family. When I pulled into my driveway at 7:00 AM, their son Ernie had set up his big stereo speakers in his bedroom window—and on cue and at top volume, he blasted the John Philip Sousa marching song to wake up the entire neighborhood.

It is a great memory and one that I won't ever forget...thanks, Ernie!

After winning an Olympic gold medal and now three consecutive Stanley Cups, people were asking me to pick lottery numbers and horse races. I guess they figured anybody with this kind of luck would be the person to ask.

This Islanders organization and team was on top of the sports world.

It was a team full of character—and characters, leaders and stars and role players. There was no bragging or resting on what had been accomplished; there was a burning desire to win, and I always admired that.

If something went against us, where other teams might yell at the refs or get taken off their game—you didn't see that with our team. We were a team that reflected our coach—stoic, focused, and methodical.

Now there was talk from the outside that we were a dynasty, but you didn't hear that talk from the Islanders. We had now won 12 straight playoff series. Summers on Long Island were incredible, but especially after a Cup win.

We had earned our rest after surviving Pittsburgh, then grinding out six games against the rival Rangers, then finishing in unrelenting fashion with series sweeps.

Respect was a big part of hockey in those days. Guys would battle and fight on the ice and then shake hands when it was over. People respected the way the Islanders played the game.

And it didn't hurt having the world's best goal scorer and 1982 Conn Smythe winner on our team!

CHAPTER 13

1983 STANLEY CUP PLAYOFFS: "I LOVE YOU GUYS"

THE SPRING OF 1983 was both different and special for a lot of reasons. We were three-time Stanley Cup champions, and the word *dynasty* was being used, not by the players but by those outside the team and in the media.

We weren't having our best season and there was talk heading into the playoffs that 1983 would finally be Edmonton's year, even though we were the defending champions.

The young, high-flying Oilers had just endured a crushing playoff disappointment in 1982 in losing to the Los Angeles Kings in the "Miracle on Manchester" series, and before that they had fallen to our Islanders team in six games in the 1981 quarterfinals.

Throughout the 1982–83 regular season and heading into the playoffs, the physical toll from all the extra hockey we had played during the previous three playoff runs, combined with the short summers to recuperate, was starting to show. Guys were missing stretches of games with injuries, and it was becoming harder to ice a consistent lineup from game to game. In 2022, during their quest to win three Cups in a row, the Tampa Bay Lightning hit a wall in the Cup Final against the Colorado Avalanche in six games. It was a remarkable run in today's NHL as their series winning streak ended at 11. Players get worn down and beaten up physically, and bounces of the puck or a hot goalie can decide a series.

Looking back to 1983, we had survived the big potential upset against Pittsburgh in 1982 and then we swept the semifinals and Cup Final that year. The perception during the 1982–83 season was that we were not quite as dominant but that we were still a very good team.

Most hockey experts had the Oilers beating us, as they were a powerhouse and dominating the Campbell Conference. They were brash and fast and high-scoring, led by Gretzky, Messier, Kurri, Anderson, Coffey, Lowe, and company.

We had a general manager in Bill Torrey and a head coach in Al Arbour who knew how to handle a veteran championship team. Bill would quietly make a couple of tweaks and additions each year and Al knew which buttons to push and when to push them during the season to keep everyone pulling in the same direction. It was always about what was best for the team, and standards were high.

As a veteran team, we came to training camp in September knowing what to expect and how to get ourselves ready for the season ahead. In those days, training camp could run for more than three weeks and there would be 10 or more exhibition games. We would begin skating on our own a few weeks before camp started, and then training camp was where you got yourself into game shape, mostly through on-ice conditioning along with riding stationary bikes off the ice. We went into the 80-game regular season knowing there would be challenges to overcome, both individually and as a team.

One of my biggest fears as a player was getting off to a slow start. You wanted the team to get some early season wins and to feel good about your own play once the season began. Coach Arbour knew when to put his foot on the gas and when to ease off. As the saying goes, it's a marathon, not a sprint.

Having said that, there are important moments and times during the season when things need to be ramped up, and the coach has to make sure that happens. Preparing the team to get off to a good start out of camp and not allowing a loss to turn into a losing streak are important as a coach. When our team was playing well, which was quite often, it seemed as easy as just opening the door on the bench and letting the guys onto the ice. One of the great strengths of our team was that we had so many leaders in the locker room. It wasn't just one or two guys; it was many.

Our captain, Denis Potvin, used to write on the chalkboard before games, "Winning is fun!" or "Scorers score, checkers check, and everybody hits."

These were simple messages, but they held true.

We finished the 1982–83 regular season with a 42–26–12 record for 96 points, second in the Patrick Division behind the Philadelphia Flyers with 106 points. Our stars had their usual stellar seasons—Mike Bossy led our lineup with 60 goals and 118 points overall.

This was his third straight season with 60 or more goals and his fourth in five. Boss was at the top of his game. He made the seemingly impossible look ordinary with his 60-goal seasons. The year before, he had become only the second player in NHL history to score 50 goals in 50 games, tying Rocket Richard's record.

Bryan Trottier had 34 goals and 89 points, and we had 11 players with at least 10 goals. We were an incredibly balanced and deep team. I played in 79 games during the regular season and scored five goals, which turned out to be the highest goal-scoring season of my NHL career.

When the 1983 playoffs started, our first opponent would be the Washington Capitals. It was their first playoff appearance and would come in their ninth NHL season. The Capitals were paced by scoring leaders Dennis Maruk and Mike Gartner and 19-year-old phenom Bobby Carpenter. They also had Rod Langway and a young Scott Stevens on the blue line. We took Washington out in four games, losing only Game 2 at home before eliminating Washington in a hard-fought series, winning 6–2 and 6–3 at the Cap Centre.

Next up were the rival New York Rangers in the quarterfinals—we were meeting them for the third straight year. This would be a six-game battle for hockey supremacy in New York against a strong Herb Brooks–coached team.

The Rangers were a tough opponent every spring, especially in 1982 and 1983.

We will get to the 1984 five-game epic later....

It was another matchup against Coach Brooks and several of my Olympic teammates, but this time I was also facing my former Bowling Green Falcons teammate George McPhee as a Ranger.

George was a heart-and-soul competitor and a tough-as-nails opponent. He had won the Hobey Baker award in 1982 at Bowling Green—an award given to the top player in college hockey, the equivalent of the Heisman Trophy in football. George was about to learn what playing for Herb Brooks would be like, something I found out three years earlier with the Olympic team.

GEORGE McPHEE
NHL executive, Bowling Green teammate

Herb was very good on the bench. He had a good feel for the game. Individually, if you were playing well, he'd find more shifts for you. Smart hockey man. He was way ahead of his time.

Of course, the Rangers proved to be a major obstacle for us again. During the early '80s, Herb's Rangers had nine players who were 5'10" or shorter, including Ruotsalainen, Pavelich, Mike Rogers, Robbie Ftorek, Eddie Johnstone, McClanahan, McPhee, Mike Backman, and Pat Conacher. Ranger fans bestowed the nickname "the Smurfs" upon them, sometimes waving blue Smurf dolls at games.

They were a pesky and fast and talented team, and they gave Philadelphia fits in the first round, shocking the division-leading Flyers in three straight games to win the series.

Former Oiler Eddie Mio was the "goalie of the hour" for the Rangers that spring and was playing some of the best hockey of his career. We took the first two games of the series 4–1 and 5–0 at home before the Rangers gave it right back to us at Madison Square Garden, taking the next two games 7–6 and 3–1.

Game 5 was at Nassau Coliseum, and it became the turning point in the series. After Trottier and the Rangers' Reijo Ruotsalainen traded goals in the first period, we took over the game by rattling off four straight goals in the second frame—with Bossy, Gord Lane, Duane Sutter, and Bourne as the goal scorers. We cruised to a 7–2 home-ice win, setting up Game 6 at the Garden.

This would be another epic clash with our hated rivals on Garden ice. The crowd was revved up at the start and even more so when Ron Duguay opened the scoring at 12:45 of the first, backhanding the puck under me as I went down to block the shot and past Billy Smith. The assist went to hustling and scrappy McPhee, who was at his best in that series.

Tonelli tied the game at 4:02 of the second, with assists to Goring and myself. Then Tonelli set up Butchie with a beautiful drop pass just 61 seconds later to give us the lead for the first time.

Then Mikko Leinonen tied the game at 2–2 on the power play at 9:31 with a goal from the high slot.

We headed into the third period of a tied game with a series win against our nemesis and a trip to the semifinals on the line. This is where our championship mettle rose to the occasion again.

BUTCH GORING
Four-time Stanley Cup winner with the New York Islanders

The Rangers were such a great rivalry. You kept waiting for the two teams to get back to the playoffs against each other. I really enjoyed the playoff games against the Rangers. Both buildings had tremendous atmospheres.

And I would get very motivated when people were making derogatory comments about me. It makes me want to win that much more.

We played our best hockey at the most important time and scored three straight goals to put the game away.

I was fortunate enough to start the play leading to the go-ahead goal, stripping the puck from a Ranger just inside our blue line before skating up ice and passing to Tonelli, who left it for Nystrom along the boards as he tangled with a couple of Rangers players. Bobby Ny sent a pass across that found Butch alone by himself in front of Eddie Mio, and in one motion the puck was in the net.

A few minutes later Brent Sutter deflected a Gord Lane shot from the point to give us a 4–2 lead. It was Goring at 5:21, Brent Sutter at 8:09, and then my first goal of these playoffs to finish the scoring at 14:09 on a wrist shot from the blue line that fooled Mio.

A dominant final 20 minutes to finish off our rivals!

"Good, clean, hard-played hockey!" exclaimed Rangers announcer Jim Gordon.

Most importantly, no seventh game!

Now we moved on to face the Boston Bruins in the semifinals. They had the best record in the NHL at 50–20–10 for 110 points. Boston would have home-ice advantage and would be the favorite going into the series, something we hadn't faced since our first Cup win in 1980.

This would be a matchup between two heavyweights, and we were missing a key player or two every game through these playoffs to injury. Clark Gillies and Dave Langevin only played in eight of 20 playoff games, Bryan Trottier missed three games, and Stefan Persson missed a couple. These all added up and made the task at hand more difficult. But we had such a strong team-first mentality and good depth through our lineup that guys would step in and fill the void admirably. This series would be another six-game slugfest against a very tough opponent.

The grind of the regular season has its ups and downs, and Al Arbour was a master at knowing when to begin preparations for the start of the playoffs in mid-April.

The emphasis was on playing our best hockey in March, getting line combinations and defense pairings together, and sharpening our attention to detail.

Both the Islanders and Bruins were known to be strong defensive teams, but surprisingly this semifinal series turned into a high-scoring affair, though none of the games were close on the scoreboard. I attribute all the scoring to the fact that both teams had a lot of offensive talent and the notion that sometimes a series can take on a life of its own.

Boston was coming off a dramatic series win over Buffalo, which ended with a Game 7 overtime goal by Hall of Famer Brad Park at Boston Garden. I always had the highest respect for Brad, who was a hero of mine. I loved the way he played. He thought the game so well and he was smooth and poised. He had all these great qualities as a defenseman and the longevity to go with them.

We opened the series with a 5–2 win on Boston ice, then the Bruins promptly tied it with a 4–1 win two nights later. The floodgates opened during the next two games on Long Island, as we won Games 3 and 4 in 7–3 and 8–3 blowouts against Pete Peeters, the very same goaltender who had been in net for Nystrom's Cup-winning goal three years earlier in the same building.

We had a bit of a scare in Game 3, as Boston had closed within 4–3 early in the third period on a goal by a young Ray Bourque, but I scored a goal a few minutes later from an unusual spot for me, right in front of the Bruins' crease, to open up a two-goal lead again.

Mike Bossy had a hat trick in Game 4. Then after getting beaten handily in Game 5 back in Boston by a 5–1 score, the "Boss" fired home four goals in the series-clinching sixth game to propel us into the Stanley Cup Final again.

If I have said it already in this book, then I will say it again—Mike Bossy is the greatest goal scorer of all time! Yes, there are players who scored more career goals, as they played more games than Mike—because his career was cut short by back injuries—but he holds the highest goals-per-game stat in NHL history at .76.

Thanks in great part to Mike's nine goals in six games, we were moving on to our fourth straight Cup Final.

We had eliminated the favored Bruins and in turn denied Park his last best chance at winning the Cup. Brad had reached the Stanley Cup Final with the Rangers in 1972 and also with Boston in 1977 and 1978.

"I never won a Stanley Cup," Park said, appearing on *The Chirp* podcast with me in June 2021. "It wasn't in the cards. I also realize that we just got beat by better teams. You've got to give credit where credit is due…. When I look at the Islander logo, I think of the two-out-of-three series [against his Rangers in April 1975] when we were supposed to beat them. After we got beat by the Islanders, they ended up dispersing the Rangers. And that's how I ended up in Boston [Park was traded with Jean Ratelle and Joe Zanussi for Phil Esposito and Carol Vadnais in November 1975]. It's their fault!"

And now, here we were playing into late spring again, an amazing time of year on Long Island. Warmer weather, being able to roll down the windows in the car, and the smell of flowers in bloom—those were the signs of playoff hockey for me.

Also the fact that it became harder and harder as the playoffs went along to climb those two flights of steps from the locker room to the lobby of the Coliseum after practices and games because my legs were worn out.

The early and mid-'80s on Long Island were a great time. The team was winning Cups and the economy was booming. There were charity golf outings and softball games all summer.

Though Long Island is densely populated, it has a unique community feel to it with its small towns, family-owned restaurants, and stores and beachfront communities, plus world-class golf courses, boating and fishing, and nearby New York City.

Most players lived along the North Shore at that time. Huntington was a great town where we spent a lot of time, as we lived in nearby Northport. Al Arbour lived in Huntington and Bill Torrey was close by in Cold Spring Harbor. Through all of the charity events I attended during my years in New York, I became friends with a lot of New York Jets players and other sports celebrities. I got to meet guys like Mickey Mantle, Willie Mays, Gordie Howe, Joe Namath, Gerry Cooney (a Long Island guy), and too many other big names to list.

Getting to have the Stanley Cup for a day or two during the summer after you win it is a great tradition unlike any other. In today's NHL, the players will take it to mountaintops or hometown parades or overseas to their home country. It wasn't that extreme back in the '80s. Most guys would host the Cup at their homes for a party and take it to their favorite restaurants or hangouts.

After winning our first Cup in 1980, we had been living in the Holiday Inn for 13 straight weeks, so I didn't get the chance to host the Stanley Cup. Thank goodness we won it a few more times. The photo ops at your favorite restaurants usually got you some free drinks and meals for awhile.

There is a funny story from one summer when I did get the Cup. I went over to Stefan Persson's house to pick up the Cup after he had his day with it. I know that nowadays security is a lot tighter, but back then I drove over to pick it up on my own. I had a smaller sedan and I laid the Cup down across the backseat.

As I made the drive back through downtown Huntington on my way to Northport, I looked in the mirror and saw a police car with its lights flashing, pulling me over. Here I am on the side of the road in busy downtown Huntington while a policeman gets out and walks over to the driver's side of my car. I knew I hadn't been speeding. He looks in the back window and says, "I thought I saw the Cup in your car."

Somehow, he had seen a portion of the Cup sticking out above the seat, and he pulled me over. So here I am sitting in my car while his lights are flashing and he and his partner are checking out the Cup and reading the names on it.

These are some of the funny and memorable moments that you don't forget.

Persson and Anders Kallur from Sweden were both so important to our team's success and were part of the core of 16 Islanders who were four-time Cup champions.

DENIS POTVIN
Four-time Stanley Cup winner with the New York Islanders

When Stefan came over from Sweden in 1977, there weren't many Europeans in the NHL. He wasn't a physical player, but he knew how to position himself beautifully, and his passing ability was terrific. I remember a playoff game against Boston in 1980 with Stef lining up against Terry O'Reilly, Stan Jonathan, John Wensink, and Al Secord. That was something. And he handled it.

Throughout the 1983 playoffs and into the final round against Edmonton, I was paired with Tomas Jonsson, another one of our Swedish guys. Tomas was an unsung and outstanding player. We complemented each other well; he was a smart and gifted all-purpose defenseman who was very good offensively, a dual threat as both a passer and shooter. He played on both the power play and penalty kill, and he could really get the puck moving up ice.

I was so lucky to have had great partners in Gordie Lane and Denis Potvin in previous runs.

As always in the playoffs, our depth proved to be so important.

DENIS POTVIN

With both Stefan and Anders, their skill sets were amazing. They added a dimension where we had so much more depth. Anders could play anywhere, and Stef became my defense partner on the power play. And we had guys like Billy Carroll who could play any position up front as well. There was no concern. That's what made our team so good. All of those guys represented depth.

In 1983, the Oilers had a much easier path in going through the Western Conference and getting to the Stanley Cup Final. They swept Winnipeg, beat Calgary in five games, and swept Chicago, rolling to an 11–1 record along the way and giving them a six-day rest before we started the final round.

We had gone six games against the Rangers and six games against the Bruins, giving us only two days of rest, which included traveling from New York to Edmonton. With the Oilers' young legs and the extra days of rest, everything seemed to be favoring their team going into Game 1 of this much-anticipated Cup Final. Additionally, Mike Bossy was a late scratch from the opening game with tonsillitis.

What did fall in our favor was that we had Billy Smith, and he proceeded to give the greatest goaltending performance I have ever seen—arguably the best in NHL playoff history—as he shut out the Oilers 2–0 in a stunning Game 1 win.

Before the game, the atmosphere in Northlands Coliseum was electric—especially with this being Edmonton's first trip to the Stanley Cup Final. With Gretzky, Kurri, Messier, Anderson, and Coffey, and all their firepower, the crowd was waiting for a goal explosion that never came.

During that opening game, Edmonton's Glenn Anderson had the puck behind our net when Smith swung his stick and struck the Oilers forward above the knee. Referee Andy van Hellemond called Smith for a two-minute slashing penalty. The Oilers, who were 0-for-7 on the power play for the night, failed to convert.

As Game 1 wound down with us holding onto a 1–0 lead and the Oilers pressuring to tie it up, I scored into an empty net with 12 seconds remaining to cement the 2–0 win. I think most people in the building were in shock because nobody believed Edmonton could be held scoreless. It was the first time they had been shut out in 199 games.

Between the first and second games, Oilers coach Glen Sather complained to the league that Smith deserved an attempt-to-injure match penalty. Sather then took his case to the media, saying, "Smith plays like a maniac. He swings that stick around like a hatchet, and if the referees don't stop it, hopefully we'll have someone on our club who will eliminate the problem."

That led to the front page of one Edmonton newspaper showing a big picture of Billy with the caption, "Public Enemy Number One," and the picture had bullet holes in it! Can you imagine if that happened today?

Game 2 of the series was another Islanders win, this time by a 6–3 score.

Edmonton tough guy Dave Semenko opened the Game 2 scoring midway through the first, but we scored three straight goals by Jonsson, Nystrom, and Bossy in the final six minutes of the period for a 3–1 lead after 20 minutes.

This was a game where our playoff experience and being battle-tested really came to the forefront. The young Oilers hadn't faced any adversity in their march through the playoffs, and you could see their frustration building, as they were used to scoring goals at will.

Kurri scored for Edmonton at 5:07 of the second but Bourne and Brent Sutter gave us a 5–2 advantage heading into the third. Anderson and Brent Sutter, with his second of the night, traded scores as we built a 6–3 lead late in the third period when another memorable incident occurred.

As Gretzky curled around behind the net with just over two minutes remaining, Smitty swung his goalie stick around the post and toward the back of the net and caught Gretzky with the heel of the stick above his knee. Gretzky went down, tensions boiled, and the crowd went into a frenzy.

The series was already heated and now, with Billy standing on his head with his play—plus the stick incident with Gretzky—more fuel was poured onto the fire. This time, after a scrum in front of the net after the play, Smith did get a five-minute major slashing penalty.

Then in the game's final minute—with Nystrom serving Smith's penalty—Dave Lumley speared Smith in the chest. Smith fell on cue and Lumley was sent with one last penalty of the night.

Now the simmering tensions would shift to Long Island.

For us to know how to dig down and stay composed and find ways to win games in the playoffs even when we were outplayed, that is what served us well in this series. Al always preached that the roof could be caving in, but we were going to play our game no matter what. You don't want that roller coaster ride and the highs and lows that go with it. Be fundamentally sound and own the ice in your own end and in those important battle areas. We also had a game plan to try and neutralize Gretzky, and it was working so far.

This young Edmonton team was still learning lessons and experiencing adversity, and through no fault of their own, they hadn't been tested much in the playoffs. We all knew this Oilers team could explode at any moment and score goals in bunches. I never felt comfortable in any of these games in this series, as no lead was safe. I have always said that fear is a great motivator, and that was true in playing against this offensive juggernaut.

I have seen interviews with Trottier and Bossy where they said their favorite Cup was this fourth one—not that the first wasn't the most special, but that the fourth was the most satisfying because many had us losing to the brash Oilers.

After sweeping both games in Edmonton, Game 3 at Nassau Coliseum was a 1–1 contest going into the third period—where again we were able to take our game to a higher level when it mattered the most. Bourne scored at 5:11 of the final period to put us ahead, and then I scored my second goal of the series and fourth of the playoffs just one minute and 10 seconds later for a 3–1 lead.

It was a classic Ken Morrow goal, similar to my goal against the Rangers earlier in the playoffs, on a wrist shot from the blue line that fooled Andy Moog.

I can picture the play—we came up ice, and Trottier pulled up along the boards and hit me with a pass just inside the blue line. I got off a quick wrist shot on the fly. It wasn't a hard shot but it was in the right spot and caught Moog off guard.

I certainly wasn't known for my shot, but I seemed to have a knack of getting shots through in the right spot and at the right time.

This one was a big goal—giving us a 3–1 lead and some breathing room. Then we scored a couple more goals after taking the steam out of the Oilers. It was a 5–1 final score, but it had been a 1–1 game in the third period.

Our Islanders team had forged a championship mentality and toughness and we were able to draw on that when it was needed most.

DENIS POTVIN

When you become a really good team—even a dynastic one like we were—a lot of those playoff series we had to come back, and we got through by the skin of our teeth. Good teams do that. In our case, losing to Toronto in 1978 showed we needed to be tougher. They took it to us physically, and we didn't respond correctly. Losing to the Rangers in 1979, we needed more structure in our game. There's no question that you learn more from your losses than you do from your wins.

The Stanley Cup playoffs are the ultimate test. No doubt it is the hardest trophy to win in professional sports. After an 80-game regular season, it is two months and four rounds of grueling playoff games, with each opponent stronger than the last. Playing through injuries is expected, and the playoff intensity is ratcheted up. You are physically drained when you get near the end, but knowing you are that close to hoisting the Cup keeps you pushing forward. Where you feel the most exhausted is when you are away from the rink; once you step on the ice for the next game you get re-energized.

Now it was time for Game 4 on May 17, 1983, with a third chance in four years to win the Stanley Cup on home ice.

None of us wanted to go back to Edmonton for Game 5. That was the fear that motivated me the most for that game.

We exploded for three goals in less than two minutes midway through the first period, breaking the game open early starting with a Trots power-play goal at 11:02 assisted by linemates Bossy and Gillies. Our stars coming through again!

Then the Banana Line (called such because they wore yellow pullovers at practice)—Tonelli scoring off a great pass from Nystrom after a strong forecheck by Merrick—made it 2–0 just 43 seconds later. That was quickly followed by Bossy's 17th goal of the playoffs at 12:39 off a great rink-wide pass from Trottier.

It was so loud at Nassau Coliseum I thought the roof might come off the barn. The fans were going absolutely crazy, but there was a lot of hockey left to be played against the stunned but dangerous Oilers. There was nothing to hold them back now and nothing for them to lose, and so we knew they would be coming after us.

Kurri scored 35 seconds into the second period, and Messier made it 3–2 in the final minute of the second frame. The Oilers had cut our lead to one goal and sent the crowd into white-knuckle time heading into the third.

At that stage of pressure and tension, you have to stay in the moment as a player and break things down into their simplest form, remembering the adage, "One shift at a time."

What some people may not understand about a playoff series is that players never feel comfortable, even up three games to none. The media

191

and fans are talking "sweep," but we all knew that momentum and an entire series can turn quickly.

If we allowed the Oilers to get back into this game and gain any momentum with a Game 4 comeback win, we would then be on a plane heading back to Edmonton facing a team that could reel off goals and wins.

We couldn't let that happen!

BUTCH GORING

We had lots of respect for them, and we worried about them, and I don't think they had any respect for us. They just thought they were going to win. Then they found out that wasn't going to happen. But we were ready for them. We didn't take anything for granted. We knew it was going to be an incredibly difficult journey.

As this pivotal Game 4 continued, Edmonton was buzzing and threatening to tie it up throughout the scoreless third period.

With under two minutes remaining and with Moog pulled for the extra attacker, Edmonton swarmed our end. I had positioned myself out in front of our goal, knowing they had two guys behind me waiting for the puck to make it to the front of the net. With just over a minute left and still plenty of time for the Oilers to press for the tying goal, Gretzky stole the puck at the top of the circle and knocked it toward the front of our goal, right to where I had positioned myself just in front of the two Oilers players near the crease. I pushed the puck ahead and skated up the middle of the ice as a sliding Ken Linseman just missed swiping the puck off my stick from behind just inside of our blue line.

My only thought was to get to the red line so any shot I would take would not be an icing. As I crossed the center red line, I snapped a shot along the ice that somehow made it between the feet of the two defenders in front of me and the puck went in dead center of the net.

No going back to Edmonton and no more games!

Nystrom still tells me his story about that play and the way it unfolded. As he and Tonelli were heading up ice and I crossed the red line, he was wondering why I was dumping the puck in and not passing it to them. He hadn't realized Edmonton had pulled its goalie.

After my shot, I ended up inside the Oilers' blue line after the puck had settled in the net. I must have jumped two feet off the ice, a height I could never have reached before or since. Then embracing in a group hug with Nystron, Tonelli, and Potvin in what was a delirious Nassau Coliseum, the words came out: "I love you guys. I love you guys. I love you guys!"

I said it three times!

Bobby, without question one of the most tenacious competitors I ever played with, has told me that it is one of his favorite hockey memories.

BOB NYSTROM
Four-time Stanley Cup winner with the New York Islanders
I was screaming at him on that one. Johnny T yelling on one side, me on the other. But Kenny just skated up the middle and calmly put it in the net. That was one of the happiest moments of my career. The best way to describe our team is the fact that we did love each other. Though I still can't believe Kenny didn't pass me the puck!

JOHN TONELLI
Four-time Stanley Cup winner with the New York Islanders
I totally do remember that hug as clear as day. That was so huge.

DENIS POTVIN

The fourth Cup was as satisfying as the first one simply because a lot of people had anointed the Oilers that year, and we battled through some tough series leading up to that. Being on the ice and just that feeling of winning again and *Thank god we don't have to go back to Edmonton* with the momentum they would have had. It was so important to pull out that fourth game.

Our fourth Stanley Cup in a row. This was one for the ages. Somehow, I outscored Gretzky three goals to none. Of course, two of my goals were empty-net goals, but we held the Oilers to only six goals in that series sweep. Unthinkable!

BUTCH GORING

That speaks volumes of how well defensively we played. Kenny had this knack. He didn't score a lot of goals but he scored timely goals.

BRYAN TROTTIER
Four-time Stanley Cup winner with the New York Islanders
Kenny was very mobile. He had a great stick. He was accurate. And in high-tension moments, he was undisturbed.

I have said many times throughout my life that I am incredibly fortunate to have taken part in so many unforgettable moments.

To be on the ice for a monumental victory and gold medal in Lake Placid and now four Stanley Cup celebrations with my teammates and the people of Long Island...truly unimaginable and remarkable!

CHAPTER 14

1984 STANLEY CUP PLAYOFFS: NEW YORK RANGERS OVERTIME GOAL

I HAVE TO SAY I AM BEHIND THE TIMES when it comes to technology, but it has been fun to rewatch so many of those epic playoff games from the 1980s that have been posted on YouTube.

In the old days, I would have had to find VHS tapes of the games, which would be nearly impossible after all these years. Being able to watch these games again brings back so many memories. The 1984 best-of-five opening-round playoff series against our New York rivals would be the most memorable of our meetings.

It was the fourth straight year we would battle the Rangers in the playoffs, from 1981 to 1984, and this was perhaps the best Herb Brooks–coached Rangers team of them all.

This was Herb's third straight season coaching the Rangers, and he had a good mix of veterans and young guys who were all buying into his system. They had scoring throughout the lineup, led by Mark Pavelich, Pierre Larouche, and Anders Hedberg, who put up big offensive numbers, while blueliners Barry Beck and Willie Huber were towers on defense.

Rounding out their defense corps were the speedy Reijo Ruotsalainen, Tom Laidlaw, rookie James Patrick, and veterans Ron Greschner and Dave Maloney. Goaltender Glen Hanlon was coming off the best season of his 14-year NHL career, with a 28–14–4 record.

BARRY BECK
Rangers defenseman and team captain

Herb was an established winner when he came to the Rangers. That gave us not only credibility but incentive. I also thought we were the second-best team in the early '80s, and that includes the Oilers. Herb was the best coach I ever had because I had to be at my best every night to play his versatile system. Herb expected that every night and so did I.

There was a lot of talent on both sides of the ice when we played against them, and there was mutual respect. We also feared the thought of losing to the enemy, which is what they were at that time.

BARRY BECK

The Islanders were strong. We needed a little luck to get by them. They had a lot of Hall of Famers and a great coach too.

With many of our core players still intact, we added a couple of new faces late in the season, with dynamic young Pat LaFontaine (USA) and big power forward Pat Flatley (Canada) joining us after the 1984 Winter Olympics in Sarajevo. These additions only strengthened our club, and the "Drive for Five" would get started with this opening-round series against the Rangers.

We finished the regular season in first place at the top of a tightly packed Patrick Division with 50 wins and 104 points.

The Rangers had a good season (93 points), led by Larouche with 48 goals and 32 from Hedberg, and a team-best 82 points from Pavelich, who was a perfect fit in Herb's system.

They finished only 11 points behind us in the standings. They were legitimate contenders with the players they had and the style they played.

We had a rough start out of the gate in Game 1 at Nassau Coliseum, as the Rangers scored first, just two minutes and 49 seconds after the opening face-off on a goal by Jan Erixon.

We were getting our chances in the first half of the game, but we just couldn't get one past Hanlon, who was standing on his head. The score remained 1–0 Rangers late into the second period in front of a nervous home crowd until we finally broke the ice with a goal from our newest addition, Flatley. Once we scored that first goal they just kept coming. Bourne scored less than a minute later, followed by two early-third-period goals by Greg Gilbert and newcomer LaFontaine, and we skated away with a come-from-behind 4–1 win.

I missed the second game of the series, which went the Rangers' way, a 3–0 shutout win on goals by Ruotsalainen, Peter Sundström, and Pavelich. I had come down with the flu on the day in between Games 1 and 2 and ended up in Huntington Hospital that night. They pumped me full of fluids through IV bags and kept me overnight so I missed Game 2 the next day. That was the only game I didn't play in the '84 playoffs.

As for the game, Potvin, Bossy, and Jonsson had 20 shots on goal between the three of them. We were getting our shots, but nothing was going in for us.

Next up was Game 3 at famed Madison Square Garden in New York City. When I watch a replay of the game, the telecast featured Jim Gordon—the longtime television voice of the Rangers—along with Phil Esposito doing the color commentary. He is a Hall of Fame player who had finished his career with the Rangers in 1981 and moved into the broadcast booth.

His viewpoints were those of a player, and he told it like it was. He and Jim were an entertaining duo calling games. Phil started the telecast for Game 3 mentioning that I had missed the last game and that he thought I was the best defensive defenseman in the league. What a great compliment and much appreciated!

The Rangers fans were fired up after their team split on Long Island, and they anticipated ending our "Drive for Five" on Garden ice with a couple of home-ice wins.

The Garden was as loud as I have ever remembered it. The start of Game 3 was wide-open and exciting hockey with both teams flying up and down the ice. Pavelich opened the scoring on a shorthanded goal 5:28 into the game and then Larouche scored with 28 seconds remaining in the first period to give the Rangers a 2–0 lead after 20 minutes of play.

The Rangers were playing their style of game, and the raucous crowd in MSG grew louder with each goal. The score wasn't close, as the home team added four more goals in the middle frame and cruised to a 7–2 final.

We now found ourselves down 2–1 in the best-of-five series, and we'd be fighting for our playoff lives the next night. This was unfamiliar territory, down in a series and facing elimination. Maybe the best thing was that we would be on the ice again less than 24 hours later—no time to think about things.

The next night you could hear and feel the energy from the crowd. The Rangers were one win from knocking off the four-time defending Cup champions. Through a scoreless first period, we had a couple of power plays but weren't able to capitalize, and Billy Smith was his usual brilliant self in goal under pressure. Larouche scored on a two-man advantage for the only goal of the second period. We found ourselves 20 minutes from elimination, down by a goal, with the crowd in a state of frenzy.

Things weren't going our way and were stacked against us, but this is where character and discipline and poise under pressure reveal themselves, things our Islanders team had in spades. Never doubt the heart of a champion. We came out of the gates and played our most dominant period of the series. Tonelli scored just 49 seconds in to tie the game at 1–1, and we kept up the relentless pressure shift after shift.

The turning point in the game and arguably the series happened midway through the period, when Flatley delivered a crushing shoulder-to-shoulder hit on Rangers captain Barry Beck in the corner, which led to a shot from the point and Brent Sutter backhanding the rebound over Hanlon for the go-ahead goal with nine minutes remaining.

Beck separated his shoulder on the play and valiantly got back to the front of the net in obvious pain as the goal was scored. Clark Gillies rifled home a long slap shot with just under three minutes left for an insurance goal, and Trottier finished the scoring in the final minute for a resounding four-goal period and 4–1 come-from-behind win.

Losing Beck for the rest of the game and the series was a huge blow for the Rangers, both for his presence on the ice as well as what must have been a psychological blow to their team. He had been a big force for the Rangers after he arrived in Manhattan in November 1979. The Colorado Rockies had traded him for five players!

So we went to a deciding Game 5, with everything riding on this one game, continuing the Drive for Five and any chance at making a run toward a record-tying fifth consecutive Stanley Cup—as well as the bragging rights for New York and this fierce rivalry.

This game lived up to its billing and is considered to be a playoff classic. It was called the best playoff overtime ever by many hockey broadcasters and media.

Regarding the game itself, credit to the Rangers for playing a heck of a game—and without their captain. They started strong and took the lead on a goal by Ron Greschner at 12:06 of the opening period. We were outplayed throughout most of the period before Bossy scored a goal that came out of nowhere, getting behind their defense and tying it at 1–1 with just 11 seconds left.

As always, Billy Smith kept making big saves and keeping us in a game in which we should have been trailing. We were like the old boxing champ who was on the ropes but continuing to hang in there. Again, we came out in the third period with the game and the series on the line and we found a way to take the lead on a goal by Tomas Jonsson at 7:56, a lead we tried to hold onto until the end.

Then, in the final minute, while we were protecting a one-goal lead and with the Rangers having an extra attacker because they had pulled their goalie, the unthinkable happened. I stood up at the blue line, as I liked to do, as James Patrick had the puck and was leading the rush. I got a piece of him, but the puck moved ahead to Pavelich, who fired a shot on the fly.

Smitty made the save and the rebound went into the air, where Don Maloney had skated toward the net. He batted the puck down and into the goal with 39 seconds remaining. The referee signaled goal, and there was no replay at the time. In looking back at video of the game it is impossible to say whether he made contact with a high stick above the height of the crossbar or not.

In today's NHL, this one would have gone to the war room in Toronto and have been looked at from many different camera angles, and I'm still not sure it would have been definitive. The result was a 2–2 tie with the game going into overtime.

DON MALONEY
New York Rangers forward
I remember a two-on-one with Mark Pavelich. He shot and the rebound came out. I hit it and it went into the net. I wasn't quite sure about the call, but I happened to lock eyes with the official, and he was pointing to the net.

It could have been hard to overcome the sudden shock, but we were a veteran championship team and we had been through adversity before. Overtime was familiar territory for us; we had been through so many during the previous four playoff seasons and we'd had great success.

As the *Hockey Night in Canada* broadcasters said back then when the overtime ended, "I have never seen hockey like this. That's the greatest overtime I've ever seen, the greatest stretch of hockey I've ever seen!" It was pure hockey at its best, intense New York rivalry with the added drama of sudden victory or sudden death, end-to-end action, and big saves by both goalies. The Rangers had a couple of great chances to end the game and end our dynasty in shocking fashion.

DAVE MALONEY
New York Rangers defenseman
The overtime was intense. I can recall Mikko Leinonen had the puck and Billy Smith dead to rights. I was at the left point and Mikko was in the left corner. The puck just hopped over his stick.

Before the overtime winner, I was on the bench when Billy Smith made one of the all-time great playoff saves on Bob Brooke, dropping to his knees and stopping what looked like a sure goal.

BOB BROOKE
New York Rangers forward
I was still getting my feet under me as a professional and had very little sense of the rivalry between the two teams. Not sure I had even played 15 games yet! But I know of the intensity now looking back and what I would give to have one chance to lift the puck over Billy Smith on my biggest chance to make an impact on that series.

Billy made it look routine. It was anything but, as 99 out of 100 of those shots are going in.

The puck then went back the other way and was dumped into the corner, where Larry Patey took it and turned up the boards. He got tripped up and Brent Sutter grabbed the loose puck and fired a low shot from a sharp angle that Hanlon saved. The rebound in front was knocked away and caromed off the boards and into the right face-off circle. I had jumped on the ice as the puck went into their end, and I skated over toward my position on the right side just as the puck bounced off the boards. The timing just happened to be right so that I was able to skate to the puck and shoot at the net all in one motion.

I never had the hardest shot—in fact, Smith used to joke that he could read "Made in Canada" stamped on the puck as my shot came at him in practice. The big thing with me was that I always tried to get my shots through and to get them on net. They didn't have to be hard, but if they got through then good things could happen—like tips and rebounds.

This overtime goal was one of those moments—a low shot along the ice that found its way through a great screen by Flatley and past Hanlon, who couldn't see it coming.

"It popped loose to the side," Hanlon told the *New York Post* at the time. "I tried to dodge traffic in front. I saw it. I saw it three times and lost it."

I didn't see my shot go in, but I heard the puck clang off the back of the goal and then I heard the roar of the Nassau Coliseum crowd. Incredible!

There was a mob scene in the corner. After the chaos I went through the handshake line and congratulated the Rangers players, especially my Olympic teammates, and then I missed the chance to shake hands with Herb Brooks, who stayed on the ice at the other end. I was totally oblivious that he was there; he was standing with Beck, who had his arm in a sling. Some of the Islanders players went to shake their hands in what was a great gesture. I got caught up in the excitement and unfortunately missed my chance to do that.

About the emotions in the handshake line, Bob Nystrom told the *New York Post* following the game, "You say, 'Good luck;' what else can you say? I would have to say they looked sad. It was the hardest way to lose. You're one shot from winning the series."

JIGGS McDONALD
NHL play-by-play announcer
That goal by Kenny against the Rangers—the big, bad Rangers, which the team and fans hated—I can understand what it meant to Kenny. That was Kenny being Kenny—the accuracy, the uncanny ability to get the puck through traffic. The rivalry was so significant. That loss was absolutely devasting to the Rangers.

To this day, when I am back in New York, I still have Rangers fans come up to me and tell me, "You broke my heart in '84."

It was a game where we got outplayed but somehow found a way to win, the sign of a champion that refuses to go down without a fight. That game truly embodied the Rangers–Islanders rivalry and would be the end of a run of four straight meetings in the playoffs and five times in six years going back to 1979. That by itself is hard to believe, as the two teams haven't met in the playoffs since 1994.

FRANK BROWN
***New York Daily News* journalist who covered every Rangers–Islanders playoff series during the 1980s**
The Rangers just didn't have the whole package. The Islanders just had it.… No one will win 19 straight series again.

If the Rangers had won that series, who knows how far they would have gone? I didn't score a lot of goals, but if you're going to be remembered in New York, this was the one to score. Thank you, Pat Flatley, for the great screen!

FRANK BROWN

I'll never forget the shot he put between Hanlon's knees to win that series and crush Rangers' souls yet again. You didn't see Morrow until he shot it, before, after, or since. You cannot overstate the specialness of the special chemistry of those Islander teams. Ken contributed to it. He helped make it happen. The dependability of his contribution was a gigantic factor.

This was a very hard defeat for the Rangers and their fans. Former Rangers captain Dave Maloney, who replaced the injured Beck in playing the 48th and final playoff game of his Rangers tenure, called it the toughest loss of his career.

Herb had done a masterful job coaching this Rangers team. I owe him a lot for helping make me the player that I had become.

BARRY BECK

Herb was demanding, but I liked that as long it was done in a professional way. He was a coach and had to win to keep his job, but it was much more than that. Herb was the last cut of the 1960 U.S. Olympic team.... When that happens, you are forever driven.

People from all across the country always want to talk about the "Miracle on Ice" game in Lake Placid. They tell me where they were and who they were with when watching the game—an incredible experience for me 45 years and counting. With that 1984 overtime goal, I get fans from both sides in New York, both Islanders and Rangers fans, wanting to tell me their story.

DON MALONEY

That series was the first time in all the years we played them that I thought we could beat them. I really felt we had the team. They had won four in a row. They had a lot of miles, a lot of hockey. I thought this was it, how it is supposed to be. We were in their home, we're going to take this game and win the Cup.

Perhaps my funniest story from all of this relates to Rangers legend Rod Gilbert, whom I got to know when we would meet at charity golf outings in the summer.

Many years later, as would happen at these events, stories get told over a beer. Rod was one of the all-time greats—a Rangers legend and one of the classiest and nicest guys I have met. He told me the following story, which was even more special in Rod's classic French accent.

"I was up in the crowded press box at Nassau Coliseum during that overtime. And the Islanders have all these scorers like Bossy, Trottier, Gillies, and Denis Potvin. And who scores the goal to beat us? Ken f—ing Morrow!"

He kept saying it over and over again. I think that pretty well sums it up for Rangers fans, as told by Mr. Ranger, Rod Gilbert.

BRYAN TROTTIER

Whenever you play a rival of that magnitude, it adds intensity to that series. So for sure it is a moment of pride for our Islander fans. We had those four years of dominance. The Rangers had great teams. They probably could have won; they probably could have won Cups those years themselves. That's how good they were. That just tells you how we had to be a little bit better. We didn't dominate. We never thought we would for a second. We had to earn it.

Even after being on the ice for Don Maloney's last-minute game-tying goal, the hockey gods smiled on me again.

I had been so blessed in my hockey career up to that point. I would ask myself, *Why am I the recipient of so much good fortune?*

DAVE MALONEY

The Islanders—like the Ken Morrow goal—always found a way to win.

MIKKO LEINONEN
1980 Finland Olympic Team forward; New York Rangers 1981–84

The 1984 playoffs against the Islanders was for sure the very best series I have played, and everybody on the Rangers knew we could beat the Islanders, but the Islanders were so good. Unfortunately, they won those important games.

All I know is that I have so many great memories to look back on.

Chapter 15

1984 Heading for Edmonton— and the End

AFTER GETTING PUSHED TO THE BRINK and surviving the epic series against the Rangers, we would now face the Washington Capitals for the second straight spring. The Caps were coming off a three-game sweep of Philadelphia in the opening round.

Washington had put together a strong 101-point season and become a force in the Patrick Division, featuring a core of Mike Gartner, my Olympic teammate Dave Christian, and young Bobby Carpenter up front, plus 20-year-old Scott Stevens and stalwart Rod Langway on the blue line. This would be another tough test for us.

The victory over the Rangers was our 17th straight series win, an amazing feat considering there were never any easy matchups in the Eastern Conference during that time. I will tell you there was no talk of the streak in our locker room. As a player, you can't get caught looking behind or ahead. You have to stay in the moment.

The Caps rallied to win Game 1 at Nassau Coliseum by a 3–2 score on a late goal by Craig Laughlin.

The second game of the series the next night featured a wild first period. We jumped to a 3–0 lead less than 10 minutes into the game, but Washington's Bengt-Åke Gustafsson scored two quick goals 50 seconds apart midway through to make it a one-goal game. Then Bossy made it 4–2 before the second intermission.

The Capitals played a hardworking and physical style of hockey under fiery coach Bryan Murray. They kept up the pressure and scored power-play goals by Stevens in the second and Gartner in the third period to force yet another overtime.

We were staring at potentially losing two games on our home ice and facing an 0–2 deficit heading to Washington if we didn't find a way to score the next goal. Thankfully, Anders Kallur stepped up to be our overtime hero, scoring at 7:35 as he sped down the left wing and fired the puck past Pat Riggin for the winner.

This is the stark reality of the playoffs. One goal can be the difference between being even in a series or down two games. Suddenly we were tied at 1–1 and the pressure was on them to win at home. We were so dominant in overtime during those 19 consecutive playoff series wins from 1980–84, going 13–2 in overtime games. (We were 11–2 during the Cup-winning years.)

Going back even further, the Islanders' playoff overtime record between 1975 and '84 was 21–5. That is astonishing!

Who is going to be the hero? was being asked again in our locker room before overtime would start.

After the Game 2 overtime win, we rolled to 3–1 and 5–2 wins in Washington and then erased an early 2–0 Capitals lead in Game 5 on Long Island with four second-period goals to capture the series with a hard-fought 5–3 win. Kallur scored a shorthanded goal halfway through the game to give us a lead that we did not relinquish.

When Greg Gilbert scored on the power play with less than two minutes remaining in the third, we had secured consecutive series win No. 18.

During this Washington series, it seemed every game we were without three or four key players due to injury or circumstance. Bourne only played in the opening game of the series, Tonelli missed the final three games, Langevin missed the last two games, and Denis Potvin missed the clinching final game of the series after the passing of his father.

Guys were playing injured and missing games, which is not uncommon in a playoff year. But we were now on our fifth consecutive run to the Stanley Cup Final, and the physical toll was showing. Thanks to our young players—LaFontaine, Flatley, Mats Hallin, Gord Dineen, and Paul Boutilier—stepping up, we continued our winning ways and moved on to the conference final against the Montreal Canadiens.

Montreal was always known for its speed and skill, and that hadn't changed, but it did play a more physical and defensive style of game under coach Jacques Lemaire.

The Canadiens were hard to play against, even though they had a losing record during the regular season. They had gone to young goaltender Steve Penney in the playoffs, and he stood on his head. They upset Boston in the first round and archrival Quebec in the second round to reach the conference final. Penney got on a roll in the playoffs and carried Montreal into the third round, four wins from the Stanley Cup Final.

For the third straight series in these playoffs, we didn't get off to a good start. The Canadiens took the first two games in the series at the historic Montreal Forum. Everything seemed to be going their way with the hot goaltender and the run they were on themselves. We were starting to show some dents in our armor in these playoffs, but our will to win and our ability to battle through adversity had become a trademark of our team.

After a 3–0 shutout loss in Game 1 and a 4–2 loss in Game 2, the Montreal Forum crowd was singing, "Na na na na, na na na na, hey hey hey, goodbye."

But we came back home, dug deep, and won two games on Long Island by scores of 5–2 and 3–1. Islanders fans were always amazing, and the Coliseum was loud and rocking. Many in the hockey media had written us off after we fell behind 2–0 in the series. As I said before, the heart of a champion should never be underestimated. Our team always found ways to overcome and to win and to play our best hockey under difficult circumstances.

Now we were faced with a pivotal Game 5 back in Montreal with the series even at two. Once again, with Billy Smith at his best and us scoring a couple of early goals, we frustrated the Canadiens and quieted their fans, grinding out a 3–1 win on first-period goals by Trottier and Brent Sutter, then Flatley making it 3–1 in the third to give us some breathing room. I can honestly say it felt very good to stick it to the Montreal fans after they were singing "Na Na Hey Hey Kiss Him Goodbye" after Game 2.

This series turned into a hard-hitting affair, uncharacteristic hockey for a Montreal team known for its high-flying style of play. This series was played in the trenches. The great Guy Lafleur didn't score a goal in the series.

We were now ready to close out Montreal on home ice, something that hadn't seemed possible after losing the first two games.

As had happened in the last game, we jumped out to an early two-goal lead as Gillies and Bossy each scored within the first eight minutes of the game. Then Flatley came up big again, making it 3–0 just 30 seconds into the third period. Bossy, with his second goal of the game, scored on the power play with less than five minutes remaining, locking down a 4–1 win.

Islanders fans were now loudly singing "Na na na na, na na na na, hey hey hey, goodbye" as the final minutes counted down, and that was great to hear. Montreal fans had been singing like it was the end of our dynasty. Instead, Islanders fans were singing to celebrate our 19th consecutive series win. We had come back to take this series by winning four straight games, another truly remarkable accomplishment for this team.

This was a testament to Bill Torrey and Al Arbour and the players who had come before and laid the foundation for all of the success that followed.

BRYAN TROTTIER
Four-time Stanley Cup winner with the New York Islanders

Without a doubt, that bond is pretty strong. Guys, to a man, feel very appreciative of each other and their contribution. There was a chemistry but also value and worth to each player and that value and worth is hard to put into words. If your penalty killer scored a goal, you blocked a shot. It didn't matter what you did in that moment, it was everybody putting on the shin pads. That is what championship teams do. When you win, when you've been on top, it's a bond that is there forever. It's deep.

We had battled our way to a fifth straight Stanley Cup Final, overcoming the odds after falling behind in all three series.

DUANE SUTTER
Four-time Stanley Cup winner with the New York Islanders

We knew the Oilers were knocking on the door. They added more size and grit to their roster. They had to change their roster to play with us. We had hurdles with injuries and through the season we had two or three fathers pass away and that trickled into the dressing room. We were a tight, tight group, and that is a major reason why we were so successful.

We lost the opener on home ice 1–0. In retrospect and in my opinion, this game was most responsible for the Oilers winning the series. It wasn't Gretzky or Kurri or any of their other stars who scored the goal—it was fourth-line tough guy Kevin McClelland with the game's sole goal early in the third period. We rebounded the next game with a 6–1 rout to tie the series at 1–1 before heading to Edmonton for three games.

215

The 1984 playoffs were the first year the NHL switched the Cup Final schedule to a 2–3–2 format: two games at home, three games away, then back home for Games 6 and 7.

Would it have made a difference if the format hadn't changed and we'd had the chance to swing the momentum back in our favor on home ice in Game 5? Who knows?

What I do know is that Edmonton was a powerhouse, and we were a beat-up hockey team. No excuses, just reality.

Once we got on Edmonton ice for Games 3, 4, and 5, we just didn't have an answer for their firepower.

The Oilers got rolling, and we suffered back-to-back 7–2 losses in Games 3 and 4. Could we possibly find a spark to ignite another comeback?

In Game 5, Gretzky scored twice in the first period and the Oilers added two power-play goals in the second. It seemed like an insurmountable 4–0 lead, heading into what could be our final 20 minutes as defending champions.

Then Pat LaFontaine scored two goals within the initial 35 seconds of the third, and this threw a serious scare into the Oilers and the crowd. Was there enough left in the tank for us to pull off an improbable comeback?

Once we got to the late stages of the game and with the score still at 4–2, it started to sink in that we might not win. I had played five seasons in the NHL, and from winning Olympic gold on February 24, 1980, until May 19, 1984, and four Stanley Cups later, I didn't know what it was like to lose. An empty-net goal by Dave Lumley in the final seconds made it a 5–2 final and ended our historic run, three wins shy of a fifth straight Cup.

Just like that, it was over.

Sitting in the locker room after this loss, it hit me hard. The noise and the bedlam in the Northlands Coliseum, looking around the room and seeing the drained faces, coming up empty after all we had put into these playoffs…now I knew how the other teams felt when we were eliminating them all these years.

Al Arbour had gone out into the hallway to talk with the media, and my memory of that moment in time is how quiet it was in our locker room. It was quiet on the bus ride to the airport and quiet on the plane ride home. The exhaustion and the shock of losing had set in. It was a terrible feeling. It was the end of an era.

RICH TORREY
Son of then Islanders general manager Bill Torrey

The ride through those Cup years was like a dream. It's why I call it our Camelot. The Islanders were never sidetracked or full of themselves. They were just in this zone, impossible to describe to my kids or anyone who wasn't around for it.

It was this perfect five-year run, and then it ended. And when it did, it was one of the strangest feelings I've ever had, like a pin stuck in a balloon. Suddenly we were back on earth after being on some long lunar mission or something.

We were worn out, even with the injection of young legs with LaFontaine and Flatley and the other young players. I was more disappointed for them than anything else. You never know if you'll ever get the chance to play for a Stanley Cup again.

When people question me about Edmonton winning the Cup in 1984, my simple answer is that it was Edmonton's time, much like it was the Islanders' time in 1980. Those Islanders had been through a couple of tough losses in '78 and '79, a hard lesson that is widely considered to be necessary in order to reach the pinnacle of winning a Stanley Cup. It was the same for the Oilers in 1981, '82, and '83. The Oilers were now a force that would have to be reckoned with.

BILLY SMITH

Four-time Stanley Cup–winning goaltender with the New York Islanders

Their team was great. They were going to win it sooner or later. Unfortunately, on the fifth, we were just beat to death.

Thinking back to all the moments where it could have gone differently, there were so many overtime games that could have swung a series the other way. That started with Game 3 in the opening round against Los Angeles in 1980 when we were down 3–1 going into the third period, continued with us escaping against Pittsburgh in Game 5 in 1982, then concluded with my overtime goal against the Rangers in the 1984 playoffs.

There were moments during our five-year run when our collective will to win combined with our character and determination simply allowed us to defy the odds and win games and win series time and time again.

BRYAN TROTTIER

Winning 19 series in a row is incredible. There's a marvel about it all that hockey fans can appreciate, especially Islanders fans. We're proud of that. We were a special group at a special time, and we all felt appreciated on Long Island. That contributed to the uniqueness of it.

Four consecutive Stanley Cups and 19 straight series wins are accomplishments that will stand tall forever. At the time, it all seemed normal. Looking back all these years later, I realize that it was not normal and what an incredible accomplishment we had achieved. Nineteen series without a Game 7, only two best-of-five series that went the distance, and both of those games had miracle overtime finishes.

As Herb Brooks would say, "The common man goes nowhere; you have to be uncommon."

And that we were!

It takes talent, some luck, and a lot of perseverance and sacrifice. As Wayne Gretzky put it, speaking about losing in 1983 on TNT during the 2023 Stanley Cup Final, "When you win the Stanley Cup, obviously there's a celebration. So in 1983 we lost four straight, got our lunch handed to us by Bossy, Trottier, Potvin, and Smith, and in the old Islander arena, the visiting team had to go by the home room and I remember…thinking, 'This is going to be the worst moment of my life. I have to listen to those guys cheering and clapping and singing and all that goes with that, right?'

"As we walked by, it was amazing to me. To win, you have to go the extra mile, and if you go the extra mile, you're beat up physically and mentally. Those guys were sitting there with ice bags on. There was not a whole lot of celebration. They were obviously in a good mood, but it was such an invaluable lesson that our team learned. We learned as hockey players how that is what it takes to get your name on the Stanley Cup."

Like Joe DiMaggio's 56-game hitting streak and our 19 straight series wins, I can't imagine either record will ever be broken.

It would take a team winning five Stanley Cups in a row. The Tampa Bay Lightning have come the closest since our run in the early '80s, winning 11 straight series and two Cups in 2020 and 2021.

But 11 is a very long way from 19.

Starting with their win in 1984, the Edmonton Oilers won the Stanley Cup five times in seven years. But they never won more than twice in a row, having been knocked out in early playoff rounds by Calgary in 1986 and Los Angeles (and Wayne Gretzky) in 1989.

BUTCH GORING
Four-time Stanley Cup winner with the New York Islanders
We are very proud of what we accomplished. We talk about the four Stanley Cups in a row. And that hasn't been done since we did it. We're still upset we didn't win the fifth one. This was never about the Oilers or whether they were good enough. They were a great hockey team. They proved it in the next couple of years. More than anything else, we love what we accomplished.

Our run of four straight Cup wins becomes more memorable and epic as time goes by. We had followed Montreal's four consecutive Cups from 1976 to '79 with our own quartet and nearly five decades later, no team has won more than twice in a row.

BRYAN TROTTIER
I think it's just great that we can all reflect on that. Those moments are special to all of us. It's obviously great joy and sense of pride. We all work toward a common goal. And so we share that history together.

We had 16 players win all four Cups, along with others who were integral parts of those Cup-winning teams. Keeping the core group together for as long as this Islanders team did was a feat all by itself.

Losing cherished teammates Clark Gillies, Jean Potvin, and Mike Bossy within three months in early 2022 really hit hard. All-time great players and character people. When I watch highlights of our games, they are forever young and always will be.

BRYAN TROTTIER

There's no way to describe that. There's no way to put it into words. I think a lot of people understand it. You understand it and you look at it and you say, that must be hard. Yeah, it's hard. It's even harder to put into words, right?

But the one thing about it is that you never stop appreciating. So we appreciate each other till we're, you know, we're not here anymore, right? They're alive in our hearts. You know, they'll always be alive. We celebrate them, like continuing to talk about them and making sure they're not forgotten in that sense, with their families and their grandchildren.

The bond with our teammates, what we went through and what we accomplished, absolutely adds to the legend.

When you are winning, the only thing you want to do is to keep winning. You don't ever want to let that feeling go.

But as we all learned, it can't last forever.

CHAPTER 16

1985–89 NEW YORK ISLANDERS

AFTER WE LOST IN THE 1984 STANLEY CUP FINAL, the page turned for all of us, and very quickly. That group of guys—the 16 players who won all four Cups—was starting to break apart.

Guys like Bob Lorimer, Garry Howatt, and Chico Resch, who were Islanders when I arrived in 1980 and won Cups, had been gone for a few years already, and midway through the 1984–85 season, Butch Goring was waived and claimed by Boston.

It had to be tough for guys like Denis Potvin, Trots, and Bossy, who had all been there since the '70s. You blink your eyes and suddenly there are new faces and new kids coming through. There is never an easy way for that to happen. You recall the memories as well as cling to the high hopes for the future, but we all saw that this was an inevitable turning of the tide into a new era.

I think once we lost to Edmonton in 1984, which had proven it was the next powerhouse, we were simply worn down. You can argue whether this team should have been given another kick at the can—but changes were still coming. Maybe remaking a team is supposed to happen that quickly...yet it still felt like it occurred seemingly overnight.

I came into camp after spending the summer rehabbing my beleaguered right knee. I had four knee operations between 1980 and 1984, with the first during the 1980 playoff series against Boston, followed by another in the '81–82 season, then one more again in 1983. I was no stranger to knee issues. I had four knee operations between April 1980 and October 1984. First was the arthroscope in the quarter-final series against Boston, which forced me to miss Game 3 against the Bruins. Then there was the second scope in May 1983 which cost me Game 5 of the semifinal series versus Boston, followed by a third scope in December 1983, which kept me out of the lineup for five games. We had tried to avoid another surgery during the summer, but I could tell at training camp in 1984 that I couldn't play on it as it was, so the decision was made that I would have major surgery on my right knee. I ended up missing most of the 1984–85 season.

I played just 15 games to finish the regular season after returning to the lineup in March. The truth is that I was slowing down, and it's a harsh reality for any player to come to terms with. Any thoughts of going up ice—as I did in May 1983 to clinch Cup No. 4—were now out the door. At this stage, I was just trying to be good defensively by taking care of my own end and to continue earning a spot in the lineup.

In my final five seasons with the Islanders, I was intent on keeping the swelling in my knee to a minimum and playing as many games as I could. The fact is that in the last two to three years of my career I was getting my knee drained regularly. Sometimes it was before the team left on a road trip and other times it was before home games. I would go out for warm-ups, then come back into the trainer's room, where they'd stick a needle into the knee joint, then squeeze around the knee to drain the fluid out, and then they would wrap it and I would go out and play. We jokingly called it "changing the oil."

It would feel pretty good after the draining, but it was temporary and would only last a few days. In the long run it wasn't the smartest choice, as it certainly shortened my career. But I did what any player would do to continue playing. All hockey players play through injuries and I would do it all over again in a heartbeat.

BOB NYSTROM

Four-time Stanley Cup winner with the New York Islanders

It was so impressive that Kenny drained his knee near every game. I don't know how he did it. It looked pretty bad, but he was tough. I never heard him complain once!

This was my regular routine those last few years. That whole 1984–85 season was so different from anything I had experienced before in my career. Not just with the knee issues and rehabbing, but with missing games, which is something no competitor wants to do.

We had three 100-point scorers that season, led by Bossy, who surpassed 50 goals again with 58 goals and 117 points. It was the eighth straight season the great No. 22 reached and surpassed the 50-goal mark.

Brent Sutter added 102 points, and Tonelli reached the 100-point mark with 42 goals and 58 assists. What a season for those three! Denis Potvin and Trots also had productive years, and Pat LaFontaine and Pat Flatley were good in their first full NHL seasons. We finished with 40 wins and 86 points, third in the Patrick Division behind Philadelphia and Washington.

For the first time in my career, the Islanders were considered underdogs in a first-round playoff series. The Capitals were first up as playoff opponents, as they came in just ahead of us in the Patrick Division standings. Mike Gartner had just wrapped up a 100-plus-point season, and Scott Stevens and Kevin Hatcher were two of the best blueliners in the NHL.

We lost the first two games at the Capital Centre but like always, we found a way and roared back strong to grab the next three, including a 2–1 series-clinching win in Washington on goals by Kallur and Brent Sutter as Smitty made an incredible 39 saves. It was another big comeback for our core group, which still included many members of the Four-Cup club. But it was the last one we had in the tank.

We next played the Flyers—for the first time since the 1980 Final—and the result was very different this time around. Philadelphia beat us in five games thanks to stellar play in goal from Pelle Lindbergh, who had two shutouts, including a 1–0 win in Game 5 at the Spectrum.

And that was it; our season was over. For the first time in my NHL career, I did not reach the Final.

Our top scorers put up big numbers as usual the following year. Bossy scored 61 goals, the ninth straight season he scored 50 or more, and Trottier chipped in another 37 goals and 96 points. LaFontaine scored 30 goals in his second full season.

In March 1986, another integral part of our Cup run departed Long Island in shocking fashion. John Tonelli was traded to Calgary for forward Rich Kromm and defenseman Steve Konroyd.

The trade ironically was finalized the morning of our game against the Flames at Nassau Coliseum. Johnny took his equipment down the hall that morning and suited up in Flames red against us that night. It was a difficult day for our team, as there was no opportunity to say goodbye.

It was very tough to see JT, a heart-and-soul Islander for so long, leave. A perennial fan favorite whose tenacity and hard-nosed style epitomized the attitude of our championship teams, John had been an Islander since 1978, with 206 regular season goals and 28 more in the playoffs. His work ethic and countless intangibles would be impossible to replace.

"JT was the worker bee, always fishing pucks out of the corners," Mike Bossy told *The New York Times* in February 2020, shortly before Tonelli had his No. 27 raised to the Nassau Coliseum rafters. "I don't think I ever saw him come away from the corner with his helmet square on his head. He was always adjusting it."

We went on to win 39 games and finish third in the Patrick Division with 90 points, but we fell to the Washington Capitals in three straight games to open the playoffs.

We lost 3–1 and 5–2 at the Cap Centre. Then, in Game 3 back home, Bossy scored our only goal in a 3–1 defeat.

More major changes were ahead.

Nystrom had played his last season in 1985–86—forced to retire due to an eye injury.

Arbour stepped down after the season and Terry Simpson became our coach, marking the first time since 1972–73 someone other than Al would be coaching the Islanders.

Gillies and Bourne left via the waiver draft in October 1986—Gillies to Buffalo and Bourne to Los Angeles.

Three major departures from our core of 16.

Despite the shake-up, we still came in third in the Patrick Division in 1986–87 with 82 points. And, once again, we met the Capitals in the first round of the playoffs.

Washington always played a hard game, and this series would not deviate from that script. How could it, considering what had led up to that Game 7 in Washington? This was the fifth straight year we'd met the Capitals in the playoffs.

Washington won the opener 4–3 at home in the dark and cavernous Cap Centre, but we took Game 2 by a score of 3–1. Back at Nassau Coliseum, we lost the next two 2–0 and 4–1 to fall behind three games to one. Fortunately for us, this was the first year the opening round of the playoffs was extended to a seven-game series.

We knew we weren't done. At that time, no team had rallied from a 3–1 deficit in a seven-game series since the Islanders did it against Pittsburgh in 1975, when they came back from a 3–0 deficit to shockingly win in seven games. That victory came on a winning goal by Eddie Westfall, the first captain of the Islanders, who won the Stanley Cup with Boston in 1970 and 1972.

We rallied back into the series winning Game 5 by a 4–2 score in Maryland, then tied the series in Game 6 with a 5–4 win at home to force a historic Game 7 at the Cap Centre on the night of Saturday

April 18, 1987, and into Easter Sunday. This game would become known as the "Easter Epic."

We knew the Capitals were loaded with stars and that this wouldn't be easy. There would be a lot of hockey fans across North America watching Game 7 on a Saturday night.

Gartner scored the opening goal for the Caps late in the first period. Then Flatley scored for us in the second to tie it before Grant Martin put the Caps ahead again 2–1. And that's how it stayed through the rest of the middle period and most of the third. Bob Mason for the Caps and Kelly Hrudey for us were playing great—shot after shot.

Finally, Trottier tied it with just over five minutes remaining in the third period on a backhand shot.

And then the frantic finish was on for both teams.

No goals were scored the rest of regulation, so we moved into overtime, where the next goal would win the series.

Greg Smith of Washington almost scored late in the first overtime, but his shot hit the right post behind Hrudey. The second overtime came and went with more of the same—quality shots from both sides but again, no goals.

On to overtime period number *three*.

Goalies Hrudey and Mason were absolutely stopping everything, allowing no goals through the extra 60 minutes of overtime.

For the first time since 1951, an NHL game was heading to quadruple overtime. The shots on goal, 36–21 in favor of the Caps after regulation time, were 74–52 in their favor after the third overtime!

Overtime just went on and on and on and it felt as if nobody was *ever* going to score another goal. I would lose five pounds of water weight in a normal game. That night, I lost more than 10 pounds. I couldn't drink enough water and Gatorade as we moved into the fourth overtime.

It was both crazy and surreal. Everything about that night was hard to fathom. It seemed like for the first five minutes of every overtime period, players from both teams had some added energy coming out of the locker room. Then, for the last 15 minutes of the overtime periods, legs would get heavy and the game would become bogged down into the trenches.

If we had been playing by today's rules, there would have been penalties almost every shift with all the clutching and grabbing, hooking and holding by both teams. The referee, Andy Van Hellemond, had put his whistle away, as was usually the case in that era. Referees didn't want to be the ones to help decide a game by making a penalty call unless it was blatant. Players knew how much they could get away with, so it was equal for both sides.

PAT LaFONTAINE
New York Islanders center, 1983–91
In the middle of that fourth overtime, I heard the organist start playing *The Twilight Zone* theme song. There was a moment where I clicked out and looked around and I thought, *Seven periods, 70-something shots—it's two in the morning. There are people sleeping in the stands! Is this really happening?*

Finally, at 8:47 of the fourth overtime—the seventh period of hockey that night—LaFontaine scored on an improvised whirl-around shot from just inside the blue line. Then it was pure adrenaline as we celebrated. Pat scored a lot of goals in his career, but never one like that.

PAT LaFONTAINE
I spun around, and I have to say, I've never shot a puck like that in my life. Ever. It was rolling and I just shot it. I believe Mason—my Olympic teammate three years earlier in Sarajevo—must have been screened. Or

231

maybe it was my teammate Dale Henry's big head helping to block his view too. But I sent the puck toward the net, I heard the post and I saw Mason drop down. It was in! Ending the longest game in Islanders history.

We didn't arrive back home until around 7:00 AM on Easter Sunday morning, and then we had to be back at Nassau Coliseum at 6:00 PM for a bus ride to Philadelphia, where we had a game the following night to start the next series.

We split the first two games of that series against the Flyers, then fell behind three games to one before rallying back to tie the series and force *another* seventh game. But we ran out of steam and fell in that final game, losing 5–1.

This was definitely the last hurrah for our group, the last *bona fide* moment of playoff celebration that spring. At least it ended with one more overtime win in the most dramatic fashion.

In 1987–88, we won the Patrick Division with only 88 points.

We hosted the upstart Devils and won the opener at Nassau Coliseum 4–3 on an overtime goal by LaFontaine. New Jersey made the playoffs that spring for the first time in franchise history on dramatic third-period and overtime goals by John MacLean in their season finale against the Blackhawks in Chicago.

New Jersey won Game 2 as two of my Olympic teammates combined on the winning goal. Mark Johnson scored it on the power play at 5:56 of the third with an assist to Jack O'Callahan. Those Lake Placid connections always seemed to pop up.

In Game 3, the Devils and Sean Burke blanked us 3–0 courtesy of two goals from Johnson and another from defenseman Ken Daneyko.

Game 4 would prove to be our last gasp, as Brent Sutter scored at 15:07 of overtime to knot the series at 2–2.

That would be my final overtime moment in an Islanders jersey.

We lost 4–2 in Game 5 at home and then 6–5 in New Jersey in Game 6. I would finish my playoff career with 11 goals, 22 assists, and a plus-37 in 127 playoff games.

New Jersey had its first playoff series win at our expense, with only four of us left from the four Cup-winning teams: Denis Potvin, Bryan Trottier, Billy Smith, and myself.

The end of an era was at hand as Denis retired that summer after 15 seasons, 310 goals, 1,052 points overall, and 185 career playoff games. He had captained us to four Stanley Cups. He had been there from the start of my NHL career from my first game on March 1, 1980, until now, so this change was seismic and emotional on many levels.

The following season, 1988–89, would be my last NHL season, and that proved to be a difficult year all the way through. I knew I had been slowing down and was trying to keep my career going for as long as I could at that stage.

We got off to a terrible start with a 7–18–2 record, at which point coach Terry Simpson was let go and Al Arbour returned behind the bench.

I had been playing more than I expected through the first couple of months of the season but ironically, after the coaching change there was a decision made to play the young guys. I had played in 33 games before the change, and I played just one game the rest of the year.

That would be in our last home game, a 4–3 loss to Buffalo on April 1, 1989. I am sure Al played me in that game out of respect, so I was able to skate in front of the home crowd one more time. No points in that game but I was a plus-2, ending my playing career on a somewhat positive personal note.

My contract was up that summer and the writing was on the wall with the Islanders, but I was still hoping to play the following year. I went through that summer of 1989 not knowing if any NHL team would sign me.

My salaries in my first three NHL seasons were $50,000, $55,000, and $60,000, with a top salary of $190,000 in my final season. Winning four championships earned us an extra $20,000 each year ($5,000 for each of the four playoff rounds) plus a $5,000 bonus for winning the Cup. That definitely felt like a lot of money back then.

I was still looking for a place to play late in the summer as it got closer to training camp, and that's when Neil Smith had been hired with the Rangers as their new general manager.

I had played against Neil in college when he was at Western Michigan and I was at Bowling Green. He had been drafted by the Islanders in 1974, then spent several seasons in the minor leagues before he started working as a scout for the Islanders. He later worked closely in the front office with the Islanders in the early 1980s. Neil invited me to Rangers training camp just a couple of weeks before camps opened, so with this as my only option I drove to Rye, New York, where the Rangers practiced.

I shed a few tears on that long drive. I was a guy who bled Islanders Orange and Blue and here I was, driving to Rangers training camp for a tryout. That was the hardest thing I have ever done in hockey.

I took my physical the next day and went and got fitted for equipment. They were going to start the on-ice portion the next day, but I was called to a hotel room with Neil and the coaches, and they said the team doctors were not going to pass me for the physical because of my damaged right knee.

You would hear about this too many times in pro sports back then—where you play your whole career and playing is the only thing that matters besides your family.

Then suddenly, it ends.

I was only 32 years old and I had no plan B. *What do I do now?*

Neil offered me a job coaching with the Flint Spirits back in my hometown in Michigan, which happened to be a Rangers affiliate that year. I stayed with my mom in Flint while Barb and our two daughters stayed back on Long Island so as not to disrupt their lives.

NEIL SMITH
Former New York Rangers and New York Islanders GM

I would have loved nothing more than to put Ken Morrow in a Rangers jersey. But he knew and I knew the end was there. You never want to admit the end being there. I liked his personality, and I liked Ken. That's why I asked if he would consider being an assistant coach in Flint.

All I could think of is that he would be great for young players, and this would give Ken a way to stay in the game. He took it and went on a path that led to many other things.

Whenever I have seen him since then it has been wonderful and friendly. He's one of the classiest, nicest guys.

I had a playing career that was taken away but had another opportunity presented to me and I took it. I was thankful for the chance Neil gave me to unexpectedly start a new career path. I signed a contract with the Spirits and not the Rangers.

I was assistant coach for a team whose roster included Mike Richter, future Cup-winning goalie for the Rangers, and defenseman Peter Laviolette, who later coached the Islanders. Laviolette won the Stanley Cup with Carolina in 2006 and took the Philadephia Flyers (2010) and Nashville Predators (2017) to the Cup Final. He has had a highly successful coaching career and became Rangers coach before the 2023–24 season, then guided them to the Presidents' Trophy and Eastern Conference Final, where they lost to the eventual-champion Florida Panthers.

Richter played only 13 games at Flint, yet his memories are still fresh. The energetic and acrobatic netminder honed his skills at the University of Wisconsin and now the NCAA Goalie of the Year award is named after him. On a personal note, Mike is one of the finest people I have had the pleasure of knowing. Not only a great goaltender but a high-character and first-class person.

MIKE RICHTER
New York Rangers 1994 Stanley Cup–winning goaltender
Everyone knew who Kenny Morrow was, what he had accomplished and how he carried himself. It was a thrill for young guys to have someone who had such a profound career. And he was so humble about it. He was a model for how to carry yourself off the ice—with humility and respect.

Our Flint team was also loaded with tough guys. Our roster included Denis Vial (351 PIMs), Rudy Poeschek (109), Jim Latos (244), Joe Paterson (198), Daniel Lacroix (128), and Peter Fiorentino (302). That was good old-time hockey and many of these guys went on to play NHL games. At the Spirits' training camp, Vial and Latos fought each other three times in the same intrasquad game! What a different era of hockey that was.

Future Tampa Bay Lightning forward Rob Zamuner led us with 44 goals and Simon Wheeldon had a team-best 83 points, including 34 goals.

The Spirits had a 40–36–6 record, but we lost to the Kalamazoo Wings four straight in the playoffs. As it turned out, this was the fifth and final season for the Spirits in Flint. The franchise moved the following year to Fort Wayne, Indiana.

It was not an easy year for me in Flint. There were some hard nights being away from my daughters and wife. I was trying to make it work both as a new career and as a way to make a living. Those early years after I had stopped playing were not easy, but I have always been grateful that I was given the chance to coach in my hometown. I am glad to know I had some impact that season as a rookie coach.

MIKE RICHTER

Kenny set a great tone. He taught defensemen how to interact with goal-tenders. He was an enormous role model. Guys would say they couldn't believe how accessible and humble he was…and to be so good with Bowling Green, win gold at Lake Placid, then the success with the Islanders. This is so rare. At some point you start to make the connection that he's not just a lucky recipient of the right place, right time. He's one of the guys making that happen. He was that good.

During that season in Flint, I met Doug Soetaert—a former Rangers goaltender who was a scout for them that year—which led to my next job. The following year, Doug was hired in Kansas City as GM/coach of the new Kansas City Blades franchise in the IHL. My good friend Bob Kaser had been hired by Doug as the Blades' broadcaster and had let Doug know I was looking for a job.

Thus, in the summer of 1991, I got a phone call from Doug asking if I would be interested in coming to Kansas City as his associate coach with the Blades. He needed an assistant who could step in when he was not able to be at practices because of his GM duties.

Consequently, my first post-playing-career coaching position in Flint led to my second job in Kansas City, a city that has been my home ever since.

CHAPTER 17

AL ARBOUR

I CONSIDER MYSELF SO VERY FORTUNATE to have played for three legendary coaches over the course of my career, starting as a freshman at Bowling Green with Ron Mason in 1975, continuing with my Olympic year in 1979–80 under Herb Brooks, and then spending most of my 10 Islanders seasons with Al Arbour behind our bench.

Arbour played as a defenseman for 14 NHL seasons and won three Stanley Cups—in 1961 with Chicago and 1962 and 1964 with Toronto. When he became Islanders coach in 1973, the team had won 12 games the previous season, its first as an expansion franchise. From that point on, Al taught the Islanders how to win and facilitated the team's quick rise in the NHL.

He developed all of the young stars who would eventually lead the Islanders to four straight Cups.

Denis Potvin arrived as the first overall pick in the 1973 draft and Islanders general manager Bill Torrey smartly acquired Denis' older brother, Jean, to help with the younger Potvin's transition.

Clark Gillies was drafted fourth overall in 1974 from Moose Jaw, and Bryan Trottier came in the second round of the same draft out of Val Marie, Saskatchewan.

Mike Bossy was taken with the 15th overall pick in the 1977 draft. Imagine 14 chances to draft Mike Bossy! To this day, it remains

241

unthinkable that so many teams passed on him. But that is what can happen at a draft.

For myself, learning from Al and playing for him from day one was a privilege and such a great fit for my game.

I believe he appreciated the defensive style of defenseman that I evolved into with the Olympic team and then playing that role after joining the Islanders in March 1980.

Al nicknamed me "Moses" almost right from the start—I'm guessing mostly because of the beard and maybe somewhat because the team was doing well. It was terrific to hear him call me that.

We had just a great mix of offensive and defensive defensemen, both with the Olympic team defense corps and then with the Islanders.

Even though I was more of a rushing and offensive guy in college, I found out there were more dangerous offensive guys than me with Bill Baker, Dave Christian, Mike Ramsey, and Jack O'Callahan on the Olympic team and Potvin, Stefan Persson, Tomas Jonsson, and Mike McEwen with the Islanders.

Al always preached "taking pride" and "owning every inch of the ice" in our end with our defensive play, and I really enjoyed killing penalties and blocking shots and being counted on in critical defensive situations.

I do believe Al saw a bit of himself in my style of play. I always likened him to a stern father-figure type of coach who you didn't want to let down—and you didn't want to get on his bad side either.

He would give you a kick in the butt when you had more to give, and he would give you a pat on the back at times you weren't expecting it. He was a big man and he had that deep voice that grabbed your attention.

He didn't have to say a lot, but he always commanded respect and he drilled the fundamentals. Those Arbour-coached Islanders teams would rarely beat themselves and opponents were going to have to earn every inch of ice.

My favorite moments with Al were when we were on the road and we would have our team pregame meal in the hotel in the early afternoon. A few guys would hang around the table after the meal, and Al would tell stories from when he played.

Hearing the great NHL names from his past and from that era and hearing the classic hockey stories was such a joy and something I won't forget.

Al was a father figure to so many of the young guys who were drafted in the early days, like Trottier, Gillies, Bossy, and the others. I certainly felt like he was a father figure to me as well.

Al was a serious guy as you would expect, but his humor would come through at times when it was unexpected. I think all the great coaches have that ability to keep players off guard.

After we won the fourth Cup in 1983, Al was quoted in an interview after the game as saying, "There's no team with greater character in any sport than this team."

That is a direct result of our coach, Al Arbour.

I wanted to share a few more thoughts from my Islanders teammates.

BOB NYSTROM
Four-time Stanley Cup winner with the New York Islanders
Al was one incredible man.

If we were going badly, he would pat us on the back, saying, "Don't worry, we're going to turn it around." Sometimes we won a game 6–5 and he'd be upset at us that we gave up that many goals and drive us hard in practice. It was exactly the opposite of what you would expect.

He also singled out stars. He would bury Denis, Boss, Trots. He would go right after them and we could go, "Wow, we better get going." Or we'd win a game, and he would skate the hell out of us.

Al just instilled that we could win any game, whatever the score was. He had a way about him. He was never negative.

I was there for 14 years, and it was very special the way Al crafted the boys. He had such a knack for what the players needed. None of us will ever forget Al. The memories we have, that's what life is all about.

DUANE SUTTER
Four-time Stanley Cup winner with the New York Islanders
A major part of our success was down from Mr. Torrey and Al Arbour and the coaching staff, their foresight into different roles and how we would fill the chemistry out to be a good team.

There are just so many different memories because each Cup was unique. The 1983 Cup run stands out because Brent, Bourney, and I had so much success together. I remember a hat trick in the '83 series against the Rangers when Brent assisted on all three goals. That was special for us.

JOHN TONELLI
We wouldn't have won without Al. He was our leader and every one of us was jumping over the boards for Al and for all our teammates. One of the things that Al did so well was that he defined everybody's role. He got everyone to play their way to the best of their ability. There was pride in not getting scored against or scoring against a top line you weren't supposed to score against.

In April 2016, many of the guys came together on Long Island for a unique memorial service for Al. He would have been proud to see the gathering of his former players and peers and longtime hockey friends.

The family and the players attended a service at St. Patrick's Church in Huntington, where they were also accompanied by the Stanley

Cup—which Al won four times with the Islanders. Arbour coached them from 1973 to 1986 and again from 1988 to 1994 during his Hall of Fame career.

The emotional outpouring from Al's players was heartfelt and especially poignant for Al's family, particularly his wife, Claire.

"To have Al's players show up and hear how they felt about him meant so much to me," Claire Arbour told *The New York Times* at the Huntington Country Club, where she once scored a hole in one, much to her ever-competitive husband's chagrin. "The tears came because there was nothing fake here. It was all genuine."

The guys—including Gillies, Nystrom, and Tonelli from the dynasty years, Garry Howatt and Gerry Hart from the early years, and Pierre Turgeon from the '90s—all wanted to honor their always caring father figure of a coach, who died in August 2015 at age 82.

Jean Potvin, the former defenseman, and Chico Resch, the Islanders' goalie from 1974–81, did short readings before Gillies—the fearsome left wing on the high-scoring Trio Grande Line with Trottier and Bossy in the team's heyday—delivered a eulogy in which he read the poem "The Dash," which considers the meaning of the time between the first and final days of life.

Clark became understandably emotional when concluding the poem by Linda Ellis:

So, when your eulogy is being read,
with your life's actions to rehash...
would you be proud of the things they say
about how you spent your dash?

"Al," Gillies added as his voice wavered and his eyes welled with tears. "Thank you for letting us share your dash."

Knowing that it was Clark who read these special words that day has even more significance, since he would pass in January 2022 at just 67.

Al returned for one more game behind the bench in November 2007, his 1,500th with the team. The Islanders' coach at the time, Ted Nolan, wanted to make sure Al had a chance to reach that milestone, and the evening turned into a celebration as the Islanders beat Pittsburgh for Al's 740th win with the team, the most by any coach with one franchise. Claire, who passed at 89 in early 2024, was of course present for one more magical night at Nassau Coliseum.

Patty LaFontaine said that coaching was only part of what defined Al Arbour—that he could be measured more in terms of being a husband, father, and family man.

"Every person has been blessed by having Al in their lives," LaFontaine said that day.

I couldn't agree more about the impact our coach had on all of us.

CHAPTER 18

EUCHRE WITH LAFONTAINE– TROTTIER–BOSSY

PAT LAFONTAINE JOINED THE ISLANDERS IN 1984 with many deserved accolades. He had broken all of Mario Lemieux's records in junior hockey and he was a heralded rookie coming into the NHL. We had a couple of connections between us. He was joining the Islanders after playing in the Olympics, similar to what I had done, and he spent time growing up in Michigan, which is where I'm from. He came to our team during our "Drive for Five" run and injected some young legs and high-end talent. He (at center) and Pat Flatley (a winger) played a big part for us in making a run to our fifth consecutive Final.

He had been under the microscope growing up and had made a big name for himself with his play and the records he was breaking. After all the attention he was getting, it was a good thing he was joining a team that had big-name stars, so the pressure on him wouldn't be as great. I believe that was welcomed by Patty.

Through our shared experiences and background, we became buddies. The Islanders organization that had been built by Bill Torrey and Al Arbour emphasized character; when you had stability and character at the top with those two, it filtered down throughout the organization. As the mid-'80s came around, our team had a good mix of core veterans and then added newcomers in the early '80s, like Brent Sutter, Tomas Jonsson, Greg Gilbert, and Rollie Melanson, then Flatley and LaFontaine, who came along in 1984. The veterans took it upon themselves to be great examples of what being a professional means and what it takes to win. I was made to feel welcome when I joined the team late in the season, and the same with Pat LaFontaine when he joined our team.

During the season, there is a lot of time spent on the road traveling to away games—so much time spent in airports and airplanes, buses and hotels, trying to keep yourself occupied doing something, reading or listening to music, doing crosswords or playing cards. It just so happened after Patty joined our team that four of us teammates started playing cards. It was Trottier, Bossy, LaFontaine, and myself. Our card game of choice was Euchre (pronounced you-ker), which was a popular card game in a handful of Midwestern states but not widely played anywhere else.

It was a big card game in Michigan, where Pat and I were from. Trots knew how to play and Bossy learned fairly quickly after we started playing. It wasn't long before the four of us were consumed by our card games. What started as a casual pass-the-time activity turned into USA vs. Canada card games, with money on the line. (It was more, "Hey, you owe me this" or "You owe me that;" we never actually paid, as it was more about bragging rights).

For a three-year span between 1984 and 1987, we played every chance we could on our road trips. We played on the bus to the airport, at the airport, on the airplane, on the bus to the hotel, and sometimes even in the room at the hotel. Al maybe occasionally noticed us playing and rolled his eyes, but it didn't go beyond that. He left us alone in "Euchreland." We would make sure to sit across from each other on the bus or plane, sometimes using a cooler or box as our table. The games were great fun, but they got competitive and the USA–Canada rivalry made it even more so.

Pat ended up having an amazing career, inducted into the Hockey Hall of Fame in 2003 and scoring more than 1,000 points before retiring in 1998—a career ended because of concussions. He is considered one of the all-time great American-born players. He played with the Islanders from 1984 to '91. Unfortunately, we weren't able to win the Cup in '84. It sure would have been nice to get that fifth Cup for us and that first one for LaFontaine and Flatley.

As a card player, he proved to be as good as he was on the ice. Of course, he was my partner on Euchre Team USA, with Trottier and Bossy representing Euchre Canada.

Euchre is a favorite card game of mine going back to high school, and my family still plays it today. Euchre emerged in the United States in the early 19th century. It most likely derived from an old game called Jucker or Juckerspiel, and Euchre is why there are jokers in the modern deck of cards. I will try my best to give a quick description of the game. Four players (two teams of two); use 24 cards (nines through aces). Each player gets dealt five cards; one of the four remaining cards gets turned up and becomes the suit for trump. Each team bids to either make that suit trump or to call another suit as trump; the object is to win at least three of the five tricks to get a point, and if you take all five tricks you get extra points. For a card game that uses only 24 cards, there is a lot of strategy and teamwork involved.

Those Euchre years with the Islanders were a lot of fun. We looked forward to playing from the moment a road trip started until we arrived back home. Patty and I wore the championship belt at the end. As you can imagine, there was some trash-talking and some shenanigans (cheating), but in the end it was the overwhelming skill of Team USA that prevailed.

PAT LaFONTAINE
New York Islanders center, 1983–91
Kenny and I were quietly ruthless. Trots and Boss were very loud, Trots being the loudest. And he had vicious nicknames for everybody.

Trottier was the sneaky one to watch out for—you had to be on your toes around him and the unsportsmanlike tricks he would pull. He got me good on one road trip in Vancouver. I had a pair of black dress shoes that I wore on most road trips. He called them my "Euchre shoes." We were at the Pacific Coliseum in Vancouver for our morning game-day skate. I wore contacts when I played but didn't wear them for the morning skate that day. At some point before practice started, he had grabbed my "Euchre shoes" from the dressing room and tied the laces together and hung them over the crossbar on one of the nets. Guys were coming onto the ice, warming up, and taking shots at my shoes dangling from the crossbar. I came onto the ice and, without my contacts in, skated around the ice a few times and shot at the shoes as well, not knowing or seeing that they were mine. Needless to say, he and everyone had a great laugh after I realized they were my shoes, with all the puck marks on them. I kept wearing them and he later named them my "lucky Euchre shoes."

BRYAN TROTTIER
Four-time Stanley Cup winner with the New York Islanders
The shoe heist was comical. I was putting my skates on next to him. He took his glasses off and he put his glasses in the shoes. I just took the shoes, put them in the net, and made them a target. We marked them up pretty good. It's all part of the lore. We loved to tease each other.

It was all great fun, and it would get competitive, and Trots and Boss might do some pouting, but they got over it.

We used two sets of "rules"—Patty and I favorited the Federated Euchre Association Rules (FEAR) and our opponents went with the Canadian Hockey Euchre Association Textbook (CHEAT).

Throughout our three-plus seasons of Euchre playing, there were a lot of accusations of cheating, from both sides, but nothing was ever proven.

When Mike retired after the 1986–87 season, we didn't bring in anyone else to play.

PAT LaFONTAINE

They cheated all the time, and they still owe us money. And with interest, they could probably buy this building [UBS Arena].

I am taking the fifth on that one.

BRYAN TROTTIER

Kenny had his lucky Euchre shoes—dark brown with pucks all over them—but he was a lightweight. And Bossy still owed him money.

Bottom line: we kicked their butts. No apologies.
Or maybe we just cheated better than they did.
Either way, Bryan still owes me a pair of shoes.
And Patty had his own stolen shoes story.

PAT LaFONTAINE

We were going back to my hometown of St. Louis, and Kenny and I had been smoking those guys. We had a plan to meet at 6:30 for dinner that night and we were feeling pretty good about our game. I'm getting ready to go down and I can't find my shoes. Trots is giving me the business about getting downstairs for dinner and I still can't find my shoes. He said, "Take a look out the window"—and my shoes were dangling from the telephone line. That was the only pair of shoes I had, so I had to wear sneakers. And I never got them back.

So clearly, Bryan owes us *both* new shoes!

* * *

For more than 40 years now, I have been incredibly blessed with the good fortune hockey has brought into my life. Having won a gold medal and four Stanley Cups, taking part in what is considered the greatest sports moment of the 20th century, and playing on a New York Islanders team that won 19 consecutive playoff series has opened up so many unique events and memorable moments that I have been able to experience. From meeting two presidents to lighting the Olympic torch in Salt Lake City, to walking the red carpet at the *Miracle* premiere, to being the Grand Marshal at two NASCAR races, to riding on a float in the Orange Bowl parade, to being at the *Sports Illustrated* best sports moment of the 20th century award show with all of the greatest athletes from every sport (and our Olympic team winning the greatest sports moment award). There have been commercials, NHL All-Star Game appearances, so many charity golf outings, charity hockey games against the Hollywood All Stars, a Caribbean cruise, a lot of reunions, and countless other events and causes that have been so much fun.

Here are some highlights of the more memorable events:

1. 1980 AmEx Commercial

It was at a restaurant in Manhattan that had been rented out for the day. It was my first experience doing anything like that. They had extras in the background and smoke in the air to give it a restaurant feel. We were all in a booth around a table—Mike Eruzione, Neal Broten, myself, Mark Johnson, Mark Pavelich, and Herb Brooks.

It was a shoot during the summer of 1980 for one of the most popular commercials at that time—"American Express, don't leave home without it."

It was a 30-second commercial, but it probably took 50 takes. Just for me to do my one line, I probably messed it up 20 or more times, I was so nervous.

We used a half-circle booth, with all the cameras and lighting and crew right there, and you are supposed to act natural? No way that was happening.

It had to be one of the most popular commercials that year, right after we won the gold medal. Just to see it on TV was so cool.

In looking back, I was so stiff! The dialogue went like this:

Eruzione: People called us heroes when we beat the Russian hockey team in the 1980 Olympics.

Pavelich: Sure, it was an upset.

Eruzione: I wasn't upset.

Morrow: The Russians…were very upset.

Johnson: Totally.

Brooks: These days, we use the American Express card—and with this, anybody can get a hero's welcome.

Narrator: To apply for the card, look for an application and take one.

Brooks: The American Express card—don't leave home without it.

All of us: We didn't!

Cue laughter.

We had a lot of fun with that for sure.

2. 2002 Salt Lake City Olympic Flame

Aside from winning the gold medal and Stanley Cups, the honor of lighting the Olympic torch in 2002 comes next on that list. When you think of how few people have had the honor of lighting an Olympic torch, it is a very short list.

The secrecy about who would be lighting the torch in Salt Lake was unreal. It was guarded like a national top secret mission. We had to sign non-disclosure agreements. We couldn't let anyone know. They wanted it to be a surprise up until the moment the torch was passed onto the stage. Somehow, it did stay a secret. Nobody knew we were lighting it until we walked out. Everyone was surprised; even the media didn't know.

We had to climb scaffolding and we came out from both sides of the elevated stage. It was held in the Utah football stadium, and they had built a stage four or five stories high. We had been waiting in the green room for three or four hours.

Sting was sitting in one corner. Reba McEntire was in another. It was all very surreal.

We climbed up, half of the team on each side, then walked out as a group in our white USA Hockey sweaters.

Eruzione was handed the torch from hockey player Cammi Granato and skier Picabo Street and we all gathered around him, just like we had on the medal stand 22 years prior.

We lit the flame and it moved up the tower until the flame burst into the cauldron at the top.

Herb was not there, as he was coaching the USA hockey team again that year. They won silver in Salt Lake City, so Herb won Olympic gold and silver as a coach.

It was a once-in-a-lifetime moment for sure!

Salt Lake brought back memories of the 1980 Opening Ceremony, but on a much larger scale and with millions more people watching.

The patriotism and pride in representing your country are hard to put into words. I grew up watching the Olympics on television every four years. I have watched the summer and winter Olympic Games throughout my life and still do to this day, cheering for Team USA.

To have walked in the Opening Ceremony of the 1980 Olympics and to take part in lighting the Olympic torch in Salt Lake are moments I will always cherish.

3. *Miracle* Red Carpet

This was another once-in-a-lifetime event I was able to experience, and even better, my family was able to take part in it as well.

Miracle, with Kurt Russell, was released in February 2004. Our team was invited to Hollywood to walk the red carpet for the premiere. Just like you have seen on TV, we walked the red carpet with reporters interviewing us, people in the stands and along the street, and Hollywood stars attending. We were able to meet Kurt Russell and Goldie Hawn.

This was another surreal moment among the many I have had the good fortune of experiencing.

A few months later, the movie won an award at the ESPYs, which took place in Hollywood, so we were back there again, going up on stage. Not long after that, my family and I got to spend a week at Disney World as VIP guests, courtesy of ESPN. We still say that is the best vacation we have ever been on!

I wanted to take this chance to set the record straight on a couple of things from the *Miracle* movie.

My character in the movie didn't have a beard, which had unintendedly become a signature of mine starting with my final college season and lasting well into my Islanders career. I was the only player on the Olympic team who had a beard; for some reason they left the beard out of the movie. After joining the Islanders, that team has been credited with starting the "playoff beard" tradition with the likes of Clark Gillies, Denis Potvin, myself, and others on the team having beards.

Also, my character shot left-handed (I shoot right-handed), and the only time my name was mentioned by Al Michaels doing play-by-play in the movie was when a Russian skater managed to put the puck between my legs and score their second goal.

That play never occurred in that game. What did happen on that goal is that Soviet player Makarov tried to pass the puck past me, and it deflected off my skate blade and right back to him where he snapped a quick shot for a goal. I have no idea why the director portrayed the goal being scored by stickhandling through me. I can tell you it is a defenseman's worst nightmare if an opponent stickhandles past you, which did not happen on that goal.

4. AMC Motors Appearance in Dallas, 1980

The summer after we won gold, five members of the Olympic team were asked to make an appearance at the annual AMC (American Motor Company) convention in Dallas. It was held at the beautiful Loews Anatole hotel. Again, this was to be a surprise appearance on the final day of their conference, where all of the AMC car dealers and their families gathered. They flew us down to Dallas two days before, with instructions to sightsee and eat and do whatever, just not to let anybody know who we were. So we had two great days of vacation without paying for anything. Then on the final day, they had everyone in a big auditorium with a stage and curtains. It was packed with people. When it came to the end of their motivational event, they had the five of us players seated on stage behind the big curtains, while they showed the final minute of the Miracle on Ice game on a big screen. People were cheering wildly as the final seconds counted down and Al Michaels' famous call could be heard. As the celebration was showing on the screen, they announced that there were five members of the team here, and they opened the curtains. People stood and cheered for two minutes. We sat there and waved and high-fived, then the curtains closed. That was all they had us do. We had a three-day paid vacation with our wives for just sitting on a stage for a couple of minutes and waving.

How great is that?!

5. Orange Bowl Parade, 1990

Our 1980 Olympic team got invited to ride in the Orange Bowl parade in 1990. The football game was played between Notre Dame and

No. 1–ranked Colorado. Notre Dame upset Colorado in the game, but Miami ended up being voted the national champions. We were invited to take part in the parade, which just happened to take place a month before the 10th anniversary of our gold medal win.

The parade was held at night and was nationally televised. They had us standing at various spots on a float. It had red, white, and blue lights and a big hockey stick down the middle that was full of lights. There were grandstands filled with people on both sides at the start of the parade route. This is where all of the television cameras were and most of the crowd. Minutes before the start of the parade, I was standing on this small square space that was surrounded by lights, near the hockey stick. I had turned to look at something and my foot slipped and I accidentally broke a couple of bulbs.

Just like on a Christmas tree, all of the lights on the hockey stick went out, right as our float started moving. We went through the parade without any of the lights on the hockey stick working. After we passed through the grandstands, the crowd thinned along the two-mile parade route, until we were eventually winding through downtown Miami on a float with parts of it falling off as we were moving through downtown. The float basically held together long enough to get past the grandstands and the crowd. We ended up in a parking lot staging area in the middle of downtown and had to walk several blocks to get back to our bus. Evander Holyfield had been on one of the floats, and we followed him back.

This was another one of those unforgettable moments.

6. Sports Moment of the Century Award Show

In December 1999, *Sports Illustrated* hosted a primetime show on CBS celebrating and counting down the top sports moments of the century. When you think back to all of the great sports moments of the 20th century, along with all of the greatest sports celebrities from all sports who were there that night, it was surreal. Whitney Houston and Garth Brooks were part of the entertainment during the show. It was a black-tie event and there was a pre-show reception in the rotunda on the lower level of Madison Square Garden, where the show was being televised from the arena. There were limousine and red-carpet arrivals to MSG, then looking across the room and seeing all these sports celebrities from each sport gathered in one room.

There were Muhammed Ali and golf greats Jack Nicklaus, Tiger Woods, and Arnold Palmer. There were basketball legends Michael Jordan, Larry Bird, Kareem Abdul-Jabbar, and Bill Russell, plus football stars Jim Brown and Dick Butkas and Joe Montana, baseball legends Henry Aaron and Willie Mays, and NHL greats Wayne Gretzky, Bobby Orr, and Gordie Howe.

Not to mention fellow Olympians Mark Spitz (swimming), Carl Lewis (track and field), and Peggy Fleming (figure skating), plus soccer icon Pele, tennis great Billie Jean King, and auto racer Richard Petty. The list goes on and on.

All of the greats of the 20th century in one place at the same time. Then having our "Miracle on Ice" chosen as the top sports moment of the century…absolutely beyond belief!

* * *

What an absolutely amazing experience it has been writing this book. I know that I have had way more than my share of wonderful moments and unimaginable events in my life that I can fondly look back on.

I also realize there have been many fateful moments that I didn't know at the time would take me down a path that I am so grateful to have followed. When opportunities are presented, you have to be prepared to take advantage of them.

As Herb Brooks would say, "Success happens when preparation meets opportunity."

I found out in the process of writing this book that there was one fateful night in December 1975 when Islanders scout Jim Devellano saw me play a game in Toronto during my freshman year at Bowling Green. Astonishing to think that this singular unplanned encounter—an off night on his schedule—led to me being drafted in 1976 in the fourth round.

Here I am, almost 50 years later, still a part of the Islanders organization. That encompasses 10 seasons as a player and more than 30 years as a pro scout since Bill Torrey offered me a scouting position in 1992 following my one season as an Islanders assistant coach.

After living apart from my family for two years while coaching, I was more than happy to accept this offer. It allowed me to keep our family based in Kansas City, which had become our temporary home when I was coaching with the KC Blades.

Having been a player, coach, and scout for all these years, I have watched hockey evolve and transform into what Herb Brooks was pushing us to play back in 1980. There were NHL work stoppages in 1992 and 1994, then a season lost to a lockout in 2004-05. There were the sluggish years of the late '90s and early 2000s when the "trap" ruled the NHL.

Then came the changes coming out of the lockout to open up the game, which highlighted speed, skill, and scoring plus the addition of shootouts following overtime to decide games.

Herb was an innovator. He was 30 years ahead of his time with his vision of how the game should be played.

North American hockey finally caught on, and the Game is in a very good place now in 2025.

AFTERWORD

MY FIRST ENCOUNTER WITH KEN MORROW was when he skated onto Madison Square Garden ice as a member of Uncle Sam's 1980 Olympic team. It was an exhibition game against the powerful Soviet national team. It was a "barometer" contest in which we in the media would judge how the American skaters would match up against what amounted to a professional team with a Russian accent.

There was little to like about coach Herb Brooks' sextet. It was men against boys and the final score (10–3) was supposed to be a portent of things to come when the official games would begin at the Olympic Village in Lake Placid.

The USA lineup may have been well-known to hockey reporters familiar with the collegiate game and the minor league variety. But, to those of us familiar only with the major league variety—better known as the NHL—Brooks' collection of stickhandlers required a program for me to know who was who, not to mention what was what.

In other words, defenseman Ken Morrow might have been Joe Doakes for all I knew of him at the time. That review would change in good time, but not in fast time.

Not having seen Morrow play for Bowling Green University, I had no idea how closely Ken's style resembled that of Hall of Fame defender Doug Harvey.

(By the way, according to the winningest NHL coach, Scotty Bowman, Harvey was the greatest blueliner he had ever seen.)

Having watched Harvey starting with his rookie season as a Canadien through his retirement with the St. Louis Blues, I agree with the assessment, "Doug could play defense in a rocking chair."

He did his job unobtrusively and without any fuss or fanfare. His trademark included a deft pokecheck with which he relieved his foe of the puck. Next, he flipped on his radar and magically found a free teammate who found the six-ounce hunk of rubber on his stick blade.

The learning cycle was apparent to hockey historians. Harvey had studied under multiple Canadiens Cup winner Butch Bouchard, while Arbour learned the moment he signed on with the Red Wings Junior A Windsor Spitfires farm team in the OHA Junior A League.

"Being across the river from Detroit, Al could watch future Hall of Fame defensemen like Red Kelly, Bill Quackenbush, and Leo Reise Jr.," said former Red Wings publicist-historian Fred Huber Jr. "By the time Arbour came to the big club, he knew defense inside and out."

For Morrow, the "Arbour Effect" was preceded by what Ken learned under Herb Brooks. While Herbie never had major league hockey experience, he imparted much of what he had absorbed from the European masters—especially the Russian possession game—to Uncle Sam's gold medal aspirants.

"In many ways Herbie was the perfect coach for Kenny," said Kevin Hubbard, author of *Hockey America*. "Brooks grew up on the east side of St. Paul, and was a standout player at St. Paul Johnson High School during the mid-1950s."

He enrolled in the fall of 1958 at the University of Minnesota, where he starred at wing and defense for the Gophers before graduating in 1962 with a degree in psychology. "Herb was like a shrink in his coaching techniques," wrote Hubbard. "It was part of his winning technique and some of that brainwork filtered down to Morrow. In time Herbie's wisdom became a part of the Morrow technique."

Having done my up-front puck work starting in 1954 when I was hired as a Rangers publicist, I could see where Arbour the player—and Al the coach—had influenced Ken.

Other reporters may have considered Morrow an instant hit on that Sunday afternoon (March 1, 1980) at Nassau Veterans' Memorial Coliseum when the Red Wings won 4–3.

But interviewed by my SportsChannel colleague Jiggs McDonald after the match, I unequivocally declared, "I don't think Morrow is ready for NHL play this year. Give him a year in the minors."

Jiggs chuckled and replied, "Maven, I think it would be wise if we gave him a bit more time. After all, going from a gold medal at Lake Placid right into the homestretch is quite a jump. Let's see what happens over the next month."

As McDonald correctly forecast—and I wrongly predicted—Morrow acclimatized himself to the major league game, and by the time the 1980 playoffs began Al Arbour's crew was ready for another crack at the Stanley Cup.

By this time the genuine experts were noticing Ken's assets.

Historian Andrew Podnieks was one who figured Morrow as a quiet genius. In his definitive encyclopedia, *Players*, Podnieks noted, "Morrow's qualities were born of talent and determination."

Podnieks could have added "clutch performances."

Within three months of joining the Islanders, Morrow became the first and only player ever to win an Olympic gold medal and the Stanley Cup in the same year.

To my utter amazement, the rookie whose ability I had once doubted defied credulity. On the one hand, his defensive play defied credulity, yet time and again he continually produced clutch goals starting in the first, 1980 Cup run.

Podnieks: "In the 1984 playoffs he scored in overtime to eliminate the Rangers. In the semifinals he earned an assist on Mike Bossy's game-winner against Montreal."

Another facet to Ken's game was his physical play.

"There was something about Ken's physique—call it raw-boned—that made you think he was skinnier than he was and even a pushover," one veteran reporter said. "But he was like Al Arbour in that respect. Nobody ever pushed Radar around, and the same held for Kenny."

Come to think of it, Herbie and Al Arbour were as opposite as broccoli and an ice cream sundae.

What made them tick?

Al turned pro when he was about 18 and had an enormously long and successful playing career; but always as a grunt would be in the infantry. He knew his limitations—mostly skating, and the fact that he wore glasses—in action. He was the archetypal defensive defenseman—beloved by coaches because "he took care of his own end."

Radar also had the *knack*. Despite his shortcomings, he played on Cup-winners in Detroit, Chicago, and Toronto while adjusting to varying coaches (Imlach included) who drove other players to distraction.

The result was that Al was adaptable, knew how the Black Aces felt, and treated superstars (Denis Potvin) as equals or was even harder on them so that *all* players knew that there was equal treatment on all Al's teams.

On the other hand, he took no nonsense while, conversely, having a terrific sense of humor.

When in his first year as Isles coach Eddie Westfall took a pumpkin pie in his face on his birthday, Al thought that was good fun because it loosened the team a bit.

But when, during the Cup years, Pat Price did the pie thing on Al during a very serious moment, it was only a matter of time before he was shipped out.

Al also was very much a family man, married to the adoring Claire, who helped hubby with early taping of games, before any other coach did it.

The dynasty Isles were an extension of Al's family. Absentmindedness was his idiosyncrasy.

The 1983 four-game Final versus Edmonton was so intense that it felt like a seven-game series. I consider it the club's most noble, toughest run-plus. And it showed on Al.

A few days after the victory, owner John Pickett threw a celebration party under a giant tent at a posh Long Island country club in a torrential downpour. Everyone on the team was there but Al.

Apparently, he was in the hospital recuperating from exhaustion.

Al saw a lot of himself in Ken Morrow and wasted no time throwing Morrow into a starting position. To Radar's credit, the way he helped Morrow was another reason for the club's success. Kenny was a quiet star overnight.

The only thing that I can think of that Herbie and Al had in common is that both were fringe players and, of course, Herbie didn't even make the cut on the U.S. Olympic team.

In contrast to Al, Herbie was well-schooled right through college and that gave him an educational leg up on Arbour; it perhaps spoiled Herbie a bit, but certainly gave him insights into how to handle American collegiate stickhandlers such as Ken Morrow.

Brooks was a master (hockey) chemist and the manner in which he blended the assorted personalities and hockey styles together was astonishing.

He also knew how to utilize his aides—as in Craig Patrick—to advantage, often disappearing and letting Patrick run the show.

Herb was the absolute perfect pilot for an underdog team, as Team USA was.

To Herbie's credit, he made the transition to the NHL very smoothly, reaching his apex in the 1984 five-game playoff versus the Islanders. It was a series some call the best ever. Herbie's problem was that Al had Billy Smith, and Herbie did not.

Brooks and I and my wife Shirley became pals.

Herbie was a delight—ditto for Al—to be with away from the rink. When Herb coached the Devils—success was fading—I did a pregame "Coach's Corner" with him and—a bit too often to suit me—he would have an assistant pinch hit for him.

My favorite memory was when he became Olympic coach the second time around in 2002. It was between games, and I was in upstate New York at my country house. The phone rings, and who's on the other end but Herb?

"Why in the world would you be calling me now?" I asked. "I just want to chat with somebody," he said, "and why not you?"

So, we chatted. I still can't believe that happened!

Yes, the gold in 1980 means even more now, in retrospect, when you consider the Soviet foes and the collegians who put them away.

Unreal!

I did many *SportsChannel* interviews with Ken at Nassau Veterans' Memorial Coliseum after he had hit the heights but, ironically, my most memorable was the one we did in his living room at Morrow's Long Island home.

What made it so special is that it was one of the first I had ever done in the quiet of Ken's home with only his wife around to schmooze with us. We talked hockey to be sure, but the no-ice ambience was more like a couple of old pals having a tuna fish salad sandwich at the deli around the corner.

It was so disarming that when I finally walked out the door, I felt as if I had spent a couple of hours with my Uncle Sid.

Picking a single favorite Ken Morrow goal is impossible. Working overtime at it, I came up with three distinctly different games.

The first took place in the best-of-five opening round against the Los Angeles Kings.

After opening with an 8–1 trouncing of the West Coasters, the Kings reawakened in Game 3 at the Forum in Tinseltown. The 3–3 tie led

268

to overtime and what could have been another playoff humiliation for the Nassaumen.

But who should "save" Al Arbour's crew but Ken Morrow's "Hail Mary" drive that catapulted the Blue and Orange on the road to the first Cup?

Mike Bossy put it best when he said, "Kenny's goal took a million pounds of pressure off everybody."

Right up there with my fave Morrow red-lighters was the fourth Cup clincher in 1983 at Fort Neverlose on Hempstead Turnpike in Game 4 of the Final with New York leading the series three-zip.

What made it unusual was the fact that Wayne Gretzky's team was the one favored to win the tourney in four games. Working the series for *SportsChannel*, I recall the Islanders winning a quick first-period 3–0 lead.

But Edmonton was not dead. The Oilers trimmed the Isles' lead to 3–2 entering the third frame; plenty of time for Gretzky/Messier/Coffey Inc. to tie the score and win in overtime.

I recall my *SportsChannel* producer commenting between the second and third period, "If the Oilers manage to win this one, I can see them coming back and winning the series."

The 3–2 Islanders lead moved to the final moments when a face-off was called deep in the Islanders' zone. A perfect time for Mister Springtime, Ken Morrow. Until Ken's biscuit crossed the Oilers' goal line, I still had my doubts about the series' outcome.

And when the red light flashed for the Islanders' fourth—and Cup-winning—goal, my stomach whirled like a hyped-up malted milk machine.

Ah, but there was just one more glorious goal; this one in the Islanders' heroic "Drive for Five."

The Patrick Division Final could not have been better choreographed by a Hollywood script writer.

The best-of-five series was down to the fifth—rubber match—at the Coliseum.

Arbour's proud skaters nursed a 2–1 lead down the home stretch when Rangers forward Don Maloney scored the tying goal on what the Islanders figured was a high stick.

But the tip-in was ruled a goal, forcing overtime.

Time and again, goalie Bill Smith had kept the home club alive with brilliant saves and now the Islanders counterattacked. John Tonelli won a battle along the left boards and sent the puck around behind the net and out along the right boards, where Morrow had an encampment.

Ken swung and destiny's puck sailed right past Blueshirts goalie Glen Hanlon.

Game, set, and match for Ken Morrow, the unlikeliest hero of any Cup Final in history.

On that dynasty winner of an unreal 19 consecutive playoff series, Ken Morrow well represented his nickname—the "Hero's Hero."

Stan Fischler, known as the Hockey Maven, is a December 2021 inductee to the U.S. Hockey Hall of Fame. He has won eight New York Emmy awards and the Lester Patrick Award for his contributions to ice hockey in the United States. He has covered hockey in print, broadcast, or online for more than 70 years and was part of Islanders broadcasts—including the four straight Cup wins—for five decades.

ACKNOWLEDGMENTS

IN EARLY 2023, I was asked whether I had ever considered writing a book. I had been asked that before and had never given it a second thought, but this time was different. A huge thank you to Allan Kreda for all his hard work and inspiration. He is the one who asked that question and without whom this book would not have happened.

Also, many thanks to his wife, Claudia, for all of her help and effort reading and re-reading the manuscript and asking insightful questions that brought out even more stories and needed context.

Through the process of writing this book, I can now call them both good friends. This endeavor has allowed me to look back in time and get to relive so many memorable hockey games and defining moments in my life.

I am grateful to Triumph Books for giving me this opportunity. Thank you Michelle Bruton and Bill Ames for your professionalism and support. And thanks to our literary agent, Doug Grad, for his guiding hand on this project.

Family and friends are the most important in my life and in that regard, I have been blessed. To my wife, Barb, who has played such an important part of this whole journey; to our daughters, Krysten and Brittany, and our son, Evan; to all of my grandkids—please know that you all mean the world to me.

To my parents, Don and Loretta; my brother, Greg; and my sister, Kathi—thank you so much for making this "impossible dream come true."

Profound gratitude to my late Uncle Cliff for always being there for me and to my cousins back in Michigan. We always look forward to our trips home and spending time with you.

To Steph and Fred, Butch and Judy, and all of Barb's family who have made me part of their family, thanks to all of you for giving me a great foundation outside of hockey.

I have so many lasting memories from my youth hockey days, having teammates and friends like the Cronks, Buckners, and Guertins and many others along the way. We will forever be bonded by hockey and friendship. Thank you to Barry Smith, my close friend in high school. You and your family welcomed this shy kid into your home.

My four years spent at Bowling Green were life-changing, both on and off the ice. I am thankful to my BG teammates and those who helped me grow both as a hockey player and a person. A special thanks to coach Ron Mason for seeing something in me and taking a chance on a raw 18-year-old kid.

To Mark Wells, who was my teammate with the Junior Red Wings, my teammate and roommate for four years at BG, and my 1980 Olympic teammate. Rest in peace, Wellsy.

To all of the special friends who are a big part of my family's life in Kansas City, which we have called home for more than 30 years. We are lucky to be surrounded by so many good people. To John Kirby, Paul McGannon, Hector Luevano, and Michelle King, your passion for hockey and community is unmatched. To Marty Raskin, Alan Mayer, and Dave Lindstrom, thank you for your friendship and our get-togethers for lunch.

Thank you to Doug Soetaert for giving me the opportunity to make Kansas City our home and to the Leshers for being such good friends.

An unexpected bonus from our 1980 gold medal win has been our annual Miracle on Ice Fantasy Camp in Lake Placid, which started in 2015 and is still going strong.

Through this camp, we have met so many extraordinary hockey people, brought together solely because of what happened during that fateful February in Lake Placid. Paul and Julia Torre have become close friends, along with many others from the camp who are all part of our expanding hockey family.

My sincere gratitude to Katie Million for all she has done and continues to do for our 1980 Miracle on Ice team.

To my 19 Olympic teammates, we walk together forever.

My heartfelt love to the Mannix family who have been and always will be our second family. To Roy and Linda Gier and their family who made us feel at home on Long Island right away and became close friends. Thank you Steve Wirth for your physical therapy expertise and your friendship.

A great big thank you to general managers Bill Torrey, Garth Snow, Lou Lamoriello, and to current Islanders owners Scott Malkin and Jon Ledecky, who have all treated me so well. Joanne Holewa, you have my admiration and appreciation for all you have done for the Islanders organization and for myself.

To Kerry and Kelly, we are forever friends. To Islanders fans and the people of Long Island, whose passion for hockey and life are unrivaled, you have my eternal respect and gratitude for letting me become a part of Long Island. I can tell you that I have Orange and Blue running through my veins!

I realize how incredibly fortunate I have been to have played for Ron Mason, Herb Brooks, and Al Arbour, three all-time great coaches.

I owe any success in my hockey career to these coaching legends and to the incredible teammates at all levels who pulled me along with them. We were able to accomplish some amazing feats at Bowling Green, a miraculous gold medal win with the 1980 Olympic team, and a record 19-straight playoff series wins with the dynasty Islanders.

Thank you to captain Denis Potvin for his effort and kind words with the foreword in this book and to Stan Fischler—the Maven—for contributing his afterword and sharing his lifetime in hockey with all of us.

To Gordie Lane, my defense partner on the ice and good friend off the ice, we have had a lot of laughs over the years. And to my Islanders teammates during my decade on Nassau Coliseum ice—through the Stanley Cup years and beyond—thank you for the incredible memories. Clarkie, Boss, and Potsy, you are dearly missed, and your legacies will live on forever.

In reflecting on the words of Herb Brooks, "Respect the game and it will respect you back."

I have been given so much by the game of hockey, and for that I am forever humbled and thankful.

—Ken Morrow

AFTER MORE THAN 35 YEARS in the writing business, I am especially grateful to be entrusted with the honor of helping Ken Morrow tell his unique story of perseverance and winning. Thank you, Ken, for your dedication and friendship throughout this journey.

Thanks to our agent, Doug Grad, for his continued support and assistance. I am glad Frank McCourt of Stuyvesant High School fame brought us together!

Thanks to Bill Ames at Triumph Books for believing in our project from the start and a standing ovation to our editor, Michelle Bruton, who did a fabulous job helping Ken and me knit this memoir together. Her guidance has been invaluable.

There is no way I could have achieved such a journalistic pinnacle without the unwavering support and love of my wife, Claudia, who has lived through endless ups and downs since we met in 1990. Like me, she has an emotional bond to the 1980 Olympic hockey team winning gold at Lake Placid. Through her outstanding organizational skills, countless reads, and insightful contributions to this manuscript, she proved as vital as any game-saving glove save or Cup-winning overtime goal.

Thank you to the iconic Stan Fischler, my hockey mentor and friend since 1985. We have shared so many hockey and life experiences through the years. I am forever grateful and honored that you are part of this book.

To my parents, Roberta and Bert, whose loving spirits are with me every day; my grandparents, Adeline and Irving, who were ardent supporters of my shift from pre-med to journalism way back when; my brother, David—my original hockey inspiration—and sister, Helene, for their complete love and support to the present day; and to my hockey-loving nieces, Danielle and Lauren, and five nephews, who always keep me young, I say thank you!

Special thanks to our puppy, Sundae, for contentedly staying by my side through countless hours transcribing interviews, editing text, and watching hockey games.

Thanks to my in-laws, aunts, uncles, and cousins and with extra special gratitude to my Aunt Gail and Aunt Evelyn for marrying into my family and being so vital to my positive life outlook!

To my many friends and colleagues over the course of my academic and professional life who have encouraged my writing, I say a supreme thank you.

To Vincent Losinno—my Brooklyn and hockey friend of more than 40 years; Jerome Minerva—dedicated Islanders fan and Associated Press colleague; and my Medill School of Journalism friends and roommates Steve Master and Jim Parenti, I have immense gratitude.

That extends to Northwestern classmates Alisa Parenti, Tad Lichtenauer, Leslie Komet Ashburn, Vicki Lo, David Voreacos, Gerti Zaccone, Ann Hayes, Thurston Hatcher, Steve Oelenberger plus the Losinno, Minerva,

Master, and Parenti families for their love and friendship through the decades.

To Jeff, Jenn, and Kaitlyn Schwartzenberg and their families, I so appreciate our years of friendship back to our days at MSG and now on OBX!

Sincere thanks to Mike Geffner for pushing me to get better from the moment I joined the AP in 1989.

And to Louis Franzetti and Larry Bauman for listening and talking when I have needed it most.

Thank you to Jon Ledecky, Marc Gold, Tom Renney, Frank Brown, Jack Durkin, Paul Curtis, Rose Jacobson, Michael Dolan, Amie Anderson, Vincent Piazza, Carlos Valladares, Mike Roth, Paul Reinhartsen, Alan Raymond, Peter Schwartz, Brad Marcus, Melissa Lea, Heather Krug, Barry Bloom, Jay Beberman, and the Bay 8th Street Boys.

Special gratitude to Robert Nappo for that first game ticket in November 1971. And to Judy and Herman Diamond for their love and support through the decades.

To Renee Rotkopf and the Soulpreneurs, heartfelt thanks.

Bonus gratitude to my Stuyvesant High School class of '82 friends, particularly Ed Newman for his stellar contribution of my back jacket photograph.

To my great teachers and professors Estelle Finkel, William McGinn, Valden Madsen, Bruce Porter, Jon Ziomek, and Jack Doppelt, many thanks. And to the spirits of Rod Gilbert, LeRoy Neiman, Jean-Pierre Trebot, Ben Olan, and Irwin Rosee, profound gratitude for encouraging me early and throughout my career.

To *all* the players, coaches, wives, siblings, parents, and friends of players I have spent time interviewing and sharing life experiences and stories with through the decades, I appreciate every one of you.

To Barb Morrow, who graciously hosted me in Long Beach, New York, during the summer of 2023 when Ken and I conducted key early interviews after which I learned the basics of Euchre, I extend my gratitude.

To the teammates, opponents, and family of Ken Morrow, I thank you for your time and input for this book. A very special thank you to the Brooks family—Patti, Dan, and Kelly—for sharing their memories of Herb and collective Lake Placid experiences. I am forever grateful.

Thanks to Katie Million, Bill Robertson, Jimmy Devellano, and Rich Torrey for their key contributions and assistance.

The 1980 U.S. Olympic hockey team, captained by Mike Eruzione, will forever be in a class all their own, and I so appreciate the opportunity to further their legacy and include their words in this memoir.

The same gratitude is extended to numerous Islanders alumni—many of whom hoisted the Stanley Cup four times—who graciously shared stories and memories of and on behalf of Ken.

Special thanks to Denis Potvin for contributing the foreword to this book. Denis and his brother, Jean, are among my all-time favorites, and the Potvin family will always have a special place in my heart.

Bonus thanks and appreciation to Jiggs McDonald and Ed Westfall, who have been friends through many Islanders decades back to the SportsChannel days.

And to Pat LaFontaine and the wonderful LaFontaine family, thank you for always being a positive life force.

This book could not have come to fruition without a self-belief that resides in one of Herb Brooks' favorite mantras: "Plan your work and work your plan."

Ken is the epitome of that mindset, and so am I.

There was a bonus moment in July 2024 when my wife and I were at the beautiful racetrack in Saratoga Springs, New York. We were mulling the racing form that Sunday afternoon when I texted Ken, who advised making a small wager in any race on No. 3 or No. 6, his jersey numbers through the years. Somehow, a colt named Itza Mirrakle was listed as No. 3 in the fifth race.

I bet him to win, and he did—with a dynamic stretch run!

Yet another moment of magic during the creative process of this book, which felt like fate from the start.

—Allan Kreda

ABOUT THE AUTHORS

Ken Morrow played 10 seasons for the New York Islanders after winning a gold medal with the U.S. Olympic team at Lake Placid in 1980.

The native of Flint, Michigan, grew up in nearby Davison. He played four years at Bowling Green State University before joining the U.S. Olympic team in the summer of 1979. He represented Team USA at the 1978 World Championships and was named CCHA Player of the Year in 1979. He then played with the U.S. Olympic team during their 61-game season heading into the Olympics at Lake Placid in February 1980.

Morrow played all seven games at Lake Placid as the U.S. team went undefeated to win the gold medal, shocking the heavily favored Soviet team in the "Miracle on Ice" game on February 22, 1980. Two days later, the U.S. squad downed Finland 4–2 to capture the gold.

Morrow was selected 68th overall by the Islanders in the 1976 NHL Entry Draft and joined the team days after the Olympics ended. Three months to the day after he earned a gold medal, he lifted the Stanley Cup at Nassau Coliseum after Bob Nystrom's overtime goal gave the Islanders their first NHL championship. Morrow would win the Stanley Cup four consecutive times between 1980 and '83. In the 1983 playoffs, Morrow tallied five goals and added seven assists in 18 games. In his regular season career, the stalwart defenseman scored 17 goals with 88 assists in 550 games.

Ken was inducted into the U.S. Hockey Hall of Fame in Eveleth, Minnesota, in 1995. He was inducted into the New York Islanders Hall of Fame in December 2011 and the New York State Hockey Hall of Fame in July 2024.

He was an Islanders assistant coach for one season in 1991–92 after spending one year as assistant coach with the IHL's Flint Spirits in 1989–90 and one year as associate coach of the Kansas City Blades in 1990–91.

Ken is currently director of pro scouting for the Islanders, a role he has had since 1992 when then Islanders general manager Bill Torrey hired him as a pro scout three years after his playing career concluded. He has been with the Islanders organization for more than 40 years.

Morrow lives in Kansas City with his wife, Barb. They have daughters Krysten and Brittany, son Evan, and six grandchildren.

Allan Kreda has spent more than three decades writing hockey for The Associated Press, Bloomberg News, and *The New York Times*.

He graduated from Brooklyn College with a degree in Biology. During his undergraduate years, he interned for Stan Fischler and SportsChannel, which gave him an opportunity to be part of game nights at Nassau Coliseum as far back as 1985. He then attended Northwestern University's Medill School of Journalism where he earned a master's degree in 1988.

Allan started his career with the *Daytona Beach News-Journal* before joining the AP in 1989, working on the sports, business, and international desks during a decade with the wire service.

He worked for Bloomberg News from 1999 to 2006 covering money and banking, then sports business, media, and the NHL, and often appearing on radio and television for the financial news outlet.

He later was senior editor of the magazine *Athletes Quarterly* for six years and has more than 400 bylines in the *Times* as a contributing hockey writer from 2013 to 2021. Allan has returned to the AP in recent years to cover home games of the New York Islanders, New York Rangers, and New Jersey Devils.

He lives in Manhattan with his wife, Claudia, and their Coton de Tuléar puppy, Sundae.

Appendix

Ken Morrow's Awards and Championships

Bowling Green
    First-team All CCHA, '75–76, '77 –78, '78 –79
    Second-team All CCHA, '76–77
    CCHA Player of the Year, '78–79
    All-American 1978

1980 Olympic gold medal

Stanley Cup champion 1980, 1981, 1982, 1983

Sports Illustrated Sportsman of the Year, 1980

Bowling Green State University Hall of Fame inductee, 1984

Flint Michigan Hall of Fame inductee, 1990

USA Hockey Hall of Fame inductee, 1995

Lester Patrick Award, 1996

KEN MORROW

No. 1 *Sports Illustrated* Sports Moment of the Century, 1999

Salt Lake City Olympic torch lighting, 2002

New York Islanders Hall of Fame inductee, 2011

Missouri Sports Hall of Fame inductee, 2022

New York State Hockey Hall of Fame inductee, 2024

Ken Morrow's Career Stats

NHL Standard

Season	Age	Tm	Lg	GP	Scoring G	A	PTS	+/-	PIM	Goals EV	PP	SH	GW	Assists EV	PP	SH	Shots S	S%	Ice Time TOI	ATOI	Awards
1979-80	23	NYI	NHL	18	0	3	3	4	4	0	0	0	0	3	0	0	19	0			
1980-81	24	NYI	NHL	80	2	11	13	19	20	2	0	0	0	11	0	0	69	2.9			
1981-82	25	NYI	NHL	75	1	18	19	53	56	1	0	0	0	17	1	0	91	1.1			AS-16,Byng-20,Norris-12
1982-83	26	NYI	NHL	79	5	11	16	16	44	5	0	0	1	10	0	1	135	3.7			
1983-84	27	NYI	NHL	63	3	11	14	25	45	3	0	0	1	10	0	1	71	4.2			AS-14,Byng-16,Norris-10
1984-85	28	NYI	NHL	15	1	7	8	5	14	1	0	0	0	7	0	0	15	6.7			
1985-86	29	NYI	NHL	69	0	12	12	21	22	0	0	0	0	12	0	0	55	0			
1986-87	30	NYI	NHL	64	3	8	11	6	32	3	0	0	0	8	0	0	52	5.8			
1987-88	31	NYI	NHL	53	1	4	5	0	40	1	0	0	0	4	0	0	50	2			
1988-89	32	NYI	NHL	34	1	3	4	-7	32	1	0	0	0	3	0	0	27	3.7			
Career		10 yrs	NHL	550	17	88	105	142	309	17	0	0	2	85	1	2	584	2.9			

NHL Miscellaneous

Season	Age	Tm	Lg	GP	Per Game G	A	PTS	GC	PIM	S	Adjusted G	A	PTS	GC	TGF	Plus/Minus PGF	TGA	PGA	+/-	Point Shares OPS	DPS	PS
1979-80	23	NYI	NHL	18	0	0.17	0.17	0.05	0.22	1.06	0	3	3	1	20	0	22	6	4	-0.1	1.2	1.1
1980-81	24	NYI	NHL	80	0.03	0.14	0.16	0.05	0.25	0.86	2	9	11	4	89	1	98	29	19	-0.6	4.8	4.2
1981-82	25	NYI	NHL	75	0.01	0.24	0.25	0.07	0.75	1.21	1	13	14	4	116	1	92	30	53	-0.2	6.1	6
1982-83	26	NYI	NHL	79	0.06	0.14	0.2	0.07	0.56	1.71	4	9	13	5	78	1	93	32	16	-0.1	5.5	5.4
1983-84	27	NYI	NHL	63	0.05	0.17	0.22	0.07	0.71	1.13	2	9	11	4	83	0	86	28	25	-0.1	3.9	3.8
1984-85	28	NYI	NHL	15	0.07	0.47	0.53	0.17	0.93	1	1	6	7	2	19	0	21	7	5	0.3	0.9	1.2
1985-86	29	NYI	NHL	69	0	0.17	0.17	0.05	0.32	0.8	0	9	9	2	77	1	89	34	21	-0.6	4.3	3.7
1986-87	30	NYI	NHL	64	0.05	0.13	0.17	0.06	0.5	0.81	3	7	10	4	44	0	65	27	6	-0.3	3.9	3.6
1987-88	31	NYI	NHL	53	0.02	0.08	0.09	0.03	0.75	0.94	1	3	4	1	41	1	64	24	0	-0.7	2.5	1.8
1988-89	32	NYI	NHL	34	0.03	0.09	0.12	0.04	0.94	0.79	1	2	3	1	25	0	56	24	-7	-0.3	1.4	1.1
Career		10 yrs	NHL	550	0.03	0.16	0.19	0.06	0.56	1.06	15	70	85	27	592	5	686	241	142	-2.6	34.5	31.9

NHL Playoffs

Season	Age	Tm	Lg		Scoring						Goals				Shots		Ice Time	
					GP	G	A	PTS	+/-	PIM	EV	PP	SH	GW	S	S%	TOI	ATOI
1979-80	23	NYI	NHL	SC	20	1	2	3	-3	12	1	0	0	1	24	4.2		
1980-81	24	NYI	NHL	SC	18	3	4	7	20	8	3	0	0	1	18	16.7		
1981-82	25	NYI	NHL	SC	19	0	4	4	11	8	0	0	0	0	30	0		
1982-83	26	NYI	NHL	SC	19	5	7	12	18	18	5	0	0	0	42	11.9		
1983-84	27	NYI	NHL		20	1	2	3	4	20	1	0	0	1	21	4.8		
1984-85	28	NYI	NHL		10	0	0	0	-3	17	0	0	0	0	13	0		
1985-86	29	NYI	NHL		2	0	0	0	-2	4	0	0	0	0	3	0		
1986-87	30	NYI	NHL		13	1	3	4	-6	2	1	0	0	0	13	7.7		
1987-88	31	NYI	NHL		6	0	0	0	-2	8	0	0	0	0	1	0		
Career		9 yrs	NHL		127	11	22	33	37	97	11	0	0	3	165	6.7		

College and U.S. Olympic Hockey Team

Season	Age	Tm	Lg	Scoring					
				GP	G	A	PTS	+/-	PIM
1975-76	19	Bowling Green University	CCHA	31	4	15	19		34
1976-77	20	Bowling Green University	CCHA	39	7	22	29		22
1977-78	21	Bowling Green University	CCHA	39	8	18	26		26
1977-78	21	United States	WEC-A	6	0	0	0		0
1978-79	22	Bowling Green University	CCHA	45	15	37	52		22
1979-80	23	United States	Nat-Tm	56	4	18	22		6
1979-80	23	United States	Olympics	7	1	2	3		6
1981-82	25	United States	Can-Cup	6	0	0	0		6